BANKING DEREGULATION AND THE NEW COMPETITION IN FINANCIAL SERVICES

BANKING DEREGULATION AND THE NEW COMPETITION IN FINANCIAL SERVICES

KERRY COOPER
DONALD R. FRASER

BALLINGER PUBLISHING COMPANY
Cambridge, Massachusetts
A Subsidiary of Harper & Row, Publishers, Inc.

International Standard Book Number: 0-88410-712-4

Library of Congress Catalog Card Number: 84-6223

Printed in the United States of America

Library of Congress Cataloging in Publication Data

Cooper, S. Kerry.
   Banking deregulation and the new competition in financial services.

   Bibliography: p.
   Includes index.
   1. Banks and banking—United States.   2. Financial Institutions—United States.   3. Banking law—United States.   4. Banks and banking.   5. Banking law.   I. Fraser, Donald R.   II. Title.
   HG 2491.C67   1984   332.1'0973   84-6223
   ISBN 0-88410-712-4

For our wives   Maryvonne
Lyn

and kids   Chris and Danielle
Eleanor

CONTENTS

LIST OF FIGURES AND EXHIBITS

LIST OF TABLES

PREFACE

This is a book about *financial change* — accomplished, ongoing, and potential change in the regulatory and economic environment in which commercial banks and other depository institutions provide financial services and serve as financial intermediaries. The scope of financial change has been enormous in recent years, and the pace of change remarkably swift. The purpose of this book is to provide the reader with a review and analysis of this recent wave of financial change, with the discussion being primarily focused on banks and other depository institutions. Deregulation, financial and technological innovation, and economic change have clearly transformed the nature of competition in the financial services industry. The authors have attempted to identify and assess the forces and events which have forged this new competitive framework, describe and evaluate its present nature, and offer insights into its possible future directions.

The literature concerned with this revolution in the financial services industry is vast. This book offers, to a substantial degree, a review of that literature as well as a current and quite complete set of references to it. Some of this literature is rather arcane in language and much of it is narrowly focused. The authors have sought to maintain a straightforward, nonmathematical, expository style and a broad scope of analysis; but readers who seek greater rigor and more detailed discussion are guided throughout to appropriate sources. It is thus the intent that the book, while comprehensible to nonacademic readers, will be useful to its academic audience due to this thorough and comprehensive integration of the material with the relevant literature.

The book consists of eight chapters. Chapter 1, "The Changing Nature of Depository Institutions," provides an introduction to the topic, describes some of the major trends present in the transformation of the financial system, and presents an initial assessment of some of the issues discussed in subsequent chapters. Chapter 2, "The Rationale and Record of Depository Institution Regulation," includes more abstract (though hopefully not abstruse) discussion than other chapters, as it reviews the conceptual case for financial regulation and the costs and benefits thereof. This chapter also describes the extant regulatory framework in a historical context.

Chapter 3, "International Trends and Influences in Financial Regulation," is a distinctive and highly useful element of this book. Many discussions of current trends in the financial system of the United States ignore international developments and influences. But U.S. financial change has never occurred in a geographical vacuum. Many developments in this nation's financial structure have their counterparts abroad—an aspect which tells us something about the nature of the root causes of such developments. (For example, high and volatile interest rates in the 1970s was an international phenomenon that evoked similar changes to the financial regulatory structure of many nations.) Further, the increasing internationalization of financial markets and financial institutions has also been a potent force for change in national financial structures.

Chapters 4 and 5 are concerned with two landmark acts of Congress: respectively, the Depository Institutions Deregulation and Monetary Control Act of 1980 and the Garn-St Germain Depository Institutions Act of 1982. These chapters discuss the origins and major provisions of these two enormously important legislative acts, and assess their significance for depository institutions. The changes wrought by these laws, in concert with market changes evolving from technological developments, innovation, and economic events, have dramatically altered the competitive framework of the financial services industry. The new competition brings with it new risks for firms in that industry and Chapter 6, "Depository Institutions Failure Risk and the Role of Deposit Insurance," focuses on this aspect of financial change. In the authors' view, deposit insurance reform is a key element in the future course of financial deregulation; thus the issue of deposit insurance is treated at length.

The title of Chapter 7, "The Changing Structure of the Financial Services Industry: Innovation, Deregulation, and the New Competition," is perhaps an adequate description of its content. Deregulatory, technological, and economic change are reshaping the financial services industry. This chapter describes the nature of this transformation, offers an explanation of why it is taking place, and attempts to look ahead to the future character of the financial services market and the role of depository institutions.

Chapter 8, "The Outlook for Financial Deregulation," offers a description and assessment of the present status of proposals for further financial deregulatory and legislative actions. This chapter serves also as a reminder of the importance of political considerations in shaping (at least in the near term) the financial structure.

1 THE CHANGING NATURE OF DEPOSITORY INSTITUTIONS

Depository financial institutions—commercial banks, savings and loan associations, mutual savings banks, and credit unions—have experienced substantial changes in their operations in recent years. These changes have perhaps been most pronounced at depository institutions in the United States, though many of the trends are worldwide in nature. To some extent these changes reflect the impact of high inflation and high interest rates, as well as rapid technological change. The developments, though, also reflect the impact of legislation, especially the profoundly important Depository Institutions Deregulation and Monetary Control Act of 1980, and the more recently enacted Garn-St Germain Depository Institutions Act of 1982. These statutes not only eliminated many of the regulatory constraints on the management of depository institutions but also allowed many institutions—especially nonbank depository institutions—to alter substantially the nature of deposit and lending services offered to their customers. As a result, numerous questions have been raised over future consequences of these developments, especially questions concerning the availability of funds to traditional customers of depository institutions, the potential for a significant increase in the failure rate of these institutions, and the scope and nature of structural change in the financial services sector of the economy.[1]

1

This chapter explores some of the major causes and consequences of recent trends at depository institutions. Changes in the sources and uses of funds at commercial banks, savings and loans, mutual savings banks and credit unions are traced, with emphasis on the increased extent of competition among these institutions. The growing competition from nondepository institutions is also discussed. The chapter provides a description of the causes of financial deregulation as well as some of the principal consequences of deregulation for banks and other depository institutions (these topics are treated more extensively later in the book).

THE EVOLVING ROLE OF DEPOSITORY INSTITUTIONS

No economic entity is static in its functions. The role played by economic entities evolves, reflecting changes in the nature of demand for products and services, changing technology, regulatory factors in industries (such as the financial services industry, in which government policy has a major influence), and various other considerations. Economic entities may flourish under one set of external factors and diminish in importance under another.

The historical evolution of depository financial institutions provides an excellent example of how changes in the size, profitability, and significance of economic entities in the financial marketplace occur in response to external factors. While the changes that have occurred in the role of depository institutions since the end of World War II have been enormous in number, two in particular are important. First, depository financial institutions have generally experienced a decline in their market shares during periods of rising interest rates and a rise in their market shares during periods of falling interest rates. There is also some, though not fully conclusive, evidence of a secular decline in the market shares of depository institutions. Second, there has also been significant "blurring and overlap" in the functions of individual depository institutions.

Declining Market Shares

Table 1-1 lists the total amount of credit provided to nonfinancial organizations by depository institutions during recent years. The

Table 1-1. Share of Total Credit Provided By Depository Financial Institutions, 1950–1982 (*percent*).

Year	Commercial Banks	Savings Institutions	Total Depository Financial Institutions
1950	26.7	13.4	40.1
1955	12.3	22.6	34.9
1960	24.7	25.6	50.3
1965	40.0	20.1	60.1
1966	25.6	11.6	37.2
1967	44.1	18.4	62.5
1968	39.4	15.7	55.1
1969	20.8	16.3	37.1
1970	36.9	18.3	55.2
1971	36.2	28.0	64.2
1972	42.4	28.4	70.4
1973	45.6	19.0	64.6
1974	34.9	14.6	49.5
1975	13.8	25.4	39.2
1976	22.8	‑27.2	50.0
1977	26.2	24.5	50.7
1978	32.3	19.0	51.3
1979	31.0	14.4	45.4
1980	28.2	16.0	44.2
1981	26.5	6.2	32.7
1982	26.1	5.8	31.9

Source: Board of Governors of the Federal Reserve System, *Flow of Funds Accounts.*

period since 1965, which encompasses an era of high and volatile interest rates, is most relevant to the present discussion. Periods of rising interest rates occurred in 1966, 1969, 1974, and 1980–81. (The 1980–81 high interest rate period was interrupted by a sharp, but temporary, decline in interest rates in the second quarter of 1980.) The share of total credit provided by depository institutions fell from 60.1 percent in 1965 to 37.2 percent in 1966. Similar reductions in the market share of depository institutions occurred in 1969, 1974, 1980, and 1981.

The declining share of the flow of funds provided by depository institutions during periods of rising rates may be explained by the phenomenon known as *disintermediation.* In periods of high and rising rates, the ability of depository institutions to attract funds (and thereby their ability to provide credit) was restricted by Regulation Q limits on the maximum interest rates payable on deposits. Since there were no such limits applicable to securities offered by non-depository financial institutions and by nonfinancial institutions, savers naturally placed their funds with these other institutions by directly acquiring corporate bonds, U.S. government bonds, state and local government bonds, and other such securities rather than by acquiring the deposit liabilities of financial institutions. In contrast, when interest rates fell, such as in 1967, 1970, and 1976, Regulation Q became less constricting, the flow of funds was *reintermediated*, and the market share of depository institutions increased.

The cyclical phenomenon of disintermediation and reintermediation with rising and falling interest rates is a well-known and well-understood phenomenon. The significance of disintermediation may have been reduced in recent years, however, by the relaxation of Regulation Q ceilings, especially the elimination of interest rate ceilings on the large (jumbo) certificates of deposit and the introduction of six-month money market and thirty-month small savers CDs, as well as by the increasing use of nondeposit liabilities not subject to Regulation Q. Moreover, disintermediation should become less significant in the future since, as a result of the Depository Institutions Deregulation and Monetary Control Act of 1980 and the Garn-St Germain Depository Institutions Act of 1982, almost all interest rate ceilings on deposit accounts have been eliminated.[2]

There is also some tentative evidence from Table 1–1 that the market share of depository financial institutions may be eroding secularly.[3] For example, depository institutions captured 70 percent of the flow of credit in 1972. In contrast, the market share of depository financial institutions was 45.4 percent in 1979, 44.2 percent in 1980, and only 31.9 percent in 1982. Each of these periods was one of high interest rates. Thus, the decline in market share may reflect cyclical, disintermediation factors rather than a secular decline in the market share of depository institutions. However, there is other direct and indirect evidence to suggest that the financial innovations developed in recent periods may have permanently reduced the market share of depository financial institutions. The direct evidence relates to the enormous expansion in financial services offered by nondepository financial institutions. The indirect evidence relates to

the differences in the burden of regulation for nondepository as compared to depository financial institutions.

Competition From Nondepository Financial Institutions

Many nondepository financial institutions have begun to offer financial services in direct competition with depository institutions. In
addition, many services offered by nondepository institutions are
prohibited to depository institutions. Perhaps the best example of
the competition from nondepository financial institutions is offered
by Merrill Lynch. Table 1–2 presents a list of financial services
offered by the nation's largest brokerage firm. These include a full
range of securities services as well as insurance, real estate lending
and brokerage, and employee relocation services. It is important to
note that many of these services are directly competitive with depository financial institutions. For example, Merrill Lynch offers credit
for real estate and related purposes and for the purchase of securities.
Moreover, with its Cash Management Account (CMA) Merrill Lynch
has created a financial instrument that is directly competitive with
checking accounts offered by depository financial institutions. Yet
Merrill Lynch is able to offer investment banking and insurance services to customers, functions traditionally prohibited to depository
financial institutions. It would not be surprising to find that these
types of innovative services offered by Merrill Lynch and other nondepository financial institutions had indeed reduced secularly the
market share of depository financial institutions.

The money market mutual fund provides another example of the
growth of nondepository financial institutions that may result in a
permanent reduction in the market share of depository financial
institutions. A money market fund is a mutual fund that invests in
short-term, high-quality money market instruments such as Treasury bills, commercial paper, and bankers' acceptances. Only about
ten years old, money market funds have grown enormously, as
shown in Table 1–3. Total assets exceeded $200 billion in early 1983
(more than three times the total assets accumulated by the entire
credit union industry in its history) and represented more than 10
percent of total household deposits.[4]

Table 1-2.   Services Offered by Merrill Lynch and Co., 1981.

Securities Services

Broker and dealer
Commodity futures and options broker
Security underwriting
Investment banking
International merchant banking
Leasing
Dealer in U.S. government and government agency securities
    and in money market instruments
Margin lending
Securities research
Investment counseling
Sale and management of mutual funds
Cash management account

Insurance Services

Mortgage cancellation life insurance
Other life insurance
Annuities
Insurance to real estate lenders against default risk
"Directed" life insurance

Real Estate and Related Services

Real estate financing
Mortgage banking
Real estate management services
Brokerage
Employee relocation

Source: Merrill Lynch and Co.

Money market funds were originated in the early 1970s in order to offer the small saver a market rate of interest at a time when the rates available at depository financial institutions were limited by Regulation Q ceilings. Moreover, many money market funds have offered a number of convenient services that have proven attractive to savers. Perhaps the most significant of these services is the ability to write checks against the value of the account. To a considerable degree, the phased elimination of interest rate ceilings and the widening of the authority to offer checkable deposits allowed depository institutions by the Depository Institutions Deregulation and Mone-

Table 1-3. Assets of Money Market Funds, 1973–1983 (*billions of dollars*).

Year	Total Assets	Percent of Household Deposits
1973	—	0.0
1974	2.4	0.3
1975	3.7	0.4
1976	3.7	0.3
1977	3.9	0.3
1978	10.8	0.8
1979	45.2	3.1
1980	74.4	5.1
1981	181.9	N.A.
1982	206.9	N.A.
1983[a]	176.2	N.A.

a. 1983 data are as of the end of the second quarter.

Source: Board of Governors of the Federal Reserve System, *Flow of Funds Accounts.*

tary Control Act of 1980 and the Garn-St Germain Depository Institutions Act of 1982 represent a response to the financial pressures placed on depository financial institutions by the growth of money market funds.

Theoretical Evidence

There is still more indirect and theoretical evidence consistent with a secular decline in the market share of depository financial institutions. This evidence relates to the rate and extent of regulatory constraints placed on depository as compared to nondepository financial institutions. If one group of financial institutions faces greater regulatory constraints than another group, it might be expected that the first group would, due to relatively diminished ability to provide innovative financial services, experience a decline in market share. Such an argument may be made for depository as compared to nondepository financial institutions.[5] For example, depository financial institutions must hold reserves against checkable deposits and against nonpersonal time deposits. Nondepository financial institutions are not required to hold reserves against their liabilities. This lack of reserve requirements is especially relevant for money market funds that offer direct competition to the savings accounts of depository financial institutions. Moreover, the importance of this "tax" arising from reserve requirements for depository institutions has increased as interest rates have risen. As another example of the differential burden of regulation, depository institutions have (until recently) faced Regulation Q ceilings on the rates they may offer for deposit funds. In contrast, nondepository institutions have faced no such limitations on the rates they pay to obtain funds. As discussed above, this was the principal reason for the phenomenal growth of money market mutual funds, and here, as above, the significance of this restraint became greater as interest rates increased.

There are numerous other examples of differing regulations of depository and nondepository financial institutions that may have contributed to a secular decline in the market shares of depository institutions. Depository financial institutions face substantial restrictions on the geographic extent of their operations. At the extreme, commercial banks in unit banking states, such as Texas, are prohibited from operating at more than one location. In addition, the pressures resulting from technological changes, such as the spread of sophisticated data processing equipment, have affected depository and nondepository institutions differently. In using this new technology, especially as it interfaces with customers, depository financial institutions have dealt with numerous regulatory burdens. No such constraints have faced nondepository institutions. As a result, nondepository institutions appear to have some cost advantages in applying electronic technology relative to the financial services industry, and these advantages may further erode the market share of depository financial institutions.

Blurring and Overlapping of Functions

Perhaps as important as the cyclical and secular changes in the market shares of depository financial institutions is the increasing homogeneity of sources and uses of funds. This homogenization of function is often referred to as a "blurring of functions" or "overlapping of functions" in the financial marketplace. (The growing overlap in functions is illustrated in Table 1–4). Whatever it is called, it repre-

Table 1-4. Financial Services Offered by Depository and Non-Depository Institutions.

Financial Services

	Banks	S&Ls	Insurance Companies	Retailers	Securities Dealers
Checking	□ ●	●	●	●	●
Saving	□ ●	□ ●	●	●	●
Time Deposits	□ ●	□ ●	●	●	●
Installment Loans	□ ●	●	●	●	●
Business Loans	□ ●	●	●	●	●
Mortgage Loans	●	□ ●	●	●	●
Credit Cards	●	●	●	□ ●	●
Insurance			□ ●	●	●
Stocks, Bonds			●	●	□ ●
Mutual Funds			●	●	□ ●
Real Estate			●	●	●
Interstate Facilities			●	●	●

□ 1960
● 1982

Source: Donald L. Koch and Delores W. Steinhauser, "Challenges for Retail Banking in the 80's," Federal Reserve Bank of Atlanta, *Economic Review*, May 1982, p. 14.

sents a remarkable change in the role of individual financial institutions. The importance of these changes for the future availability of credit from depository institutions will be discussed below in the chapters devoted to the implications of the Depository Institutions Deregulation and Monetary Control Act of 1980 and the Depository Institutions Act of 1982. However, numerous changes have already occurred in the role of these institutions, changes appropriate to discuss at this point.

It is important to recognize that each depository financial institution in the United States began as a highly specialized organization designed to fulfill very specific financial demands.[6] *Commercial banks* began as institutions designed to provide financial services to businesses. Funds were provided by demand deposits from businesses, and loans were made for short-run operating purposes to business firms. Savings deposit funds were generally not sought from individuals nor were consumer loans made in any quantity. In addition, permanent real estate loans were usually viewed as outside the province of the banking function. Other depository financial institutiont exhibited similar degrees of specialization.

Savings and loan associations were originally formed as temporary cooperative building societies. Members pooled their funds and drew from the pool when they built a house. When all of the members had exhausted their financing needs for home ownership, the pool was disbanded. Later, these building societies were established on a more permanent basis, but their functions remained the same—to channel the funds of small savers into credit made available for the purchase of real property, primarily single family dwellings. In many ways similar to savings and loan associations, *mutual savings banks* had become important as a financial intermediary earlier in the U.S. history, but their growth has been much less significant. Formed primarily to provide an outlet for the savings of "new immigrants" during the 19th century, mutual savings banks placed a substantial proportion of their funds in real estate, primarily single family mortgages. The degree of concentration of their portfolio, however, has never been as great as for savings and loans. In addition, the growth of mutual savings banks has been retarded by the lack of explicit chartering legislation in most states. Mutual savings banks operate under state charters, and only a few states—principally those in the northeastern portion of the nation—have legislation allowing their operation.

The fourth and final depository financial institution is the *credit union*, the newest and the smallest of the nation's depository financial institutions. Founded in the early 20th century, when it was transplanted to the United States from Europe, credit unions were designed to fill a void in the financial services industry in that consumer credit—usually small personal loans, often unsecured—was generally available from financial institutions at acceptable rates. While pawn shops and illegal "loan sharks" were sources of personal loans, commercial banks, savings and loan associations, and mutual savings banks were unable or unwilling to provide this type of credit. Credit unions concentrate on various types of consumer credit, with emphasis on durable goods such as automobiles, and finance these loans and other uses of funds with savings deposits and small certificates of deposit accounts.

Each of the four types of depository financial institutions was created to fulfill a particular demand for a special type of financial service. Yet with changes in the nature of the economy and changes in the regulations that govern the operations of individual financial institutions, as well as with developments in technology, the demands for financial services have been altered. An agrarian society with limited technology will necessarily demand different financial services than a sophisticated industrial society with advanced technology and electronic methods of communications available. Changes in the demands for financial services as the U.S. economy has developed and expanded have produced profound changes in the roles of the individual depository institutions. Some of these changes are illustrated with the use of Tables 1–5 through 1–8 which show the change in the portfolio composition of depository financial institutions from 1950 through 1982. Figure 1–1 represents some of the important changes in the composition of assets of depository institutions.

Commercial banks have experienced some major changes in their sources and uses of funds, reflecting changes in the demands for financial services at these financial institutions. Examining first their sources of funds, perhaps the most significant impact (as shown in Table 1–5) has been the sharp drop in demand deposits and the related increase in time and savings deposits. At one time demand deposits were the principal source of bank funds (both absolutely and relatively), but the composition of deposits has changed markedly. The passbook savings account has shrunk dramatically as Regulation Q ceilings made this vehicle unattractive, while various types of time deposits—especially the six-month market and large certificates of deposit and more recently the money market deposit account—have come to dominate the deposit structure of commercial banks. Reflecting these changes in sources of funds, as well as other considerations, bank asset composition (uses of funds) has also changed substantially. Holdings of U.S. government securities (abnormally large at the conclusion of World War II) have been reduced, while banks have acquired large amounts of state and local government issues in order to reduce their effective tax burden. Total loans have increased as a percentage of total bank assets, responding to strong loan demand and the willingness of bank managers to accept a higher risk portfolio. Equally significant, the composition of the loan portfolio has diversified. The traditional emphasis on

Figure 1–1. Distribution of Financial Assets of Depository Financial Institutions, 1960 and 1981.

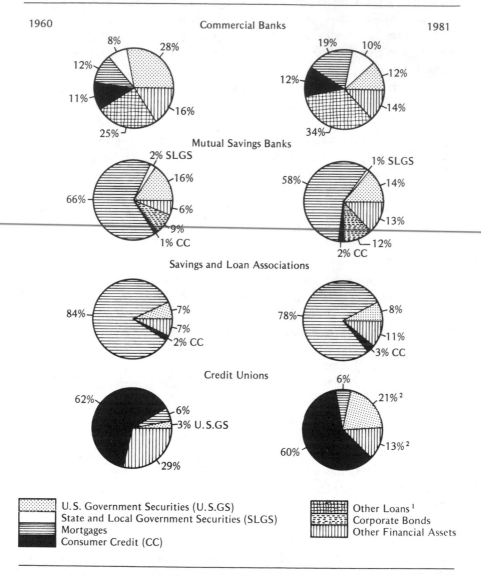

U.S. Government Securities (U.S.GS)
State and Local Government Securities (SLGS)
Mortgages
Consumer Credit (CC)

Other Loans[1]
Corporate Bonds
Other Financial Assets

1. Primarily business loans.

2. The shift in credit union assets from other assets to U.S. Government Securities resulted primarily from a shift out of deposits at S&Ls.

Source: B. Frank King, "Depository Institutions: Trends Show Major Shifts," Federal Reserve Bank of Atlanta, *Economic Review* (June 1983), p. 49.

Table 1–5. Portfolio Composition for Commercial Banks, 1950–1982 (percent of total assets).

Year	U.S. Government Securities	State and Local Government Securities	Mortgage Loans	Consumer Loans	Demand Deposits	Time Deposits
1950	42.9	5.4	9.0	4.9	63.8	24.6
1955	34.5	6.8	11.1	7.0	60.8	26.7
1960	27.7	7.6	12.5	8.9	54.2	32.0
1965	19.2	11.3	14.4	10.3	43.2	42.9
1970	14.8	13.5	14.0	10.4	36.6	44.9
1975	13.7	11.8	15.6	10.3	27.8	52.2
1980	12.6	10.9	19.4	12.9	23.6	56.1
1981[a]	13.2	11.4	21.1	13.2	25.4	59.3
1982[a]	14.2	10.8	20.5	12.9	24.9	61.8

a. For 1981 and 1982, demand deposit data includes *all* checkable deposits.

Source: Board of Governors of the Federal Reserve System, *Flow of Funds Accounts.*

short-term, self-liquidating commercial loans has been sharply curtailed. Increasingly, the attitude of bank managers has been to make
any legitimate loan that meets appropriate risk levels. This change
in attitude, as well as strong demand, has produced a substantial
increase in mortgage and consumer loans as shown in Table 1–5.
Yet, as commercial banks have increased their commitment to mortgage loans, they have become more like and more competitive with
savings and loan associations. Similarly, as commercial banks increased their emphasis on consumer loans, they have become more
like and more competitive with credit unions. Both developments
provide excellent examples of the "blurring of function" among depository institutions that has been occurring for decades, though at
a more rapid rate in recent years.

Similar, though less pronounced, changes have occurred at savings
and loan associations, as shown in Table 1–6. In terms of sources
of funds, the principal change has been the marked reduction of
the passbook account and the phenomenal increase in certificate
accounts, especially the explosive growth of six-month money market certificates. The Depository Institutions Deregulation and Monetary Control Act of 1980 allowed savings and loans and other nonbank depository institutions to offer negotiable order of withdrawal
(NOW) accounts nationwide for the first time. These liability powers
were further broadened with passage of the Garn-St Germain Deposi-

Table 1–6. Portfolio Composition for Savings and Loans, 1950–1982
(*percent of total assets*).

Year	Mortgages	Consumer Credit	U.S. Government Securities
1950	80.1	1.2	8.8
1955	83.4	1.3	6.3
1960	84.0	1.4	7.1
1965	85.0	1.0	6.3
1970	85.0	1.2	6.2
1975	82.4	0.9	6.7
1980	80.0	2.8	7.4
1981	78.2	3.1	8.1
1982	68.3	2.9	12.5

Source: Board of Governors of the Federal Reserve System, *Flow of Funds Accounts.*

tory Institutions Act of 1982, under whose authority the money market deposit accounts were created to compete with money market funds.

The principal changes in the portfolio of savings and loans have occurred on the asset side of the balance sheet, as shown in Table 1-6. Cash assets and U.S. government security holdings (except in 1982) have been reduced as a percentage of total assets, reflecting the rising interest rate environment of recent years. Mortgage loans have maintained their dominance of the uses of funds at savings and loans, though the types of mortgage loans made by the industry have broadened. An increasing amount of mortgages has taken the form of mortgage pools (such as the "GNMA" issues, insured by the Government National Mortgage Association), rather than locally originated mortgages. (These mortgage pools are treated as U.S. government securities in Table 1-6 and account for the increase in 1982.) Moreover, consumer credit has begun to account for a more significant share of the total uses of funds. Until recently, most of the consumer credit extended by savings and loans was for housing-related purposes. However, under the Depository Institutions Deregulation and Monetary Control Act of 1980 and the Depository Institutions Act of 1982, the industry has much wider consumer-lending powers. In terms of functional overlap and competition with other depository institutions, the ability to offer checkable deposits in the form of NOW accounts obviously provides substantial overlap with commercial banks that have traditionally had a monopoly of transactions accounts. Similarly, as savings and loans penetrate consumer lending more actively, they become more like and more competitive with commercial banks and credit unions.

Mutual savings banks and credit unions have perhaps experienced less change in sources and uses of funds than commercial banks. Both institutions have experienced shifts to savings certificate accounts as at savings and loans, and both now offer transactions accounts. At mutual savings banks, cash asset holdings have remained a relatively small fraction of total assets. As shown in Table 1-7, mortgage holdings have also fluctuated cyclically, while holdings of U.S. government securities have declined (except in 1982). At credit unions, consumer credit continues to dominate the uses of funds, though mortgage loans have some significance, as shown in Table 1-8. Both financial institutions are now in direct competition with commercial banks for checking accounts. Moreover, the recent authority to

Table 1-7. Portfolio Composition for Mutual Savings Banks, 1950-1982 (*percent of total assets*).

Year	Mortgages	Consumer Credit	U.S. Government Securities
1950	36.8	0.3	48.4
1955	55.1	0.3	26.7
1960	65.0	0.5	16.9
1965	75.5	0.9	10.7
1970	73.0	1.4	6.7
1975	63.7	1.5	8.9
1980	57.8	2.4	8.0
1981	57.0	3.1	8.1
1982	54.2	2.5	13.7

Source: Board of Governors of the Federal Reserve System, *Flow of Funds Accounts.*

Table 1-8. Portfolio Composition for Credit Unions, 1950-1982 (*percent of total assets*).

Year	Home Mortgages	Consumer Credit	U.S. Government Securities
1950	6.9	61.7	9.4
1955	6.0	57.6	4.6
1960	6.0	62.5	3.1
1965	5.3	66.4	3.1
1970	4.3	72.2	7.6
1975	4.3	68.5	13.6
1980	6.1	62.2	19.2
1981	6.5	62.6	19.3
1982	6.2	53.3	13.1

Source: Board of Governors of the Federal Reserve System, *Flow of Funds Accounts.*

offer permanent, long-term mortgage loans for credit unions increases the degree of competition between credit unions and savings and loans, and indeed between credit unions and all other depository institutions.

This brief review of some of the major portfolio changes at depository financial institutions should make clear the profound homogenization in function that has been occurring at depository financial institutions. This homogenization is likely to proceed further as the result of regulatory changes mandated by the Depository Institutions Deregulation and Monetary Control Act of 1980 and the Depository Institutions Act of 1982. Depository financial institutions are more alike today than they were at the end of World War II, and they are likely to become more alike in the future. Whether they will ever become identical, however, remains to be seen. Developments discussed in succeeding chapters of this book have important implications for that question.

CAUSES OF FINANCIAL DEREGULATION

There are a large number of factors that, in cumulative and progressive fashion, have produced the trend toward financial deregulation. These pressures have been building for many years. They resulted in numerous unsuccessful attempts prior to 1980 to enact legislative reform of the financial services industry. Finally, in 1980 and again in 1982, the pressures were sufficiently large to overcome legislative inertia, and major reform legislation was passed by Congress and signed by Presidents Carter and Reagan, respectively.

K. W. Colton has pointed to the following groups pressing for change in the financial system as being instrumental in the ultimate passage of the legislation: (1) the federal government, especially the U.S. Congress; (2) regulatory agencies; (3) concerned industries (including financial institutions and the housing industry); (4) technological innovations; (5) public and consumer pressure; and (6) changing economic and market conditions.[7] Many of these factors may overlap (and there may be other factors of substantial importance), but these six pressures appear to be of major significance.[8]

Federal Government. The federal government, through its legislative and executive branches, is obviously greatly concerned about the functioning of the nation's depository institutions. Indeed, the financial system of the United States could not work effectively unless the major depository institutions were performing their deposit-taking and credit-making functions effectively. The concern of the federal government with depository institutions is especially pronounced during periods of uncertainty and stress on these institutions. It is not surprising that the high and volatile interest rate period that began in 1966 stimulated the federal government to adopt a strategy of reform in regard to its control of financial institutions (though it perhaps is surprising that this strategy involved deregulation).

The initial actions of the federal government toward financial reform concentrated on the production of formal studies of the financial system. These included the Hunt Commission study in 1970, and the Financial Institutions and the Nation's Economy Discussion Principles prepared by the House Banking Committee in 1975.[9] While their proposals were quite similar to those ultimately adopted in the 1980 and 1982 bills, there was insufficient concern by Congress (most likely reflecting insufficient pressure on Congress by special-interest groups) to pass such legislation. Not until the extraordinarily high interest rate period from 1979 to 1981, and the serious problems of the thrift industry that accompanied it, was the federal government able to pass significant reform legislation.

Banking Regulatory Agencies.   Pressure for passage of reform legislation also came from the bank regulatory agencies. These agencies are naturally concerned with the viability of the institutions that they regulate. In particular, the Federal Home Loan Bank Board—the principal regulator of savings and loan associations—took an active role in pressing for financial reform legislation. While the prosperity of commercial banks was less affected by the high and volatile interest rates, the Federal Reserve nevertheless took a particularly strong position in seeking financial reform. This position reflected the existence of the "Fed membership problem" that refers to the diminished significance of member versus nonmember banks and the alleged negative effects of this trend for the ability of the Federal Reserve to control the nation's money supply.

Concerned Industries.   The passage of financial reform legislation also reflected the pressures on Congress from concerned industries. Depository institutions as a group sought legislative changes that would allow them to compete more effectively with their less regulated or unregulated competitors. The competitive position of depository institutions, relative to money market funds, was especially significant to managers of depository institutions who argued that Congress either should regulate money market funds (including imposition of reserve requirements) or deregulate the depository institutions. Managers of savings and loans, in particular, were active in seeking adjustments in the scope of the activities allowed their institutions as they feared the extinction of the industry under existing economic conditions and statutory limits on their powers. In addition, representatives of the housing industry often supported legislation that would liberalize the powers of savings and loans, the principal supplier of credit to the housing industry (though they also feared that such liberalization might cause the savings and loan industry to direct its credit outside of the housing industry).

Technological Change. Technological change was clearly one of the motivating factors producing major reform legislation. That the geographic scope of many financial institutions has traditionally been quite small reflects, in part, limitations of communication and transportation. With the developments that have occurred in electronic communication and transportation (loosely referred to as electronic funds transfer systems or EFTS), the geographical scope of the market for financial services has broadened greatly, encompassing the entire nation and, in some instances, the entire world. Yet the ability of depository institutions to install the latest electronic equipment available to the financial services industry has been reduced (at least as compared to nondepository institutions) by the existence of regulatory constraints.

Consumer Groups. Pressures by public and consumer groups on Congress also played a role in producing financial reform. This pressure was especially applied by spokesmen groups for the elderly (such as the Gray Panthers) who correctly argued that Regulation Q ceilings discriminated against the small saver (such as elderly people). They advocated elimination of Regulation Q so that depository institutions could pay market rates of interest. Yet it is difficult to justify deregulation of the liabilities of depository institutions without also deregulating the assets of these institutions. To some extent this consumer pressure reflects the extraordinary rise in financial sophistication of consumers of financial services. Spurred by rising levels of wealth and a higher level of education, households have become much more adept at managing their funds. There is little "lazy" money left in a high interest rate environment.

Economic Environment. The final factor that appears to have played a role in producing financial reform legislation is the turbulent economic and financial environment of recent years, characterized by high and volatile interest rates. The increased volatility of interest rates appears to stem, at least in part, from the change in October 1979 to a reserves-based operating policy by the Federal Reserve. The existing system of regulation and authority for depository institutions has clearly been less relevant in this environment. Volatility in the economic and financial environment appears to require flexibility in the powers of depository institutions. The volatility in economic and financial conditions also was much more easily dealt with by the less regulated nondepository institutions than by the tightly regulated depository institutions. Coupled with the unstable economic and financial environment has been the growing internationalization of the financial system and increasing competition by foreign depository institutions that usually are subject to considerably less regulation than domestic depository institutions. Additional discussion of these factors is provided in Chapter 3.

HIGHLIGHTS OF RECENT LEGISLATION

The two major pieces of legislation that have affected depository institutions are the Depository Institutions Deregulation and Monetary Control Act of 1980 (DIDMCA) and the Garn-St Germain Depository Institutions Act of 1982. (Background for these regulatory developments is provided in Table 1-9.) Since the details of the acts are discussed in later chapters, it is necessary here only to outline the basic features of the legislation. The 1980 DIDMCA provided, among other things, for the following:

Uniform Reserve Requirements. Once fully implemented, all depository institutions will be subject to the same reserve requirements; only the size and type of deposit will be relevant in determining reserve requirements.

Fed Services. Services provided by the Federal Reserve must, following passage of the 1980 legislation, be offered to all depository institutions and must be priced based upon the Fed's production costs plus a "normal" profit margin. Prior to passage of the legislation, the

Table 1-9. Regulatory Developments.

1972	NOW accounts were authorized for thrift institutions in Massachusetts. In the next few years, all New England thrifts were allowed to issue NOWs.
1973	The wild card experiment: The first use of ceiling-free, small denomination certificates of deposit. The certificate had a minimum maturity of four years; the experiment lasted four months. All depository institutions were allowed to participate.
1975	California state-chartered savings and loans were authorized to issue variable-rate mortgages. At the same time, a few national banks in California began to issue variable-rate mortgages.
1978	6-month money market certificates were authorized nationally for all depository institutions. California federally-chartered savings and loans were authorized to issue variable-rate mortgages.
1980	Authorization of the 2 1/2-year small saver certificate for all depository institutions. Passage of the DIDMCA: Extension of reserve requirements to all depository institutions. Creation of the DIDC. Allowed thrifts to invest 20 percent of assets in consumer loans. Allowed mutual savings banks to make business loans and accept business deposits.
1981	Introduction of nationwide NOW accounts. Introduction of the ceiling-free Individual Retirement Account. Introduction of the tax-exempt All Savers certificate of deposit.
1982	Several new accounts paying market-related rates were introduced: 91-day money market certificate 3 1/2-year ceiling-free deposit. 7-to-31 day time deposit. Passage of the Garn-St Germain Act: Capital assistance for ailing thrifts. Authorization of the money market deposit account. Increase allowable consumer loan percentage at thrifts to 30 percent. Authorized savings and loans to issue business loans and accept business deposits.
1983	Introduction of the Super NOW accounts. Lowering of minimum deposit on short-term certificates of deposit to $2,500 Elimination of ceiling rates on remaining time deposits.

Source: Daniel J. Vrabac, "Recent Developments at Banks and Nonbank Depository Institutions." Federal Reserve Bank of Kansas City, *Economic Review* (July–August 1983), p. 35.

Fed provided its services only to member banks and then generally without explicit cost.

Regulation Q.   The legislation began the process of eliminating interest rate ceilings on deposit accounts at all depository institutions. It created the Depository Institutions Deregulation Committee with instructions to phase-out interest rate ceilings and to eliminate those ceilings completely no later than early 1986.

Negotiable Orders of Withdrawal (NOW) Accounts.   The legislation authorized all depository institutions to offer interest-bearing transactions accounts, generally in the form of NOW accounts. For the first time on a nationwide basis, the traditional monopoly by commercial banks of transactions accounts was broken. Also, for the first time in almost fifty years, explicit interest payments on transactions accounts were allowed.

Savings and Loans.   The lending powers of savings and loans were broadened with passage of the 1980 legislation. In particular, the savings and loans were allowed to commit a substantial fraction of their assets to consumer loans. They were also given trust powers. The reforms of the powers of savings and loans contained in this legislation went a long way toward the creation of a "department store of family finance."

Usury Laws.   As interest rates rose throughout the 1960s and 1970s, those state laws that limit the interest rate charged on certain types of loans (commonly referred to as usury laws) became increasingly binding. Such laws particularly affected the flow of credit to the residential real estate market. The 1980 legislation pre-empted state usury ceilings for a number of types of loans (most notably for mortgages).

Turning to the Garn-St Germain Depository Institutions Act of 1982, the provisions of this legislation may be viewed in some respects as dealing with the problems that had not been resolved by the 1980 legislation. The earlier legislation had attempted to deal with the thrift institutions problem and to provide a gradual elimination of Regulation Q ceilings. By 1982, the thrift institutions problem had become a thrift institutions crisis, and it was becoming apparent that—in the extraordinarily high interest rate environment of 1981–82—a more rapid lifting of interest rate ceilings was necessary. Also, regulators needed additional flexibility in dealing with troubled depository institutions. As a result, the bill provided for:

FDIC/FSLIC Assistance for Floundering and Failing Institutions. In past years, the regulatory agencies had been constrained in arranging the purchase of a floundering or failing institution by restrictive laws on interstate acquisitions. The Act allowed interstate acquisitions of failing institutions according to the following priority schedule: (1) same type institution, same state; (2) same type institution, different state; (3) different type institution, same state; and (4) different type institution, different state.

Net Worth Certificates. The 1982 legislation provided for an exchange of debt (called net worth certificates) between depository institutions and the regulatory agencies. While of substantial legal significance in maintaining an adequate capital position for floundering and failing depository institutions, the economic importance of this portion of the 1982 legislation is quite small. Few institutions have sought such assistance.

Additional Thrift Institutions Restructuring. Savings and loans and other thrifts were given further powers to offer deposit-taking and lending services. Savings and loans were permitted to offer demand deposit services to qualified commercial, corporate, and agricultural customers, as well as to expand their consumer lending and to engage in a limited amount of commercial lending.

Money Market Deposit Accounts. Perhaps the most significant feature of the 1982 legislation was the provision instructing the Depository Institutions Deregulation Committee (DIDC) to create (within sixty days) a money market deposit account equivalent to and competitive with money market mutual funds. The DIDC did create such an instrument effective in December, 1982, as well as the Super-NOW account effective in January, 1983.

CONSEQUENCES OF DEREGULATION

Moving now from the causes of financial deregulation and the specific provisions of the major acts, we turn from description to speculation. Existing evidence of the effects of deregulation in other industries and the logic of the competitive model do, however, provide a basis for reasonable prediction. It is important to note that, at the same time that depository institutions are obtaining additional management discretion, they are also finding a change in the nature of remaining regulation and in the nature of the regulatory agencies that they confront. Perhaps the best example of such change is the broadened power of the Federal Reserve to set reserve requirements. Also, these remarkable changes in the financial services industry have not occurred in a domestic vacuum. They are a part of a worldwide trend that is changing the basic functions of financial institutions. These domestic and international developments interact, with developments in one country obviously having important implications for developments in another. With these considerations in mind, let us turn to some of the specific consequences of deregulation.

Functions of Depository Institutions. It appears highly likely that deregulation will result in a marked change in the functions of individual financial institutions. Certainly, savings and loan associations will become more like banks, and conversely, banks will become more like savings and loans. (Britain currently provides an excellent example of this merging of function between the thrifts and the commercial banks.) Whether this merging of functions will ever result in total overlap of services is questionable, though, since savings and loans appear to have some comparative advantage in the origination of mortgages and mortgage-related credit, and commercial banks to possess a corresponding advantage in commercial lending. At the same time that depository institutions are becoming more alike in their deposit-taking and credit-providing services, the depository institutions will become like other financial service firms. For example, the division between commercial banking and investment banking (a division that is unique among major nations to the United States) is rapidly being eroded. Unless checked by additional and more restrictive legislation, it appears likely that these functions will merge in the near future. The rapidity with which the gap between commercial and investment banking is being closed provides ample evidence of the validity of the adage that "bankers can innovate faster than regulators can regulate."

Prices and Availability of Financial Services. Certainly, the movement toward financial deregulation will affect the price and availability of financial services—to the benefit of most, though not all, consumers. A greater number of firms offering a given financial service should produce greater competition with resultant benefits to consumers. Removal of Regulation Q ceilings permits consumers to receive market rates of interest on their deposits. Similarly, greater competition in the credit market should produce a greater availability of credit at lower cost than would otherwise be the case in the absence of deregulation. At the same time, some consumers of financial services—those that have not been paying their own way—will be made worse off by deregulation as depository institutions reprice their services.

Profitability and the Number of Depository Institutions. If the expectation of greater competition, higher deposit rates, and lower loan rates is realized, then there should be substantial pressure on the profitability of depository institutions. While spreads should fall with growing competition for deposits and loans, it is not at all clear what the magnitude of the decline in profitability should or will be. It may be, for example, that declining spreads will be more than offset by more efficient operations in other areas of the institutions. In past years, restrictions on competition produced by regulation should have resulted in reduced efficiency (and higher cost) in providing financial services. Growing competition associated with less regulation should, to some extent at least, reverse this process.

To the extent that profitability is reduced by growing competition, however, the number of independent depository institutions should shrink as high-cost firms find it impossible to make an acceptable profit. (As shown in Table 1-10, the United States has a very large number of depository institutions.) The pricing flexibility offered to managers of depository institutions may also contribute to this reduction in the number of institutions. Managers of depository institutions under deregulation have greater flexibility in making decisions, greater opportunity to make correct decisions, and also greater opportunity to make incorrect decisions. Some of these incorrect decisions will result in failure of the organization, thereby reducing the number of independent entities.

It thus appears very likely that there will be consolidation among depository institutions. The question of the extent of such consolidation for depository institutions in general and for individual groups of depository institutions, however, remains. The extent of consolidation may be quite different, for example, for commercial banks as

Table 1-10. Number of Depository Financial Institutions (Insured and Noninsured) in the United States.

Year	Commercial Banks Number of Charters[a]	Banking Units[b]	Mutual Savings Banks[c]	Savings and Loans[d]	Credit Unions[e]	Total Units[f]
1960	13,484	13,105	515	6,320	20,456	39,936
1965	13,818	13,403	506	6,185	22,119	42,213
1970	13,705	12,931	494	5,669	23,699	42,793
1971	13,804	12,951	490	5,474	23,284	42,199
1972	13,950	12,837	486	5,298	23,115	41,736
1973	14,194	12,630	482	5,170	22,999	41,281
1974	14,488	12,642	480	5,023	22,964	41,109
1975	14,654	12,688	476	4,931	22,703	40,798
1976	14,697	12,708	473	4,821	22,615	40,617
1977	14,740	12,750	467	4,761	22,407	40,385
1978	14,741	12,753	465	4,725	22,177	40,120
1979	14,738	12,815	463	4,684	22,002	39,964
1980	14,870	12,787	460	4,592	21,731	39,570
1981	14,882	12,693	441	4,347	20,814	38,235

a. Includes 480 banks not insured by FDIC in 1981.
b. Banking Units = (Commercial banks + bank holding companies – bank subsidiaries of bank holding companies).
c. Includes 111 banks not insured by FDIC in 1981.
d. Includes 568 savings and loan associations not insured by FSLIC in 1981.
e. Includes 3,581 credit unions not insured by NCUSIF in 1981.
f. Banking units, savings and loan associations, mutual savings banks, credit unions, and securities dealers.

Source: B. Frank King, "Depository Institutions: Trends Show Major Shifts," Federal Reserve Bank of Atlanta, *Economic Review* (June 1983), p. 50.

compared with savings and loans. What the resulting structure of the depository institutions industry will look like after the consolidation has been completed is also open to question.

There are a number of different estimates of the ultimate degree of consolidation. For example, the bank consulting firm of Golembe Associates sees a potential decline in the number of commercial banks of from 30 to 50 percent. This would leave roughly 7,000 to 10,000 commercial banks in the United States, though a lesser number of independent entities. In contrast, consolidation among savings and loans would be less substantial (in view of the prederegulation consolidation that has already occurred) so that the number of savings and loans may shrink only by about 10 percent. Additional evidence is provided by the consulting firm of McKinsey and Company. Drawing upon experience with deregulation in other industries, they envision the banking and financial services industry as evolving into a three-tier structure, encompassing a few national financial institutions offering a wide range of financial services. It would include some highly specialized, low-cost producers and a number of firms specializing in less price-sensitive markets.

It is important to note that neither of these studies implies that small community banks will fail in this deregulated environment. Given the evidence that economies of scale in providing most financial services are quite limited, any cost disadvantages of community banks (and thrift institutions) are likely to be quite small. As long as financial services remain highly personal in nature, the ability of well-run community organizations to survive and prosper appears unthreatened.

Depository Institutions Failure. With diminishing profit margins, growing competition, and with increased management discretion permitting managers to make greater mistakes, the incidence of failure should rise, at least relative to what it would be in the absence of deregulation. The incidence of failure will obviously be greatly affected also by the stability of the economy and the level of interest rates. If the failures are limited to small institutions, the effects on the financial system should be limited. However, if, as appears likely, a significant number of large depository institutions fail, this could be the trigger that ultimately produces interstate banking (which appears now to be coming more rapidly than had earlier been thought). Failures of large organizations will also place great pressure on the federal deposit insurance system and may produce fundamental changes in the nature of deposit insurance, possibly including changes in pricing, scope of coverage, and in the operating procedures of deposit insurance agencies.

Regulatory Consolidation. As depository institutions become more alike (and this appears certain, with only the degree of similarity open to question), it becomes less and less reasonable to have multiple overlapping federal regulatory agencies. Some consolidation among the regulatory agencies may thus be expected. One step in this direction may be the merging of the FDIC and FSLIC insurance funds. More fundamentally, it seems reasonable to expect that the regulatory functions of the Federal Reserve will at some point be merged with those of the FDIC, the Comptroller of the Currency, the FSLIC, and the National Credit Union Administration. What the resulting agency may resemble is uncertain, though its shape will most likely be determined as much by political as by economic considerations.

Interest Rates and Monetary Policy.   It also appears likely that the deregulation phenomenon will have some important effects on the operations of monetary policy. In past years, when Regulation Q was fully operative, the Federal Reserve could restrain the economy through a combination of availability and interest rate effects; that is, the Fed was able, partially though not completely, to curtail the availability of credit from depository institutions by making it difficult or impossible for these institutions to acquire new funds. With the elimination of Regulation Q, however, the Fed must rely entirely on the interest rate to restrain the demand for credit. As a result, it seems likely that, in periods of tight money, interest rates will rise further than they would have before deregulation. This volatility of interest rates (made more volatile by the October 1979 change in operating procedures by the Federal Reserve) certainly has important domestic implications. It also has international implications since the volatility of interest rates may produce more volatile exchange rates between the dollar and important foreign currencies.

There are other implications of the deregulation and reregulation movement for the conduct of monetary policy. As noted earlier, the 1980 legislation sharply increased the powers of the Federal Reserve in its central banking function. With its control over reserve requirements for all depository institutions and its additional powers to acquire assets, the Fed now has greater power to pursue the "right" monetary policy (and also a greater degree of discretion to pursue the "wrong" policy).

CONCLUSIONS AND IMPLICATIONS

The basic role of depository institutions in their deposit-taking and credit-granting functions has changed dramatically in recent years.

Competition among different depository institutions and between depository institutions and nondepository financial institutions has intensified dramatically. As a result, depository institutions have become much more alike.

The major factors producing these changes include pressures from the Congress, the regulatory agencies, and the involved industries. Fundamentally, however, the changes in the role of depository institutions reflect market forces—high and volatile interest rates and rapidly changing technology in particular. A tightly regulated, limited-function financial institution may have been the appropriate type of firm in a period of stable interest rates and static technology. Clearly, though, such a system is inappropriate for an economy experiencing volatile interest rates and rapidly changing technology.

Two major pieces of legislation have substantially altered the ground rules under which depository institutions operate, the Depository Institutions Deregulation and Monetary Control Act of 1980 and the Garn-St Germain Depository Institutions Act of 1982. Taken together, these pieces of legislation will undoubtedly revolutionize the financial services industry, affecting depository institutions directly and nondepository institutions indirectly. There is little doubt that depository institutions will operate with lower levels of profitability, that there will be consolidation in the number of institutions (partially through the failure of existing institutions), and that the regulatory system will itself have to undergo fundamental change.

NOTES TO CHAPTER 1

1. A more extensive discussion of the changes that have occurred in the role of individual depository (and nondepository) institutions may be found in the following: Robert O. Edmister, *Financial Institutions: Markets and Management* (New York: McGraw-Hill, 1980); Murray Polakoff, *Financial Institutions and Markets*, 2nd edition (Boston: Houghton-Mifflin, 1981); and Peter S. Rose and Donald R. Fraser, *Financial Institutions*, 2nd edition (Dallas: Business Publications, Inc., 1984).

2. On October 1, 1983, all time deposit rate ceilings were removed on accounts with maturities greater than thirty-one days. Only deposits with maturities less than thirty-one days and minimum balances of less than $2,500 remained regulated.

3. Contradictory data was provided by the Federal Reserve Bank of Minneapolis in its 1982 annual report. Computing a five-year, moving average of total

credit market debt claims against nonfinancial sectors, this report shows a relatively constant market share for commercial banks from 1965 to 1982. Nonbank savings institutions gained market share in the 1950s and 1960s, and maintained their market share in the 1970s. As a result, the market shares of depository institutions as a group actually increased over the period. However, taking a longer perspective, Berger points out that the share of the banking system in total financial intermediation has declined sharply since the early 1930s. See: "Are Banks Special?" *Federal Reserve Bank of Minneapolis, 1982 Annual Report*, pp. 2–24; and Frederick Berger, "The Emerging Transformation of the U.S. Banking System," *The Banker* (September 1981), pp. 25–39.

4. Money market funds accounts are, in substance, deposits even though they legally are equity shares. As such, it might be justifiable to view money market funds, as economic institutions, to be depository institutions even though the traditional definition of a depository institution does not en compass money market funds

5. For a more complete discussion of this argument see Thomas A Lawler, "On the Nature and Causes of Financial Innovations by Nondepository Firms" (Paper presented at the 1981 Western Finance Association Meeting).

6. Additional information on the historical evolution of depository institutions is available in a chapter entitled "The Evolution of U.S. Money and Capital Markets and Financial Intermediaries," in Murray Polakoff, *Financial Institutions and Markets*, pp. 33–54.

7. Kent W. Colton, *Financial Reform: A Review of the Past and Prospect for the Future* (The Office of Policy and Economic Research, Federal Home Loan Bank Board, September 1980).

8. Silber points to the following factors that have contributed to rapid financial innovation: (1) inflation, (2) volatility of interest rates, (3) technology, (4) legislative initiative, and (5) internationalization. Cargill and Garcia [*Financial Deregulation and Monetary Control* (Stanford, Ca.: Hoover Institution Press, 1982)] point to the following structural problems that ultimately produced financial deregulation: Regulation Q; the monopoly by commercial banks over demand deposits; restrictions on entry in a number of financial markets; restraints on the uses of funds by financial institutions; and state-imposed usury laws and other interest rate ceilings. See also: William L. Silber, "The Process of Financial Innovation," *American Economic Review* (May 1983), pp. 89–95.

9. It is interesting to note that the recommendations of these two groups were very similar to those adopted in the Depository Institutions Deregulation and Monetary Control Act of 1980 and the Garn-St Germain Depository Institutions Act of 1982. For example, the Hunt Commission recommended that nonbank depository institutions be allowed to offer transactions accounts and that they receive broader lending authority. In addition, the

Hunt Commission recommended that Regulation Q be eliminated, though only gradually and over a ten-year period. With regard to reserve requirements, the Hunt Commission recommended mandatory membership in the Federal Reserve System for all state chartered banks and for savings and loans and mutual savings banks that offered transactions accounts. In addition, the Financial Institutions and the Nation's Economy Discussion Principles recommended the following: (1) permission for all depository institutions to offer transactions accounts; (2) broader powers for thrifts, particularly in making consumer loans and issuance of credit cards and trust power; (3) Federal Reserve requirements applicable to all depository institutions, though with a five-year transition period; and (4) elimination of Regulation Q ceilings with no more than a five-year delay from passage of the proposed legislation.

2 THE RATIONALE AND RECORD OF DEPOSITORY INSTITUTION REGULATION

Since their emergence as significant economic organizations, banks and other depository institutions have generally been highly controlled and regulated by governments. The root cause of such government intervention in banking almost certainly lies in the financial power wielded by banks. Beginning with European monarchies, governments sought to tap the financial power of banks to preserve and enhance their political power. One reason these governments restricted banking was in order to preserve the government monopoly on the creation of money. The purpose of retaining this particular government monopoly was unrelated to the modern macroeconomic objective of money supply control. Rather, governments sought to gain *seignorage* —the difference between the cost of producing money and its value as a means of exchange. Governments also regulated early banks in order to tax them and to gain access to low-interest loans.[1] Indeed, central banking evolved out of this early recognition of the inherent power that resided in the ability of banks to provide credit and create money.

Both the means and purposes of banking regulation have changed greatly since its inception. The purpose of this chapter is to review and assess the reasons for regulating depository institutions, relating the economic rationale for regulation to the events that forged the present regulatory structure in the United States. Effects of regulation—both intended and unintended regulatory consequences—are identified. While we begin rather abstractly and theoretically, our discussion of the historical development of regulation will include reference to more concrete arguments that have characterized the discussion of banking regulation in the political arena. The theoretical discussion will establish an analytical framework for the policy perspectives addressed in the latter part of this book; concrete examples will serve as a bridge to the political realities (including the pleadings of special-interest groups) that inevitably loom larger in the forging of public policy than abstract economic theorizing.

THE ECONOMIC BASIS FOR REGULATION

The case for free, unfettered markets as a mechanism for allocating scarce resources and otherwise directing economic systems is made in almost all introductory texts on economics published in this country. We need not review the general market model here. Rather, we need only note how an unregulated banking system would function—and note also the conspicuous contrast to the regulated reality.[2]

Model of a Competitive Banking System

A free banking system would necessarily include unrestricted entry and exit of banks. Banks would enter the market until excess profits (profits greater than necessary to maintain the presence of an optimal number of banks) were competed away. The market for banking services would assure that the pricing and availability of such services were in harmony with public demand for them. Free exit of banks would assure that relatively inefficient and superfluous banks would be flushed out of the system.

Banks would also operate without geographic or portfolio restrictions, free to branch where they pleased and borrow and invest as they pleased. Capital structure would be the prerogative of management. Only the imperatives of the market would operate to direct branching, investment, and funding decisions. Competition would limit branches to the number congruent with public preferences. The cost of a bank's funds would be determined by its business and financial risk profile. And, of course, the penalty for either excessive or inadequate expansion of risk-taking would be failure.

"Free banking," at least in its pure form, requires the absence of a central monetary authority. At a minimum, the exercise of monetary control almost certainly results in an aggregate *level* of banking assets and liabilities different from that which would emerge from a truly free banking system. In the application of monetary powers, central banks have invariably acted so as to affect the *composition* of bank assets and liabilities as well. Conceptually, however, none of the principal tools of monetary control utilized in this country—reserve requirements, open-market operations, or Fed discount window policy—need unduly compromise the competitive model. ("Moral suasion" and credit controls, however, are respectively an outgrowth and a means of direct regulation.) Reserve requirements constitute a tax on the banking system but, if equitably applied, do not interfere with the market mechanism any more than other uniformly applied taxes.

Out of a competitive, market-directed banking system would emerge the least-cost producers of the quantity and type of banking services desired by consumers. New technology would be embraced and put into place wherever and whenever consistent with the former outcome. Competition in the industry would be solely on the basis of the pricing and quality of service. Funding of banks—particularly the placement and pricing of deposits—would be consistent with the individual and aggregate risk-return preferences of the suppliers of funds. Similarly, the allocation of these funds to ultimate borrowers would reflect optimal risk-return outcomes. In sum, the "invisible hand" would have served to assure that the banking sector of the larger market economy was operationally and allocationally efficient.[3]

The Limits of the Market Model

The foregoing scenario could be a reality only if a number of implicit assumptions are valid. The most important of these assumed conditions depends on the relationship of firm size and cost structure, information availability (and credibility), and perceived and actual validity of contractual relationships entered into by transacting parties in the banking system. Certain assumptions bearing on these items must hold if any unregulated banking system is to result in an optimal allocation of resources (allocational efficiency) with a minimum expenditure of the resources required to bring about such an optimal allocation (operational efficiency). Departure from the assumed conditions means that some degree of "market failure" exists (the invisible hand wobbles). Flaws in the market model, however, are not necessarily the signal to institute regulation; the public policy issue is whether the costs imposed on society by these market imperfections are greater or less than the direct and indirect costs of a regulatory framework.

Economies of Scale

Competition is essential for a free banking system to operate in optimal fashion. Assuming away the government restrictions on entry that actually exist, there must be no barriers to entry or operating restrictions of *economic* origin. The existence of significant economies of scale in banking operations would be a "natural" competitive constraint. (Other non-government barriers to entry—sharply differentiated products and very large capital requirements—clearly do not exist in banking.) When operating economies of scale exist, total costs increase less than proportionately to output—average unit costs decrease as output increases.[4] Substantial economies of scale would lead to a concentration of banking and the withering away of the competitive environment necessary for maintenance of optimal cost-price structure and quality and availability of services. New, small banks could not enter the industry to compete with larger, established banks, and the latter would have a continuing incentive to grow larger through mergers and acquisitions in order to further lower their unit costs and enhance their competitive advantage. Anticompetitive collusion among the shrinking number of banks would likely prove an irresistible temptation. Another possible undesirable aspect of the banking consolidation that economies of scale would precipitate is a concentration of political and financial power in a relatively small number of banks.

Information

If the competitive banking model is to be economically viable, information relevant to the risk-return profile of individual banks must be fully and freely available to the public and must be used by all parties contracting with banks. In particular, suppliers of funds to banks—depositors, other creditors, and shareholders—must be aware of all aspects of the bank's financing and investment activities. Further, the benefits to the suppliers of bank funds of securing and analyzing such financial information must at least equal the costs of information search and analysis. Only if these conditions hold can there be assurance that the returns offered by banks to suppliers of funds is commensurate with the business and financial risks assumed by banks. In the absence of such information efficiency relative to banking activities, the market model will be a failure in this realm of the economy.

There are two principal market failure possibilities for financial information markets (each of which has several corollaries).[5] The first pertains to the nature of the information as being a "public good," that is, its provision to a single individual makes it equally and costlessly available to other individuals. Public goods lack the *exclusion* attribute of private goods: nonpurchasers cannot be excluded from consuming the good in question. Further, public goods possess *joint consumption* characteristics: one person's use of the good does not reduce the quantity or quality of the good that is available to other users. (National defense, parks, and museums are classic examples of the "joint consumption" attribute.) Since the absence of the exclusion attribute precludes functioning of the price mechanism, there is little or no incentive for private production of a public good, such as national defense. Even when the exclusion attribute is present (fees can be charged for admission to parks and museums), the joint consumption attribute means that a suboptimal amount of consumption of privately produced public goods will occur. If financial information is a public good, in the absence of government regulation (such as disclosure requirements), the amount of its production and dissemination would fall short of the quantity necessary for the informed investment decisions necessary for optimal resource allocation in the economy.

The second major information market failure possibility involves the *asymmetry* (unevenness) in the distribution of financial information among producers and users of the information. Asymmetric information may result in problems of the so-called "moral hazard" and "adverse selection" variety, familiar concepts in the field of risk and insurance. "Moral hazard," to an insurer, relates to the mental attitude of the insured party and that party's resulting behavior regarding the probability of a loss; the insured party knows this but the insurer does not. "Adverse selection" pertains to cases in which those individuals most likely to incur a particular type of loss are the only members of some larger group who apply for insurance protection against the loss. Moral hazard and adverse selection are thus both symptomatic of an asymmetry in the distribution of information between insurers and applicants for insurance, and this asymmetry increases uncertainty to the point where execution of insurance contracts is jeopardized.

The possibility that a similar asymmetry exists in the market for financial information is a potential source of market failure (or inefficiency) in this market. The fact that firms may have an incentive to withhold information or to issue fraudulent information has the same potential impact on the market for financial information as "moral hazard" and "adverse selection" on the market for insurance. Conceptual discussions of the adverse selection issue as it pertains to information markets usually refer to Akerlof's important paper on "lemons."[6] The sale of "lemons" (i.e., products with actual quality characteristics of less value than those perceived by the buyer at the time of purchase) increases product uncertainty and may lead to the collapse of a market as, in a variant of Gresham's Law, the bad goods or "lemons" drive out better goods.

While it is not universally agreed that concerns regarding the efficiency of a free market for financial information are valid, these concerns have led to an extensive regulatory framework for corporate financial disclosure in this country and other industrialized nations.[7] The Securities Acts of 1933 and 1934, which established the Securities Exchange Commission and mandated numerous financial disclosure requirements, are the basis for governance of the nature and extent of required disclosure of corporate activities.

The regulation of depository institutions, however, extends in scope far beyond the disclosure requirements that have been imposed on nonfinancial and financial corporations alike. One reason is that the implications of an imperfect information market (especially information asymmetries) are much more severe for financial intermediaries than for other business organizations. This is best understood by relating the information environment issue to that of contractual validity in the context of the market model of the banking system.

Agency and Contractual Problems

Why is the problem of asymmetric information presumed to be so much more acute for depository institutions than for other business corporations? While nonfinancial corporations must adhere to the statutory and regulatory framework regarding disclosure of information about their activities, their investment and financing decisions (with the exception of the "natural monopoly" industries such as utilities, communication, and transportation) remain largely the prerogative of management. Why not banks?

The difference lies in the very nature of the relationship between depository institutions and depositors. These financial intermediaries exist because of the unique characteristics of the assets they afford depositors—demand deposits (money) and highly liquid savings and time deposits. These deposits supply a combination of services and offer an interest return while providing liquidity and minimal risk to the depositor. The contractual relationship between the depositor and the depository institution assumes that funds deposited in demand accounts will indeed be available on demand and that other deposits (at face value) will be available to the depositor according to specified conditions.

Validity of contractual relationships is critical in a market system. While fraud, embezzlement, and other forms of contract violation inevitably occur, their occurrence must not be so frequent or pervasive as to jeopardize the general willingness of individuals and organizations to enter into contractual agreements, or market failure will ensue. In addition to the threat posed to contractual validity by these "expropriation" means, there exists what economists call the "problem of agency." The agency problem concerns performance by an agent under an agency contract such as that between depositors and depository institutions.

The problems of asymmetric information and moral hazard clearly hold for agency relationships. A party to a contract with an agent wants the agent to perform according to the contract but at the same time is aware that the agent's performance will be largely unmonitored. It is generally costly to monitor the behavior of an agent, even when government disclosure requirements mandate "free" provision of financial information. Thus a valuable feature of an agency contract is the right to withdraw (at the first sign of trouble) from the contractual arrangement.

Convenient and immediate exit from reliance on a particular agent is not always available to a contracting party, but it is certainly a feature of the depositor-depository institution relationship. A depositor can immediately withdraw demand funds *at their face value*, and time and savings deposits are also readily available. The cost of such withdrawals is minimal and certainly far less than the cost in time and money of monitoring activities of the institution in which funds are deposited. Further, the cost of withdrawal is surely less than diversifying across agency relationships by holding deposits in a number of banking institutions.

In this context, the "runs on banks" that have marked financial "panics" of past eras can be viewed as economically rational responses by depositors to real, apparent, or merely possible difficulties of banks. During such periods, when *some* banks experienced difficulty or outright failure (perhaps due to some violation of the agency accord, whether of the expropriation variety or simply overzealous pursuit of profitability at the expense of liquidity), depositors in other institutions lacked access to credible assurances that *their* banks were solvent. Thus they acted to obtain their funds, and triggered difficulty and failures for otherwise solvent institutions. This "domino effect" is a type of *external diseconomy*, as economists label such phenomena, stemming from the failure of banks.

To recapitulate, depositors place funds with banks and other depository institutions in order to secure deposit services and returns. In general, depositors lack convenient access to timely and relevant information about the financing and investing activities of institutions or the willingness and incentive to seek such information, or a combination thereof. Depositors must rely on the institution's management to maintain a degree of liquidity that assures the safety of their funds. They have no control over the actions of the management or knowledge of management's plans and intentions. Management has an incentive to pursue institution profitability, perhaps at the risk of maintaining adequate liquidity. In this situation, and in view of the depositors' right to immediate access to their funds, it is both understandable and inevitable that they will exercise that right when they become concerned about the viability of their bank. And the exercise of the withdrawal right by enough depositors will precipitate the bank difficulties or failure that was previously only a possibility.

The Economic Significance of Banking Market Failure

The special aspect of bank deposits that makes banking so susceptible to market failure—the immediacy of their availability—is also the source of banking's special economic significance. Bank demand deposits are the principal component of the money supply. The transactions accounts offered by banks and other depository institutions offer the liquidity, mobility, and acceptability necessary for our economy's payments system to function with ease and efficiency. Further, banks are the primary source of liquidity for other financial institutions and serve as the "transmission belt" for the implementation of monetary policy. A safe and sound banking system is thus viewed as essential for a nation's monetary system and financial marketplace.

The distinction between failure of an individual bank and difficulties in the banking system should be noted. Thousands of firms fail each year in the United States and the employees, owners, suppliers, and customers of these failed firms all suffer in varying degrees. Only when industrial firms on the brink of failure are very large (such as Lockheed and Chrysler) is there likely to be government intervention to save them.

It has been observed that, in many respects, a bank's failure is less injurious to affected parties than failure of other types of business ventures.[8] Bank employee skills are readily transferable, and customers generally have readily available alternatives. In the absence of government protection of depositors (such as deposit insurance), the households, business firms, and governmental units holding deposits in a failed bank will likely suffer losses, but this is true of creditors of any failed firm. What makes bank failure different is its contagious nature. There is ample historical evidence that widespread bank failure inflicts damage on the entire economy, and in an unregulated banking system, bank failures tend to spread in domino fashion. It is presumed that this social cost exceeds the direct and indirect costs of regulating bank failure risk.

EVALUATION OF THE ECONOMIC CASE
FOR BANKING REGULATION

The one dominant reason for government intervention in the banking sector is thus the prospect of failure in an unregulated banking market and the economic instability that would result. The "Task Group on Regulation of Financial Services," established in 1982, chaired by Vice-President Bush, and charged with the task of reviewing the current financial regulatory system and recommending changes, stated the following as the first of four goals of regulation: "Assuring safety and soundness of financial institutions, and of the financial system as a whole, both to protect individual depositors and to avoid or limit secondary effects of a failed institution."[9]

The other three goals as stated by the task group can also be related to the economic rationale described in the preceding pages: "avoiding conflict of interest, fraud, and consumer abuses; promoting orderly markets to encourage savings and capital formation and to support macroeconomic stability; and avoiding excessive concentrations of economic and financial resources." The second of these four goals is clearly a reflection of the possibilities for expropriation stemming from problems of agency and asymmetric information in the market for banking services. The third, "promotion of orderly markets . . . ," is closely linked to the first goal, but has implications for nonbank financial institutions beyond the latter goal. The fourth and final goal reflects the continuing concern about economies of scale in banking that would cause bigness to begat bigness.

The goals stated by the task group break no new ground, but rather reflect past and prevailing sentiments regarding the regulatory framework for depository institutions. Certainly most, if not all, elements of the extant regulatory structure can be traced to these goals. The next section of this chapter describes this structure and its historical evolution. Before moving to this topic, however, one aspect of the economic rationale for banking regulation—presumed monopolistic tendencies of banks—warrants one further note.

Banking Competition and Concentration

Economies of scale are believed to exist in the production and provision of communication, transportation, water, and power services.

All of these industries are regulated (in varying degrees) for this rea-son. Much of the regulation of depository institutions is attributable to supposed efforts to prevent the concentration that could result from possible economies of scale in banking, but is of a different nature than the regulation of transportation, communication, and public utility firms. Regulation of the latter firms is intended to pro-duce the pricing and quantity-of-production results of a competitive market. Regulation of banking is aimed at creating a competitive environment as well as simulating a competitive outcome, but with-out the exit aspects (failures) of truly competitive economic sectors. Charter, merger, and branching restrictions and other regulatory pro-visions are the principal instruments of this policy.

Entry restrictions regarding the establishment of new banking institutions are justified as preventing "overbanking," which presum-ably creates a threat to depository institution solvency (and thus "market failure") as well as being injurious to operational efficiency (excessive amounts of resources devoted to banking activities). Entry into the financial marketplace by new competitors is thus controlled by regulators. For example, to obtain a bank charter (a permit to operate commercial banking functions) an applicant must, among other things, establish that: (1) there is a need for a new bank; (2) the new bank will be profitable within a reasonable time; and (3) the chartering of the new bank will not cause substantial harm to exist-ing banks in the market areas. The last requirement appears to be rather anomalous in a competitive system. Not only must those who wish to start a new bank show that there is a need for a new firm (for most industries such need is demonstrated after the fact by the mar-ket test), but they must also show that no harm will be done to their competitors (in most industries the objective *is* to harm competitors). The purpose of such restrictions on entry is, of course, to limit bank failure stemming from competition, even though the result is likely to reduce the efficiency of the financial system's operations. Al-though this reduction in number of competing firms does limit the extent and significance of failures, the limitations on entry provide existing firms with the opportunity to earn a higher risk-adjusted return than would be possible with fewer restrictions on entry. In effect, restrictions on entry allow inefficient firms to earn "normal" profits.

Entry restrictions pertaining to expansion through branching and merger are similarly justified. Although "preservation of competition" is usually the principal argument here, risk of failure (as well as the overall performance of firms) is obviously affected by the number and size distribution of depository institutions ("structure" of the industry). In evaluating requests by existing firms to merge or establish branches, as well as by organizers of new firms to establish additional competitors, the regulatory authorities evaluate the impact of these developments on the safety and stability of other firms in the industry. Limitations on branching and attitudes toward mergers affect the degree of concentration (the share of the market controlled by a few firms) and thereby the stability of individual institutions.

It is clear that policies aimed at preventing banking concentration also have an underlying goal of preventing market failure. But it is well understood that attainment of the latter goal does not require restrictions on banking structure. Such restrictions can, in economic terms, be defended only on the grounds of preventing banking consolidation stemming from economies of scale.

Do significant economies of scale exist in banking? Probably not. There have been numerous empirical studies of this question,[10] and no definitive evidence has emerged that economies of scale exist to such a degree as to justify fears of the inevitability of massive banking concentration in the absence of regulatory restrictions on entry, merger, and branching. Then why is there so much regulation aimed at avoiding excessive concentration of economic and financial power? The answer lies not in theoretical considerations, but rather in the history of our banking system, the attitudes and beliefs of our citizens and their political representatives, and in the perceived economic interests of various groups in our society.

It has been suggested that much of the distrust that surrounds concentration of banking stems from the importance (and nature) of agriculture in the U.S. economy, and the special significance of access to credit for farmers.[11] Since the late nineteenth century, U.S. agriculture has been characterized by conditions of growing capital intensity and a chronic scarcity of capital resources. American farmers came to view a decentralized banking system of many small banks as most amenable to their financing needs. The concern was that large banks would drain funds from agricultural areas and use them for industrial financing. Agricultural interests certainly played a large role in the successful effort in the early part of this century to restrict branching by banks and to otherwise limit consolidation of the banking structure.

Concerns of agricultural interests about undue attention to commerce and industry (at the expense of farm financing) by banks contributed also to the emergence of a strong body of opposition in this country to affiliation of banks with nonfinancial enterprise. Such opposition was part of a broader concern over the concentration of economic power—a concern strongly rooted in other sectors of society in addition to agriculture. In time, the view that bank involvement in nonbanking activities would result in increased risk to bank depositors developed as a further argument for limiting the scope of allowable bank activities.

Much of the regulatory framework for U.S. depository institutions thus reflects social and political (as well as economic) phenomena, and this framework can best be assessed in light of the historical evolution of the American financial system.

EVOLUTION OF THE REGULATION OF DEPOSITORY INSTITUTIONS IN THE UNITED STATES

The American system of depository institution regulation is unique, and its peculiar structure reflects broader differences in the political and economic system of this country relative to the rest of the world. The importance of the individual states in our political structure, for example, accounts for a *dual* (federal and state) system of chartering and regulating depository institutions. The potent and pervasive concern over the concentration of power that can be traced to this nation's origins has played a central role in shaping the means and ends of U.S. financial regulation. Further, in a nation so philosophically committed to the free market ideal, regulation has been (and remains) viewed as, at best, a necessary evil.

The first real commercial banks in the United States were founded in the 1780s. Their "chartering" required special acts of the state legislature, a requirement that held until the "free banking" charter laws of various states were passed in 1837 and 1838. Even so, there were more than 300 commercial banks by 1830.

The First Bank of the United States (1791–1811) and the Second Bank of the United States (1816–1836) constituted this country's first tentative experiments with central banking and national influence on private sector banking operations. The banks served as a significant check on the issue of state bank notes by periodically presenting such notes for payment in specie, either coined gold or silver. (In this pre-checking-account era, each bank made loans by issuing its own notes, which were supposedly redeemable in specie.) The end of both banks (nonrenewal of their twenty-year charters) stemmed from opposition by banks and cheap-money advocates to this practice and from those who feared the concentrated financial power embodied in these national banks. The demise of the Second Bank marked the end of federal regulation of banking until 1863.

The Free Banking Era

In 1837, Michigan enacted a free bank chartering law; New York and Georgia followed with similar legislation the following year. By 1860, eighteen of the then thirty-two states in the United States had passed free banking statutes (see Table 2-1). While there were variations among the states, these laws essentially allowed banks to be chartered by any parties providing a prescribed amount of capital and securing notes of the new bank with a specified amount of bonds. The bonds were deposited with an agent of the state who would sell the bonds to satisfy calls for note redemption should the bank fail to do so.[12]

The free banking era gave rise to the term "wildcat bank" to describe the fact that many banks of the period were located in isolated, backwoods (and intentionally inaccessible) locations more agreeable to wildcats than to people trying to redeem bank notes in specie. Wildcat banking has now come to mean fraudulent banking, with banks being formed to issue notes that the bank organizers never intended to redeem in specie. The notes were simply printed and circulated, and the bank would be closed after they had all been distributed.

Irrespective of wildcat banking, the free banking era is considered to have been a failure insofar as the provision of a safe and stable banking system is concerned.[13] For example, of the 709 banks that opened for business under the free banking laws of New York, Indiana, Wisconsin, and Minnesota, only 370 remained in operation in 1863 (most of the failures occurred in the last three states). However, some states had few bank closings and maintained a stable banking system during this period. Notably, such states generally had some system of monitoring banking operations and less liberal entry requirements.

Table 2-1. A Majority of the Thirty-Three States in the Union in 1860 Had Some Form of Free Banking.

Eighteen States Had Explicit Free Banking Laws:		Twelve States Had No Form of Free Banking:	Three States Did Not Allow Free Entry, But Did Have Bond-Secured Note Issue:	
State	Year Passed Law	State	State	Year Passed Law
Michigan	1837[a]	Arkansas	Kentucky	1850
Georgia	1838	California	Virginia	1851
New York	1838	Delaware	Missouri	1858
Alabama	1849	Maine		
New Jersey	1850	Maryland		
Illinois	1851	Mississippi		
Massachusetts	1851	New Hampshire		
Ohio	1851[b]	North Carolina		
Vermont	1851	Oregon		
Connecticut	1852	Rhode Island		
Indiana	1852	South Carolina		
Tennessee	1852	Texas		
Wisconsin	1852			
Florida	1853			
Louisiana	1853			
Iowa	1858			
Minnesota	1858			
Pennsylvania	1860			

a. Michigan revoked this law in 1840, but passed another in 1857.

b. In 1845, Ohio passed a law that allowed "Independent Banks" with a bond-secured note issue.

Source: Hugh Rockoff, *The Free Banking Era: A Reexamination* (New York: Arno Press, 1975), p. 3.

The emergence of state insurance plans for banknotes and deposits also characterized this period. New York was the first (1829), followed by Vermont (1831), Indiana (1834), Ohio (1845), and Iowa (1858). In New York and Vermont, the note/deposit guarantee programs were operated by the state governments; in the others, the systems were based on mutual agreements among the participating banks.

The National Banking System

The problems of the state banking system were well recognized long before 1863, when the National Banking Act, which served to address many of these problems, was passed. The pressure of financing the Civil War proved to be more effective than concerns about the safety and soundness of the banking system in prompting Congress to act. The *national banking system* emerged as a consequence of the 1863 act and succeeding legislation. Under this series of statutes, the federal government began chartering national banks subject to reserve requirements, a portion of which had to be held in U.S. Treasury bonds.[14] A tax on state bank notes was instituted to "encourage" state banks to convert to national charters.

The tax on state bank notes was initially effective; there were more than 1,600 national banks (and less than 400 state banks) by 1866. A decade later, however, the growing use of checking accounts (rather than bank notes) had caused the tax on bank notes to become increasingly irrelevant. As a result, state banking enjoyed a resurgence, and by 1888 there were 1,500 state banks. This country's present dual system of both national and state banks was thus in place.

The National Banking System inaugurated formal federal regulation of banks.[15] The National Banking Act established the office of Comptroller of the Currency to administer the law and supervise and examine national banks. While bank chartering requirements were liberal (though stricter than the state free-banking laws) and no specific authority to regulate bank entry was included in the act, the Comptroller soon began the exercise of discretion in approving or rejecting applications for national bank charters. Further, the act placed restrictions on the types and amounts of loans national banks could make and established a system of reserve requirements. A significant measure of noteholder protection was provided by the requirement that national banks deposit with the comptroller an amount of government bonds equal to the amount of "national bank notes" (printed in uniform fashion by the Treasury) received by the banks for issue. If a national bank failed to redeem its notes, its bonds could be sold to pay the noteholders.

The National Banking System provided the country with a uniform currency and a more stable banking system. However, it did not provide a mechanism for ensuring that the quantity of money would be appropriate for the economy's needs. Note issue was based on the amount of government securities outstanding, and thus the quantity of national bank notes depended on the size of the federal debt, which was generally shrinking during the late nineteenth and early twentieth century. The quantity of "specie" (and of paper currency backed by it) was a function of the fortunes of miners and the country's balance of trade. This apparent currency inelasticity in the national banking system, its inability to provide an "elastic" money supply that would expand and contract with the needs of industry and commerce, along with the problem posed by the interbank holding of required reserves in "pyramid" fashion, was blamed for the financial "panics" of 1873, 1884, 1893, and 1907. The latter led to the founding of the Federal Reserve System, the primary purpose of which was the provision of an "elastic currency" to end the periodic bank liquidity crises that characterized the national banking system.

Establishment of the Federal Reserve System

Established primarily to accomplish the macroeconomic objective of monetary stability, the founding of the Fed in 1913 was also a milestone in the history of bank regulation. The Fed's role in directly regulating the country's banking system was to be enlarged to its present significance only in subsequent years; its immediate effect on the regulatory structure was relatively minor. Indeed, some observers view the failure of the Federal Reserve Act to include provisions for strengthening the state banking system to be the major weakness of the 1912 legislation.

Membership in the Federal Reserve System was mandatory for national banks but voluntary for state banks. This sop to "states' rights" was surely unfortunate, creating a number of problems, some of which persist to the present day. An immediate effect was to encourage state bank chartering by banks seeking to avoid membership (and its costs) in the Federal Reserve System. Since nonmember banks were subject to state rather than Federal Reserve requirements, a system of nonuniform reserve requirements was allowed that continued until the DIDMCA of 1980.

To encourage national bank chartering (and thus Fed membership), Congress passed the McFadden Act in 1927. This act, the name of which has become the code word for geographic restriction on banks (prohibition of interstate banking), was actually intended to liberalize the branching and investment powers of national banks. The legislation allowed national banks to establish branches where permitted by state law,[16] increased the limit that could be loaned to a single borrower, and broadened national bank investment powers to include corporate bonds, certain other securities, and expanded real estate lending.

Until 1922, national banks were not allowed to branch by a series of Comptrollers of the Currency who interpreted the National Banking Act to prohibit branching. This placed national banks at a competitive disadvantage relative to state banks in states where branching was permitted. By the end of the nineteenth century, branching had become a fiercely debated issue. In 1922, then Comptroller of the Currency David Crissinger ruled that national banks in states permitting branches could establish branches. The ruling was hotly disputed, and only the McFadden Act clearly established the branching powers of national banks.

The Banking Crisis of the 1930s

The Federal Reserve Act had no implications for bank entry, and the number of banks in the United States continued to increase—passing the 30,000 mark in the early 1920s. Bank failures were common during the 1920s—more than 5,700 banks failed between 1921 and 1929. Most of these failed banks were state banks in rural, agricultural communities. Failures and mergers (many of the latter serving to forestall failure) had winnowed the number of commercial banks to about 25,000 in 1929. The economic collapse known as the Great Depression began in that year.

More than 10,000 banks closed their doors between 1929 and 1933. From June 30, 1929, to June 30, 1933, the number of commercial banks declined from 24,970 to 14,208 and total bank deposits dropped 35 percent (from $49.4 billion to $32.1 billion).[17] The U.S. banking system appeared to be teetering on the verge of collapse. In late 1930 and early 1931, serious banking crises developed. A third "panic" erupted in 1933, after President Roosevelt had taken office. Roosevelt responded with the famous "banking holiday," and a wave of bank reform actions were set in motion.

The Banking Acts of 1933 and 1935, two banking acts of great importance in U.S. financial history, were passed by Congress. The Banking Act of 1933 (Glass-Steagall Act) separated commercial and investment banking, gave increased regulatory authority to the Federal Reserve System, prohibited payment of interest on demand deposits, and raised the minimum capital of national banks. But most important of all, the 1933 law established the Federal Deposit Insurance Corporation (FDIC).

The small number of state deposit insurance plans were all defunct by 1930, and opponents of federal deposit insurance (which included many banks) predicted similar failure for a national system. But the FDIC had many key advantages relative to the state programs. One was that so many weak banks had already failed under the terrible crunch of the Great Depression. The FDIC thus had responsibility for a nationally diversified pool of banks at least strong enough to have weathered hard times. The FDIC had supervisory and examination powers over insured banks (though, in practice, the Comptroller and Fed perform the primary supervisory and examination function for national banks and state member banks) that could be used to avert bank failure. Most importantly, as a federal agency, the FDIC had behind it the monetary power of the central government, and with that implicit guarantee came public confidence. The role of deposit insurance in the U.S. regulatory framework is so great that it warrants attention in a separate chapter. Thus, further discussion of this feature of the 1930s banking reform measures is deferred until Chapter 6.

Another highly significant aspect of the Banking Act of 1933 was the section that prohibited commercial banks from underwriting issues of corporate securities and nonguaranteed revenue bonds of state and local governments.[18] At the time, commercial and investment banking were almost totally integrated. The new law thus obliged the numerous institutions performing both functions to choose either commercial or investment banking as their line of business and divest themselves of the other. The author of this legislation (Senator Glass) had sought passage of similar measures before the 1930s and the banking crisis of the latter period served to win him enough support to make it part of the 1933 reform package. The separation of commercial and investment banking was viewed as a means of reducing the risk of the former (as were most features of the 1933 Act), and thus was intended to help restore public confidence in commercial banks. Further, some legislators were swayed by alleged abuses (of the conflict-of-interest variety) stemming from mixture of the two functions. And, as always, there was concern about the concentration of financial power in institutions exercising commercial banking, investment banking, and trust powers.

The Banking Act of 1935 was primarily intended to strengthen the Federal Reserve System and its monetary management power. The act gave the Federal Reserve Board expanded reserve requirement authority and the power to regulate the rate of interest paid by member banks on time deposits. To strengthen the board's independence, the Comptroller of the Currency and the Secretary of the Treasury were removed from membership on the board.

The 1935 act also marked the end of free banking in this country that had held sway for a century. The Congress, seeking to curb the high rate of bank failure that had long characterized the American banking system, gave the Comptroller greater authority to exercise discretion in the granting of national bank charters. Applicants for a charter were henceforth to demonstrate the need for the proposed bank and make the case that the new bank would be successful without significantly injuring existing banks. If the applicant's case is not convincing to the comptroller, or if the comptroller's own investigation of these issues raises reasons for denial, the charter will not be issued.

Another element of the termination of free banking was the establishment of the FDIC. The FDIC does not charter banks, but it has discretion concerning which banks shall obtain deposit insurance. When a national bank is chartered, the FDIC can be expected to insure deposits of the new national bank. However, *state* bank applications for deposit insurance are carefully scrutinized and evaluated. To the extent that banks regard deposit insurance as essential for their operations (and the deposits of about 96 percent of U.S. banks are insured), the FDIC thus has a virtual veto power over the granting of state charters for banks.

The effect of greater restrictions on bank entry is evident in the record of new bank charters (see Figure 2–1). During the 1920s, new bank charters granted averaged about 360 per year. From 1935 until the U.S. entry into World War II, an average of only about fifty new banks were chartered each year. While this sharp reduction in the rate of new bank chartering in large measure reflected depressed economic conditions (and thus a decline in requests for charters), it also

Figure 2-1. Commercial Banks in the United States (*number, by class*).

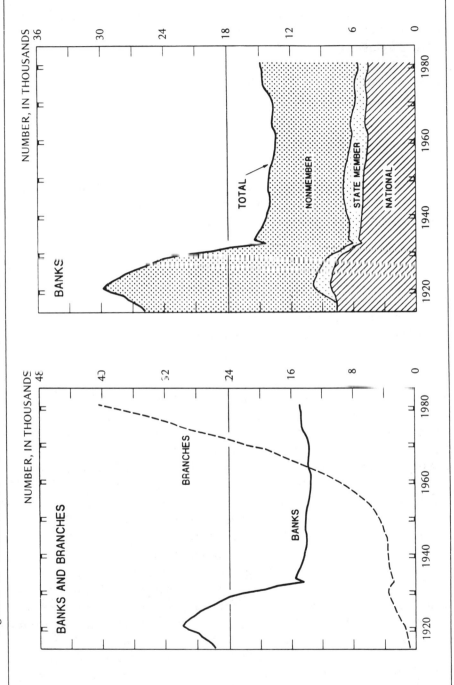

Source: Board of Governors of the Federal Reserve System, *Historical Chart Book*, 1982.

reflected the fact that charters were more difficult to obtain. In the postwar expansion (1945–1960), the annual average of new bank charters remained below 100. Not until James Saxon became Comptroller of the Currency and relaxed national bank charter restrictions did new bank chartering approach pre-1935 levels. From 1962 to 1965, for example, 514 national banks were chartered.

A New Regulatory Framework

The 1933 and 1935 acts, in conjunction with previously existing regulation, thus served to set in place a regulatory structure that placed the following constraints on banks:

1. Restrictions on pricing of deposits
2. Restrictions on entry and expansion
3. Restrictions on scope and nature of activities
4. Restrictions on leverage (minimum capital requirements) and other balance sheet elements
5. Restrictions on geographic expansion

Some of these restrictions stem from the traditional American concern over concentration of financial power, with vociferous support in more recent decades from groups likely to suffer economic injury from relaxation of these restrictions. Branching and merger restrictions are, of course, the primary example of this aspect of U.S. regulation, but a number of activity restrictions are related to financial power concerns (and fears of competition) as well as failure risk.

The bulk of the restrictions on the formation and operations of U.S. depository institutions relate to curbing failure risk. The purpose of this framework, law, and set of regulations was to limit the degree of risk that a depository institution could take in the assets it acquired and in the securities it offers to the public in order to raise funds. These limitations are most severe for the depository financial institutions—commercial banks, savings and loans, mutual savings banks, and credit unions—but they also apply to many nondepository financial institutions. Although there have always been regulatory limitations on the degree of risk that can be assumed by financial institutions, the restrictions became much more severe following the banking legislation of the early 1930s. In recent decades, when failures among the nation's financial institutions have been infrequent, some of these limitations on the risk exposure of individual institutions have been relaxed to some extent.

A few examples may be useful in explaining the limitations on risk produced by the regulation of different financial institutions. Commercial banks may extend credit only through acquiring financial assets that are "nonspeculative" in nature. If municipal securities in the portfolio are rated by one of the rating agencies (such as Moody's or Standard and Poor's), they must be at least of "investment grade." And if financial assets in the portfolio are not rated, then management is responsible for maintaining adequate credit files to demonstrate to the regulatory authorities that their credit extensions represent "sound credit." Not only are there limitations on the quality of individual financial assets held within the portfolio of the financial institution, but there are also restrictions on the fraction of the portfolio devoted to any borrower. For example, national banks may not lend more than 15 (only 10 until 1982) percent of their capital to any one borrower. In addition, national banks may not have real estate loans that exceed their total capital position or 70 percent of their time and savings deposits, whichever is larger.

From a broader perspective, the bank regulatory agencies periodically evaluate the liquidity position of the bank, the adequacy of the capital base it has available to offset losses, the quality of its management, and other dimensions of the bank that bear on the risk of default and thereby on the riskiness of the securities offered to the public by these financial institutions. And, of course, a bank or savings and loan association cannot even receive a charter unless it meets minimum capital standards established by the regulatory authorities. Similar types of restrictions on risk-bearing and supervisory oversight also apply to other depository institutions.

Still another aspect of risk regulation is the tradition of outside examination. Periodic and unannounced inspections or examinations by officials of the regulatory agencies (examiners) occur at all types of depository institutions. The purpose of these examinations is to appraise the "quality of management" of the organization in both its financial and its nonfinancial dimensions. More specifically, the purpose of the examinations is to identify problem areas within the organization and eliminate the problems before they threaten the viability of the organization. The adequacy of internal controls to prevent the theft of assets is evaluated. The extent to which the institution is conforming to the detailed regulations designed to reduce risk and achieve other objectives is examined, and the quality of the asset portfolio is scrutinized. Loans are evaluated as good, substandard, doubtful, or loss. If any asset is of unsatisfactory quality ("loss"), the institution is forced to write off the asset against its capital account. And if the capital account proves inadequate, the institution is forced to raise additional capital through the sale of stock or through other means, such as greater retention of earnings (as opposed to the payment of cash dividends to stockholders).

At the federal level, supervision and examination responsibilities for commercial banks are shared by the Office of the Comptroller of the Currency (OCC), the Federal Reserve system, and the FDIC. The OCC has primary responsibility for national banks; and the FDIC, for insured nonmember state banks. (In the case of state banks, surveillance jurisdiction is shared with state agencies.) The essence of the supervision process is reflected in the bank rating system developed for the Uniform Financial Institutions Rating System. Called CAMEL (for the rating components of capital, asset quality, management, earnings, and liquidity), this rating system results in a composite rating of 1 to 5 for banks. (CAMEL is also used for federally regulated nonbank depository institutions.) An institution with a composite rating of 1 is considered sound in every respect, and, at the other end of the rating spectrum, a composite rating of 5 applies to institutions considered to be on the verge of failure. The purpose of the rating system is to help identify institutions that warrant special supervisory attention and concern.

Regulation Since the Bank Reforms of the 1930s

The structure and nature of American banking changed dramatically in the 1930s as a result of the wave of bank failures and the reform legislation it evoked. The reduction in the number of banks proved to be enduring, partly as a result of increased entry restrictions. Figure 2–1 indicates a pattern of declining numbers (except for a postwar blip of expansion) until recent years. An expanded, tighter net of regulation was cast over depository institutions. Deposit insurance became a salient and (indeed, central) characteristic of the U.S. banking system. Bank failures became rare.

Most of the changes wrought by the banking reforms of the 1930s remain in place today. Some (such as the prohibition of interest-bearing transactions accounts) were undone by the DIDMCA of 1980. Others, such as the separation of commercial and investment banking, are under significant pressure for change. But the increased authority of the Federal Reserve Board, deposit insurance, and other features of the banking acts of 1933 and 1935 appear to have become permanent fixtures of our financial system.

After the reforms of the 1930s, banking entered a relatively tranquil period. Banks, like the rest of the U.S. economy, remained generally depressed until World War II. Not until the late 1940s did banking regain its pre-Depression vitality. The ratio of bank loans to assets (only 16 percent in 1945 as compared to a 1925 ratio of 63 percent) began to rise steadily throughout the 1950s. This resurgence of banking continued in the vigorous economic expansion of the 1960s, with banks becomingly more aggressive, competitive, and less averse to risk. Dramatic expansion of foreign banking activities by U.S. banks occurred, and banks sought new avenues of profitable growth outside traditional banking.

The renewed aggressive and energetic posture of banking inevitably created tensions within the regulatory framework shaped in the 1930s. Banks sought, often successfully, to circumvent regulatory restraints through various organizational and financial innovations. Table 2-2 indicates a few selected financial and technological innovations. The most important organizational innovation was the formation of holding companies by banks in order to enter service and

Table 2-2. Selected Recent Financial and Technological Innovations of Commercial Banks.

Innovations	When Introduced
Consumer time certificates	1950s
Eurodollars	1960s
Credit cards	1960s
Leasing	1960s
Federal funds	1960s
Repurchase agreements	1960s
Certificates of deposits	1961
Variable rate term loans	1970s
Remote service units	1974
Money market certificates	1978

geographic markets from which banks were barred by state or federal legislation.

Bank Holding Companies. The Banking Act of 1933 included provisions for Federal Reserve Board supervision and regulation of bank holding companies that held Federal Reserve member banks, but these limited powers did not pertain to formation and expansion of such companies. Not until the Bank Holding Company Act of 1956 was legislation enacted for significant federal regulation over the formation of bank holding companies and their acquisition of additional banks. The act defined a bank holding company as an organization owning 25 percent or more of the stock of two or more banks (thus excluding "one-bank holding companies"). The Fed was given power to supervise bank holding companies, and Fed approval was required for both new acquisitions of banks and the formation of new holding companies. The legislation listed factors to be considered by the Fed in evaluating proposed holding company acquisitions. These factors included the current and prospective financial condition of the holding company and bank in question, needs of the community, and "preservation of banking competition."[19] Further, the 1956 Douglas Amendment to the Bank Holding Company Act prohibits bank holding companies from acquiring an affiliate bank in another state unless the latter's laws permit such entry.

The 1956 legislation was intended to halt interstate banking expansion (existing holdings were "grandfathered"), separate nonbanking activities from bank holding company activities, and avoid concentration of financial resources in holding companies. However, in a classic example of the sometimes perverse consequences of regulatory action, the effect was quite different.

It seems surprising that relatively few bank holding companies were formed prior to the 1956 legislation, considering their freedom from the geographic and activity restrictions that characterized bank regulation. (In 1954, there were only forty-six BHCs or bank holding companies.) The reason the device was not used more often lay in the uncertain status of bank holding companies. The pressure for new restrictive legislation from unit banking groups and others and the Fed's stated position on regulation of bank holding companies made it clear that such legislation was likely. Since severe restrictions or even abolition were possible consequences of a new statute, bankers were wary of the holding company form of organization. When the new legislation did emerge in the Bank Holding Act of 1956, it was hardly draconian and mainly served to clarify the status of BHCs. As a result, it actually *encouraged* their formation and expansion as a means of overcoming geographical and functional barriers.

There was also a major loophole in the 1956 act—bank holding companies controlling only *one* bank were not included. Since such exclusion of one-bank holding companies (OBHCs) continued their freedom to engage in nonbanking activities, a large increase in the number of OBHCs resulted (more than 1,000 existed by 1970). OBHCs could establish loan affiliates across state lines, sell debt instruments not subject to interest rate ceilings, and otherwise engage in activities proscribed to individual banks and (after 1956) multibank holding companies (MBHCs). This loophole was closed with a 1970 amendment of the Bank Holding Company Act of 1956, which brought OBHCs under the purview of the latter act. (Most of the 1973 surge in number of registered holding companies shown in Table 2-3 stems from inclusion of OHBCs.) The 1970 amendments also authorized the Fed to develop a new (somewhat liberalized) list of allowable activities of BHCs.

By 1982, the bank holding company form of organization had become predominant in U.S. commercial banking, with the nation's 4,557 BHCs accounting for about 84 percent of all domestic bank deposits (according to the Fed's 1982 *Annual Report*). BHCs had also become a powerful engine of financial innovation and resistance to regulatory restraints.

Consumer Protection Regulation

In the 1960s and early 1970s, a wave of environmental, worker protection, equal opportunity, and consumer protection legislation was enacted by the Congress. Virtually all business firms in the United States were affected, including depository institutions. The principal legislation directed at the financial services industry concerned borrower protection and potential discrimination by lenders. The Truth in Lending Act of 1968 required full disclosure of credit costs and terms on consumer loans. The act also provided for regulation of the content of credit advertising. The Fair Credit Billing Act of 1974

Table 2-3. Number of Registered Bank Holding Companies, Banks and Branches Controlled, and Total Deposits (for selected years 1957-1981).

End of Year	Number of Registered Holding Companies	Banks Controlled	Total Branches	Time Deposits (billions)	Total Deposits as Percent of Total U.S. Commercial Bank Deposits
1957	50	417	851	$ 15.1	7.5%
1963	52	454	1,278	22.5	8.2
1968	80	629	2,262	57.6	13.2
1970	121	895	3,260	78.1	16.2
1973	1,677	3,097	15,374	446.6	65.4
1975	1,821	3,674	18,382	527.5	67.1
1977	1,913	3,903	20,340	624.3	66.4
1979	2,478	4,280	23,765	744.7	67.8
1981	3,702	5,689	28,044	937.8	74.1

Source: Board of Governors of the Federal Reserve System, *Annual Statistical Digest*, various issues.

regulated credit card distribution, terms, and cardholder liability. The Fed's Regulation Z details the features and administrative aspects of these laws.

Other financial service consumer protection legislation followed. The Fair Credit Reporting Act of 1970 provided for regulation of credit reports furnished to creditors, employers, and insurers. The Real Estate Settlement Procedures Act of 1974 (as amended in 1976) required mortgage lenders to provide borrowers with a detailed statement of lending charges. The Right to Financial Privacy Act of 1978 limited external access to banking records of depositors.

The Fair Housing Act of 1968 forbade mortgage lenders to consider race, color, religion, gender, or national origin in loan decisions. The Equal Credit Opportunity Act of 1974 (as amended in 1976) broadened this antidiscriminatory provision to all credit provisions. The Community Reinvestment Act of 1977 (in effect) forbade discrimination by home lenders on the basis of age or location of buildings and requires regulators to consider the degree to which an institution is satisfying community credit needs when evaluating requests from that institution to branch or merge.

This aspect of the regulatory framework of depository institutions is largely independent of the rest of the structure. While some of these regulations have conceptual support, given the existence of agency problems and asymmetric information in the financial markets, they generally stem from political and social (rather than economic) objectives. To the extent that society accepts and endorses pursuit of these goals, the relevant economic issue is how they can most efficiently be achieved. It is not at all apparent that existing financial services, consumer protection, equal opportunity, and similar regulations meet that test.

REGULATION OF NONBANK DEPOSITORY INSTITUTIONS

To this point, our discussion of the nature and evolving scope and structure of depository institution regulation in this country has focused on commercial banks. By and large, the regulatory system for nonbank depository institutions parallels that for commercial banks and has evolved for much the same reasons and in the same manner. However, there are a number of important differences in regulatory features for the latter group of financial institutions. Before discussing these particular differences, however, a comparison of the conceptual rationale for regulation of banks and nonbank depository institutions is of interest.

Many of the economic arguments for bank regulation hold as well for nonbank depository institutions and other financial intermediaries. Certainly, agency and asymmetrical information problems exist and, at a minimum, can be used as a basis for justifying disclosure requirements and perhaps public agency supervision and examination as well. But, as noted earlier, the much greater reach of regulation that exists requires further justification. In the case of banks, the danger of market failure and the special, disastrous macroeconomic implications of such failure serve as such justification. Does this rationale hold for nonbank depository institutions?

Claims on nonbank depository institutions (deposits or shares) are highly liquid and generally subject to immediate withdrawal. As with banks, this aspect of nonbank depository institution operations (combined with agency and asymmetrical information problems) makes them prone to market failure. Unlike banks, however, it is not at all apparent that a market failure problem for nonbank depository institutions has any serious macroeconomic implications that do not hold for major nonfinancial industries that are not subject to extensive regulations. Until the DIDMCA of 1980, most nonbank depository institutions could not issue transactions accounts. (The exception was the NOW accounts issued by mutual savings banks in a few states, and this practice did not emerge until the 1970s.) Thus, nonbank depository institution failures posed no direct threat to the money supply (transactions balances).

The potential of any nonbank depository institution difficulties spreading to commercial banks is, of course, a possible justification for regulating the former groups as extensively as the latter. But only in recent decades (after the present regulatory framework for all depository institutions was largely in place) has the nonbank depository institution industry been large enough to evoke major concern along these lines. Nor can concern about concentration of financial power among these institutions be persuasively invoked as a rationale for extensive regulation.

How then can we justify (or explain) the fact that a system of regulation exists for nonbank depository institutions that closely parallels the one for banks? The reason lies in the fact that the claims issued by these two types of institutions are very similar and are highly substitutable. Given the effect of the nature and extent of bank regulation on the *risk* of claims on banks, similar *risk reduction* is necessary for nonbank depository institution claims, or the latter would be competed out of existence. Consider, for example, deposit insurance. After the FDIC was established, what would have been the effect on thrift institutions if deposit insurance had not been available to them? In fact, of course, the Federal Savings and Loan Insurance Corporation (established a year after the FDIC) provides deposit insurance to savings and loan associations, and mutual savings banks have access to both FDIC and FSLIC insurance. In a very real sense, deposit insurance for banks made deposit insurance for nonbank depository institutions necessary. And, as we discuss at length in Chapter 6, the existence of federal deposit insurance assures extensive federal regulatory oversight.

More generally, it is clearly the sense of the U.S. Congress and (somewhat less clearly) the sense of the people represented in Congress that the existence of nonbank depository institutions is in the public interest. Whereas regulation of bank operations is primarily aimed at *curbing* their activities in order to assure their performance of key macroeconomic functions, regulation of nonbank depository institution operations is aimed at *protecting* these institutions and *channelling* their credit-granting activities to support a presumed socially beneficial purpose—housing construction.[20]

The Regulatory Structure

The important nonbank depository institutions are, of course, savings and loan associations, mutual savings banks, and credit unions. A brief discussion of the regulatory structure for each type of institution follows.

Savings and Loan Associations. The dual system of bank chartering and regulation also exists for savings and loan associations (S&Ls). The proportion of state and federal chartering is roughly half and half. More than 90 percent of all savings and loans are insured by the FSLIC, and these insured institutions account for more than 98 percent of all deposits in savings and loan associations. Federally chartered institutions are regulated and supervised by the Federal

Home Loan Bank Board or FHLBB (established in 1932) on the basis of charter. The FHLBB also regulates federally insured, state chartered institutions (since the FSLIC is part of the FHLBB and also since many state chartered S&Ls choose to belong to the FHLB system). State chartered savings and loans are also regulated and supervised by state commissions with various titles.

The regulatory system functions much like the one for commercial banks. Interstate branching is forbidden, and intrastate mergers and branching are subject to approval. (In general, restrictions on the latter are much less stringent than for banks.) A similar system for supervision and examination exists, with institutions (like banks) being subject to capital requirements and portfolio restrictions.

Until recent years, savings and loans have been obliged to operate within a framework of severe portfolio restrictions aimed at concentrating lending of these institutions in the form of residential mortgages. Such mortgages, as a result, have come to constitute about 80 percent of all savings and loan assets. The FHLBB also required maintenance of prescribed minimum liquidity ratios, loan-loss reserve ratios, and net worth ratios.

Entry restrictions on S&Ls are very similar to those imposed on commercial banks. As noted above, branching regulations are more liberal than for banks. The FHLBB's policy has been to permit branches for federally chartered savings and loans, unless the state of residence prohibits branches for *all* depository institutions (not just state chartered S&Ls).

Savings and loan associations have been favored by law and regulation in several respects. Until 1966, S&Ls were not subject to Regulation Q-type ceiling interest rates, and their imposition (by the Interest Rate Adjustment Act of 1966) was meant to protect the institutions from rate competition. The S&Ls were allowed to pay interest rates 0.25 percent higher than commercial banks could offer for deposits. Further, the FHLBB has been a significant supplier of funds to S&Ls through what are called *advances*. Unlike Fed discount window lending to banks, which is viewed as temporary, the FHLBB funding is quasi-permanent.

The savings and loan industry has also been the recipient of various tax breaks. It was not until 1952 that S&Ls (and mutual savings banks) were made subject to the federal corporate income tax. Even then, these thrift institutions generally avoided federal income taxes until 1962 by means of loan-loss reserve adjustments. However, tax legislation in 1962 and 1969 significantly increased S&L payments of corporate income tax, although a relatively liberal loan-loss deductibility provision remained available to S&Ls having a specified percentage of their total assets in residential mortgages and liquid assets.[21]

Mutual Savings Banks.   Although chartered and generally supervised by states, most mutual savings banks (MSBs) have availed themselves of FDIC deposit insurance and FHLB system membership. Thus, federal regulation and supervision reaches many MSBs through their association with these federal agencies. As in the case of savings and loans, MSBs have been viewed as primarily mortgage-lending institutions and regulated accordingly. Entry and branching restrictions, while varying somewhat from state to state, generally parallel those of S&Ls. MSBs also share the tax advantages available to S&Ls.

Mutual savings banks in New England (along with credit unions in that region) had the distinction of serving as subjects of an experiment in interest-bearing transactions in the 1970s. At this time, MSBs in Massachusetts and New Hampshire began offering negotiated order of withdrawal (NOW) accounts and won state court tests of their right to do so. The U.S. Congress then passed legislation limiting NOW accounts and credit union share drafts to New England. In 1980, of course, NOW accounts were permitted nationwide.

Credit Unions.   The National Credit Union Act of 1970 established the National Credit Union Administration (NCUA) for the purpose of insuring, regulating, and supervising credit unions. Credit unions may be either federally chartered (about 13,000 since 1934) or state chartered (about 9,000 in forty-six states). All federally chartered credit unions must now have NCUA share insurance. Not quite one-half of the state chartered credit unions have NCUA insurance, but many are insured through state plans or private insurance companies.

Until recently, the lending and investment powers of credit unions were highly restricted and essentially limited to short-term consumer loans, U.S. Treasury securities, and insured accounts of thrift institutions and commercial banks. In 1977, amendments to the Federal Credit Union Act liberalized lending powers to include residential mortgages, mobile homes, and home improvements. Further liberalization came with the DIDMCA of 1980.

CONCLUSION AND IMPLICATIONS:
TOWARD A REGULATORY CRISIS?

In retrospect, it is clear that three principal policy goals have shaped the regulatory system for depository institutions in the United States:

1. To prevent banking market failure;
2. To prevent concentration of financial power; and,
3. To use nonbank depository institutions for limited, specialized purposes—specifically, residential mortgage lending in the case of savings and loan associations and mutual savings banks.

Until the near-collapse of the banking system in the 1930s, government regulation focused primarily on the second goal listed above. Free banking and restrictions on mergers and branching were the principal means to this policy end. The result of these policies has been a very large number of depository institutions and the establishment of vested interests that can always be counted on to oppose measures likely to broaden the geographic (and functional) span of competition.

The banking crisis of the Great Depression led to greater emphasis on bank safety in regulation. The main thrust of the 1930s "reforms" was anticompetitive in nature and (with the exception of the termination of free banking) did little to disturb the system of restrictions already in place. The 1930s legislation simply broadened and tightened the regulatory net and, by instituting deposit insurance, gave the federal government a direct and enduring interest in the risk profile of most banks.

The third objective emerged to become highly significant in the postwar period as a response to the public demand for housing. In addition to the shaping of an expanded number of S&Ls to serve this purpose, deposit rate controls were employed as an instrument to this end. It is likely that the regulation-spurred expansion of these institutions came at the expense of commercial banks.

Out of these goals and the means employed to achieve them, and mixed with the U.S. federal system and pluralistic power structure, came a very complex and fragmented regulatory system monitoring and seeking to control a complex and fragmented financial system. Neither system was constructed to withstand the strong gales of major economic and technological change. Out of such change has come crisis, new legislation, and perhaps the beginning of transformation (some would say, rationalization) of the American financial system and the framework of financial regulation.

NOTES TO CHAPTER 2

1. For a discussion of the historical evolution of banking regulation, see George J. Benston, "Federal Regulation of Banking: Analysis and Policy Recommendations," *Journal of Bank Research* (Winter 1983), pp. 216–244.

2. Free banking is not entirely a historical abstraction. In many states in this country, free banking was permitted in the period between 1836 (when the charter of the Second Bank of the United States expired) and 1863 (when the National Banking System was established). Scotland also provides a case study in unlimited bank entry.

3. The concepts of allocational and operational efficiency are related but not identical. *Allocational efficiency* is attained when the quantity of output of a good or service desired by society is produced with the minimized use of productive resources. *Operational efficiency* is a necessary condition for allocational efficiency and pertains to a minimal consumption of resources in the markets for resource allocation.

4. For an excellent discussion and empirical analysis of economies of scale in banking, see George J. Benston, "Economies of Scale and Marginal Costs in Banking Operations," *National Banking Review* (June 1965). Reprinted in *Studies in Banking Competition and the Banking Structure*, The Administrator of National Banks, United States Treasury, 1966, pp. 355–394.

5. See Kerry Cooper and Gerald Keim, "The Economic Rationale for the Nature and Extent of Corporate Financial Disclosure Regulation: A Critical Assessment," *Journal of Accounting and Public Policy* (September 1983), pp. 189–205.

6. George A. Akerlof, "The Market for Lemons: Quality, Uncertainty, and the Market Mechanism," *Quarterly Journal of Economics* (August 1970), pp. 488–500.

7. Two notable critics of required disclosure are Professors George Benston and George Stigler. See, for example, Benston's *Corporate Disclosure in the U.S.* (Lexington, Mass.: D.C. Heath & Co., 1976), and Stigler's paper, "The Effectiveness and Effects of the SEC's Accounting Disclosure Requirements," in H.G. Manne, ed., *Economic Policy and the Regulation of Corporate Securities* (Washington, D.C., The American Enterprise Institute, 1969).

8.   See George J. Benston, "Deposit Insurance and Bank Failures," Federal Reserve Bank of Atlanta, *Economic Review* (March 1983), pp. 4–17.

9.   Golembe Associates, Inc., "Regulatory Reform—Some Observations on the Bush Task Group," *Golembe Reports*, vol. 1983–1.

10. For reviews of these studies, see George J. Benston, "Economies of Scale in Banking," *Journal of Money, Credit, and Banking* (May 1972), pp. 312–314; and George J. Benston, Gerald A. Hanweck, and David H. Humphrey, "Operating Costs in Commercial Banks," Federal Reserve Bank of Atlanta, *Economic Review* (November 1982).

11. Dwight B. Crane, Ralph C. Kimball, and William T. Gregor, *The Effects of Banking Deregulation* (Washington, D.C., Association of Reserve City Bankers, 1983), pp. 17–20.

12. Since checking practices were not yet widespread, banks made loans by issuing notes that could (hopefully and usually) be used as a means of purchasing power. The notes were sometimes (but not always) redeemable in specie. During this period, the U.S. money supply was largely a crazyquilt collection of state bank notes, amounting to over $200 million in 1860.

13. A recent study suggests that wildcat banking was not a primary source of widespread bank closing during the period, but rather adverse economic developments—particularly large declines in prices of bonds held by banks—were responsible. See Arthur J. Rolnick and Warren E. Weber, "Free Banking, Wildcat Banking, and Shinplasters," Federal Reserve Bank of Minneapolis, *Quarterly Review* (Fall 1982), pp. 10–19.

14. This provision explains the timing, at least, of the legislation. Since national banks had to hold government bonds as capital reserves and collateral for note issues, the market for federal debt was expected to be significantly strengthened. The actual effect was minor.

15. A history of national bank supervision is offered by Ross M. Robertson, *The Comptroller and Bank Supervision* (Washington, D.C.: Office of the Comptroller of the Currency, 1968).

16. The 1927 legislation restricted branching to the home city. This restriction was removed in a 1933 amendment.

17. Board of Governors of the Federal Reserve System, *All Bank Statistics, United States 1896–1955* (Washington, D.C.), p. 37.

18. Franklin R. Edwards, "Banks and Securities Activities: Legal and Economic Perspectives on the Glass-Steagall Act," in Lawrence G. Goldberg and Lawrence J. White, eds., *The Deregulation of the Banking and Securities Industries* (Lexington, Mass.: Lexington Books, 1978), pp. 273–291.

19. For a detailed description of the 1956 act and other aspects of bank holding company regulations, see M.A. Jessee and S.A. Seelig, *Bank Holding Companies and the Public Interest* (Lexington, Mass.: Lexington Books, 1977).

20. The contrast is apparent when one observes how the principal regulator of savings and loan associations—the Federal Home Loan Bank Board—acts to *promote* the interests of these institutions and, indeed, helps finance them via "advances."

21. The S&Ls and MSBs can add up to 40 percent of taxable income to loan-loss reserves tax free if 82 percent (for S&Ls) or 72 percent (for MSBs) of assets are held in qualifying form. The 40 percent deduction is reduced by 0.75 percent for each percentage point below 82 and 72 percent, down to 60 percent (at which point there is no deduction).

3 INTERNATIONAL TRENDS AND INFLUENCES IN FINANCIAL REGULATION

We have concerned ourselves thus far with the nature and extent of the changes sweeping the financial system of this country, with special attention being focused on depository institutions. However, financial innovation and change—both of the market-generated and government-mandated variety—is not confined to the United States but is evident, in varying degrees, in most economically advanced nations. This chapter reviews recent developments in the financial systems of a few selected countries and assesses how the growth in international banking has spurred and shaped financial change in this country. Our discussion strongly suggests that recent and prospective changes in the U.S. financial system stem from deeply rooted technological and economic developments that span the global financial system. Further, it is apparent that the internationalization of the U.S. financial system that has occurred in recent years has contributed significantly to recent regulatory (and deregulatory) developments.

A CLIMATE FOR CHANGE

Depository institutions and most other major components of the financial systems of the world's nations have been subject to a significant degree of government control since their inception. The pur-

pose and rationale for the existence and pervasiveness of such financial regulation was the subject of detailed discussion in the previous
chapter. But certainly the universality of government intervention
in the banking sector is striking. Depository institutions in many
nations are government owned, and privately owned institutions in
all nations are subject to a high degree of regulation and supervision.

Economic events and trends of recent years have caused many
Western nations (and Japan and Australia) to reexamine their financial regulatory frameworks. Various committees and commissions
were established for this purpose in these nations and were known by
the name of their chairmen—"Wilson" in Britain, "Mayoux" in
France, "Gessler" in Germany, and "Campbell" in Australia. (The
formal title of Britain's "Wilson Committee" is worth noting as an
example of English literalism—"The Committee to Review the Functioning of Financial Institutions.") A less formal review in Canada
resulted in the Canadian Bank Act of 1980. Even Japan, in the 1981
revision of its Bank Law, liberalized its banking system somewhat.[1]

While this book is concerned with the United States experience,
this experience is linked to corresponding developments in other
nations, even when outcomes differ. Various common causes of
financial change exist, the most important being perhaps the high
and variable market interest rates of recent years (spawned by high
rates of inflation). But there are other significant factors—the international economic malaise, technological change, overseas banking
expansion, and changing attitudes concerning banking risks.

High and Volatile Interest Rates

As noted in Chapter 1, financial distortions develop when market
interest rates rise above mandated ceiling rates—the most notable
being "disintermediation." When the differential between returns
offered by the "indirect securities" of financial intermediaries (such
as time deposits) and the returns offered by securities of nonregu-
lated (or less regulated) institutions expand, funds flow out of the
intermediaries. The implications for intermediaries are apparent (witness the plight of the savings and loan associations in the U.S.), and
less obvious but equally distressing ramifications occur throughout
the economy. The basic lesson learned by all nations attempting to
regulate the financial system via deposit rate ceilings is that this form
of price control is unworkable when market interest rates surge up-

ward. Government could respond only by either seeking to control *all* rates of return on saved funds or by moving to eliminate ceilings on deposit rates. It is surely fortunate that the latter course has been chosen.[2]

The increased volatility of interest rates within the past decade— separate and apart from their level—has revealed other shortcomings of regulation. In particular, problems have emerged in those countries (such as the U.S.) where regulatory restrictions and such means as tax incentives have been used to encourage specialization by financial institutions. Such specialized institutions, in effect, developed balance sheets that reflected accustomed relationships between short-term and long-term sources and uses of funds as well as adjustment to the regulatory environment. Frequent changes in interest rates altered familiar relationships between short-term and long-term flows of funds, causing lenders to become much less willing to acquire long-term, fixed-rate securities.

General Economic Malaise

Economists continue to debate the cause of the worldwide slowdown in economic growth that has characterized the past decade (for example, the extent to which more expensive energy is responsible), but there is no doubt that most countries have been in the grip of an economic malaise for much of the period since the late 1960s. Most major industries have been affected, and financial institutions are no exception. Tight monetary policies in the United States and Western Europe have made credit a dear commodity, with generally negative implications for the profitability of financial institutions. Constrained credit and slowly growing markets have intensified jealousies among groups of institutions of the real and perceived regulatory advantages of competitors. Increasing demands on the part of regulated institutions for a "level playing field" gave impetus to a drive for deregulation.

Technology

Increasing acceptance and utilization of new technology by financial institutions and their customers have made many regulatory restrictions—particularly those of a geographic nature—appear archaic. The marriage of telephone (and telex) to computer in banking operations, the advent of automated teller machines, electronic funds transfer systems, and other technical innovations have had a dramatic impact on financial systems in many nations. One of the major effects is to augment and expand competition for banking services.

Changing Attitudes Toward Banking Risk

In most nations, much of the financial regulatory framework was erected with the intent of averting any recurrence of the financial panics of the 1930s and earlier eras. Memories of such crises are fading, the unregulated Eurocurrency market has functioned relatively smoothly despite a number of political and economic shocks, and the success of deposit insurance in the United States and West Germany and interbank liquidity assurances among European banks have reduced fears of falling-dominoes-style bank failure. The world banking system coped quite satisfactorily with the disturbances of 1974 (including the failure of Bankhaus I.D. Herstatt in Germany and Franklin National Bank in the U.S.) which resulted in strengthened confidence and improved liquidity arrangements.[3]

Certainly, many investors and depositors appear to be only marginally concerned about institutional failure (witness the shift of almost $200 billion in the U.S. from insured bank deposits to uninsured money market funds). Further, it has become apparent that regulation can spawn its own crises. The recent difficulties of U.S. savings and loan associations (with their asset portfolios overloaded with fixed-rate mortgages) are essentially the result of their regulation-induced specialization in mortgage lending. More diversified institutions are obviously less susceptible to damage from the winds of economic change—an observation that supports deregulation in favor of competition and nonspecialization.

The recent emergence of the so-called "Third World debt problem" triggered new concerns about bank failures, but of a different nature than lingering memories of the Great Depression banking collapses. While this development will almost certainly result in new restrictions and new required disclosures concerning overseas lending by banks, the nature of this new concern suggests that many aspects of the existing regulatory framework are ineffectual, if not archaic. Further, the danger to the solvency of some large banks that international debt poses can be eased only by international cooperation and concerted action.

The Internationalization of Banking

The increased presence of foreign banks in the United States has played a significant role in bringing about change in this country's banking laws. Foreign financial competition has similarly disturbed the financial regulatory structure of other nations—Great Britain, for example. Further, the growth of international banking has brought to the attention of regulators and regulated alike the fact that there is nothing sacrosanct about the shape of any particular financial system. Finally, the Euromarkets have served as a salient example of how an unregulated, competitive financial market can function.

The above developments are truly international in scope. Individual nations, of course, have various specific reasons for deregulating (and perhaps for *not* deregulating) their financial systems. In the United States, for example, deregulation is perhaps the most rational means of correcting problems stemming from past regulation—such as excessive specialization in mortgage lending by savings and loan associations. While the path of deregulation may vary among nations because of differing economic and political circumstances (as well as differences in the present structure of their financial systems), it is equally apparent that there is now a *world financial system* and that national financial systems can exercise total independence from it only by imposing upon the larger economy a highly significant cost.

COMPARATIVE FINANCIAL FRAMEWORKS

When the financial systems of other nations are compared to that of the United States, striking similarities and striking differences emerge. The pervasiveness of banking regulation is one of the major similarities. Like the United States, most of the world's advanced nations greatly increased the scope of financial regulation in the 1930s as a response to the economic disorder of that era. Economic depression spawned a rejection of the hitherto accepted view (in democratic nations) of the efficacy of the competitive marketplace and resulted in an increase in government presence in all areas of the economy. In the case of the financial system, the responses to bank failures and other manifestations of financial crisis were remarkably similar among Western nations. Interest rate ceilings, for example, or similar anticompetitive measures were adopted in an attempt to establish financial stability and "channel" capital into desired avenues.

Increased governmental intervention in the financial system as well as the changes in the nature of financial regulation that characterized the era of the Great Depression and its aftermath were part of an overall expansion of the economic role of government. However, for reasons discussed in the previous chapter, the financial segment of virtually all national economies has been regulated by the central government throughout modern economic history. Differences in the nature and extent of the financial regulatory framework among countries largely reflect differences in their political and economic systems, as suggested by the following brief descriptions of a few selected nations' financial systems and principal depository institutions. The United Kingdom and West Germany are given the most attention due to similarities with the United States and their importance in the world financial system.

The United Kingdom

Great Britain's financial system is markedly similar to that of the United States, particularly with regard to its specialized depository institutions. There are, however, notable differences. These differences stem largely from a relative lack of concern in Britain regarding financial concentration and from the much greater role that international banking played in the evolution of the British banking system.[4]

Commercial Banking. Commercial banking in the United Kingdom is highly concentrated, and is dominated by the so-called "clearing banks"—the banks belonging to the Committee of London Clearing Bankers. Until 1968, there were eleven clearing banks, but mergers in 1968 and 1970 reduced this number to six (and only five are independent). Four of the London clearing banks—Barclays, Lloyds, Midland, and National Westminster—account for 95 percent of total bank deposits and operate more than 12,000 branches. These banks have been quite profitable in recent years, consistently ranking high in the ratings of all international banks in return on assets. While their primary role remains in providing the main payments mechanism for England and Wales and performing other commercial banking functions, the London clearing banks have broadened the scope of their activities in recent years.

There is no statutory counterpart in the United Kingdom to the U.S. Regulation Q or the prohibition of interest payment on demand deposits. Until recent years, the clearing banks acted as a cartel in setting deposit and loan rates—a practice unofficially condoned by the government. Much of the nonprice competition practiced by U.S. depository institutions (and attributed to deposit rate ceilings) had its U.K. counterpart. To the extent that price competition existed among the clearing banks, it was largely confined (until recent years) to their subsidiaries.

Commercial banking in Great Britain was significantly affected by the enactment of the 1971 Competition and Credit Regulations of the Bank of England. These regulations, which ended the "Collective Agreements" on interest rates of the clearing banks, removed all controls on lending, and instituted a revised system of reserve requirements, amounting to a new system of financial control intended to provide more equitable treatment of institutions and stimulate competition in the banking system.[5] In its "rationalization" and equity aspects, the 1971 regulations were, in considerable degree, a precursor to some of the provisions of both the U.S. International Banking Act of 1978 and DIDMCA. It is generally agreed that the regulatory system set in place in 1971 did serve to encourage bank competition and to further stabilize the U.K. securities markets. Certainly the clearing banks responded to the new system with more vigorous competition among themselves and with other financial institutions. Further, the banks have broadened the scope of their activities, narrowing the differences between them and other types of British depository institutions.

Other U.K. Banking Institutions. The business of banking in the United Kingdom is shared among the London clearing banks and other British banks, overseas banks, merchant banks ("accepting houses" and "issuing houses"), savings banks, discount houses, building societies, and finance houses. *Other British banks* include the Northern Ireland and Scottish clearing banks and their subsidiaries and the smaller British banks with majority U.K. ownership. Some of these banks are highly specialized in the investment and international fields. The overseas banks maintain a London office but conduct their main business outside the U.K. Numbering about 200, the overseas banks include foreign-owned banks—particularly American and Japanese—as well as British.

The British *merchant banks* have a long history. Most began as accepting houses (and are still so labeled), financing nineteenth century overseas trade, and many still play a large role in accepting bills of exchange arising from international commerce.[6] But accepting houses also conduct business in foreign exchange, the gold and silver bullion market, and investment management, advise clients on mergers and acquisitions, and act as trustees. They also participate in new domestic and overseas security issues as underwriters and in other roles. ("Issuing house" is the term for the merchant banks whose principal activity is the sponsoring, underwriting, and flotation of security issues.)

Discount houses are peculiar to the U.K. financial system, but are similar to government security dealers in the U.S. They borrow from banks and invest in U.K. Treasury instruments and other short-term paper. The discount houses function primarily as an intermediary between the clearing banks and the Bank of England and, in that role, are useful in the conduct of monetary policy.

Savings banks include the National Savings Bank (formerly the Post Office Savings Bank) and Trustee Savings Banks. These institutions offer interest-bearing accounts at competitive rates and invest in public sector securities (although a limited amount of short-term lending to customers occurs). Since 1968, the National Giro System has offered the payments services available in most Western European countries.

Building societies are similar to U.S. savings and loan associations and mutual savings banks. They are nonprofit mutual associations and specialize in mortgage lending. There are about 300 building societies in the United Kingdom, down from over 2,000 at the turn of the century due to mergers. Approximately 80 percent of the assets of building societies are mortgages. Shares and deposits (interestingly, but not significantly, a distinction is made between the two, unlike the U.S. counterpart) now in building societies exceed the total deposits of the London clearing banks.

Finance houses specialize in consumer credit, particularly of the installment loan variety. Deposits by financial institutions and business firms supply the principal source of funds for these institutions. Accounts held by individuals with finance houses are of considerably less significance. Financial houses have suffered from increased competition for consumer finance in recent years.

Financial Regulation in the U.K. The Bank of England is the sole supervisory and regulatory authority for the British financial system. Compared to the U.S. financial regulatory framework, British regulation has long been notable for its relative flexibility and lack of formal structure.[7] While steps were taken in 1976 toward a more formal system of control over bank entry, licensing, branching, mergers and acquisitions, and dissolution, the regulatory system remains relatively unstructured. As is true of so much of the British political and social structure, the weight of tradition plays a central role. There are several significant banking laws, but no formal statutory framework for bank supervision, examination, and regulation.[8] The Bank of England generally prefers the use of informal "suggestions" to banking associations or individual bankers, rather than formal directives.

Despite its informality and flexibility, the regulatory power of the Bank of England over British banking organizations should not be underestimated. For, while the Bank of England's regulatory approach has been termed "informal but precise,"[9] the relative concentration of British banking makes "moral suasion" a more potent technique than in the United States. Since 1974 (following failures of a number of small banks), the Bank of England has established a separate regulatory department and set forth a revised regulatory policy that featured a significant increase in bank disclosures. While the examination process, capital adequacy determination, and other elements of bank supervision remain somewhat nebulous, this does not mean that they are taken lightly by banks.

Changes in British Banking. Many recent changes in British banking have arisen without benefit of either Bank of England mandate or parliamentary action, but rather as a response to economic events. In particular, the level of competition among depository institutions has intensified considerably in recent years. The U.K. clearing banks are now competing actively for savings deposits both among themselves and with the building societies. As a result, British savers now have a choice of a wide variety of time deposit maturities and features. Further, the clearing banks are moving actively into home mortgage lending (the traditional territory of the building societies) for the first time. In 1981, banks had garnered about 15 percent of the new home loan market. The motivation for this encroachment was not so much a search for new *uses* of funds by the clearing banks as a desire to retain *sources* of funds. The building societies often link home loan availability to savings deposits held with them, and the result has been a net outflow of deposits from the clearing banks to the building societies in the past two decades. By 1979, the societies held a larger amount of sterling deposits (£45 billion) than the clearing banks (£37 billion). Further, since mortgage lending in Britain is solely of the variable rate variety, the move by clearing banks did not appreciably increase exposure to interest rate risk. Clearing banks have also begun to embrace some merchant banking functions, competing with accepting houses in various activities.

Numerous other banking changes are taking place in Britain. The temptation is great for the building societies to get into, if not the checking account business, then the cash availability business. Only slightly more than half of all Britons have a "current" (checking) account, and consequently much of Britain's retail transactions are on a cash basis. An aggressive move by the building societies to expedite withdrawals from depositor accounts with teller terminals and automated teller machines (ATMs) could doubtless both coax deposits from presently nonbanking Britons and attract transfers of deposits from bank current accounts. Several of the larger societies are considering precisely that action.

Foreign banks in Britain have also begun to compete more fiercely with domestic banks for both deposits and loans. And the Scottish clearing banks (all of which are wholly or partially owned by the London clearing banks) have begun to compete for more "little England" business. Finally, the nation's "trustee saving banks," as a result of relaxation of governmental restrictions and a trimmed structure (a reorganization from 73 to 16 regional, largely autonomous banks), have begun to compete aggressively for loans and deposits.

Thus in the United Kingdom, as in the United States, the trend in the financial system is clearly toward increased competition and diversification among depository institutions. There does not appear to be any sentiment for regulatory or legislative resistance to this trend. The 1983 reelection of the Conservative government assures at least five more years of rule by a Parliament favorably disposed toward a more competitive, less regulated financial system.

West Germany

Commercial banking in West Germany is dominated by the *Gross-banken*—the six largest commercial banks (including Deutsche Bank, Dresdner Bank, and Commerzbank) accounting for almost as much business as the approximately 120 regional banks.[10] While not so concentrated as the United Kingdom, it is apparent that German banking is much more concentrated than in the United States. The activities of the commercial banks span the realm of commercial and consumer banking and many own substantial interests in private mortgage banks (Hypothekenbanken). There is no legal (as in the U.S.) or traditional (as in the U.K.) separation of investment banking and commercial banking in Germany, and German banks actively engage in securities underwriting and trading. A further contrast is in German bank ownership of equity securities; in fact, ownership by banks of large shares of German industrial firms is common.

Other depository institutions are of major importance in West Germany. There are more than 600 municipally owned and managed *savings banks* and *Giro banks*, and their aggregate deposits considerably exceed (by one-third) the amount held by the commercial banks. The third major banking group—the *cooperative banks*—is also a strong competitor of the commercial banks and holds assets exceeding $180 billion. The boundaries between these groups have largely disappeared in recent years due to a trend that began with legislation in 1967 aimed at the development of a more competitive banking environment. Indeed, most Germans think of the savings and Giro banks in the same way Americans think of commercial banks.

West German banking conditions, relative to those of the United States and other nations of Western Europe, have been characterized by a high degree of competition and freedom from regulatory restraints. (Germany's unfortunate history in the 1930s and 1940s put the country on a somewhat different path than its neighbors in the development of its financial system.) Even so, West Germany geographically restricts operations of its depository institutions and provides regulatory protection for its major mortgage-lending institutions—mortgage banks and building and loan associations.

Interest rates have been unregulated in West Germany since 1967. "Universal banking"—full availability of a wide range of financial services at a single institution—is the norm.[11] As might be expected,

West German consumers have benefited from the high level of competition among the nation's full-service banks. Users of financial services enjoy ease of access (one branch for every 1,400 West Germans), competitive deposit and lending rates, and a range of services unique in the world. (For example, many German banks offer a *Plus-Sparen* account that automatically transfers end-of-month customer demand deposit balances to a savings account as soon as the customer's payroll check is deposited.) For depository institutions, however, such competition entails relatively thin profit margins—an aspect of German banking to which the country's comparatively slow-paced adoption of automation is attributed. The financial difficulties of a number of German banks are also attributed to intensive competition, but the country's scheme of deposit insurance and other "safety net" devices has served to avert the development of any "crisis of confidence" in the German financial system.

Under the amended Banking Law of 1961, bank regulation and supervision are the shared tasks of the Deutsche Bundesbank (the central bank) and the Banking Supervisory Office. Bank entry is supervised by the regional branches of the Bundesbank (which is organized much like the Federal Reserve System), with licensing requirements being administered by banking federations. Bundesbank branches also handle such routine supervisions as periodic examination of credit reports and financial statements. Audits are performed when there are concerns about possible (or apparent) irregularities. The Banking Supervisory Office is empowered to close a bank or take other measures when laws are violated or failure looms. Banks are required to maintain a prescribed minimum ratio of capital to outstanding credit (presently about 5.5 percent).

West Germany has had a voluntary deposit insurance plan since 1976.[12] All private and public deposits (except interbank deposits) are covered up to an amount equal to 30 percent of bank capital. Participating banks must pay an annual fee (a fraction of a percent of deposits) and allow special audits of their books. The insurance fund is administered by the Federal Bank Supervisory Authority, which can close a failing bank and pay off its depositors (or take over its operation). All German banks and most foreign banks belong to the system.

The German deposit insurance plan provides almost full deposit coverage because of the high maximum limit of coverage. Adoption of the plan also resulted in an extension of the regulatory powers of the Federal Bank Supervisory Authority and imposition of stated lending restraints on participating banks. The amount that banks can lend to any one customer and the amount of single loans are limited to a stated percentage of capital.

Other Western European Nations

The financial systems of other Western European nations, with the exception of France, bear strong resemblances to those of the United Kingdom and West Germany, although each possesses its own peculiar features.[13] The French banking system, now largely nationalized, is notable for its specialized banks and highly structured and formalized system of regulations. The purview of France's regulatory umbrella will soon widen with the establishment of a new banking commission with even broader powers than the current Banking Control Commission, and with authority over virtually all depository institutions in France. Italy's financial system is complex and features a much less concentrated commercial banking sector than its neighbors. The Netherlands' largest bank is an agricultural cooperative, but the Dutch banking system is otherwise typical of Western Europe—a highly concentrated commercial banking system alongside a less concentrated system of savings banks, the Post Office giros, and cooperatives. In these and other nations in the region, few bank failures are permitted and depositor losses are covered by the government.

Italy's relatively unconcentrated but highly regulated banking system is under severe pressure from foreign bank competition. The Bank of Italy has long restricted competition among Italian banks and has seldom allowed them to branch outside their regional bases. Further, a 1936 law constrains commercial banks from lending for longer than eighteen months. Any medium-term lending is limited to 8 percent of total bank deposits, and matching maturities are required. As a result, most commercial banks own in whole or in part special credit institutions that are authorized to make medium- and long-term loans. These and other restrictions have made Italian banks especially vulnerable to competition from huge foreign banks unfettered by restrictions on their lending maturities. As a result, serious attention is being given, for the first time, to an overhaul of the country's financial regulatory structure.[14]

In general, Western European banking systems are changing in the direction of increased competition and a broadened scope of activities by constituent institutions that is steadily eroding past specialization. In retrospect, the German banking reforms of 1967 were a harbinger of things to come in Western Europe. In the majority of the region's nations, interest rate controls have been removed and interest-bearing checking accounts have emerged. In some nations, such as Austria, geographical and functional restrictions have been removed. Also in Austria, the country's savings banks are now allowed to enter a wide range of new lines of business, thus becoming much like their German counterparts. And, since the 1981 collapse of the traditional interest rate cartel among Austrian banks, banks and thrift institutions have competed fiercely for deposits on a price basis.[15] An increased level of competition is also notable in the small nations of Northern Europe, and a number of innovative approaches to retail banking have emerged in the Netherlands, Sweden, and Denmark.

Especially notable in the retail banking market in Western Europe is the embrace of new technology by banks in most nations. France's Credit Agricole, for example, has the largest automated teller machine network in the world—more than 12,000 ATMs. More than $350 billion has been spent on ATMs by European banks, and pooling arrangements are common on these and other automated banking devices. In Britain, Barclays Bank cited automation as the reason for a 1983 decision to reorganize its branch system (consisting of about 2,900 branches) over a seven-year period—thus closing 150 branches and reducing services at 700 other branches. One of European banking's largest successes is more in cooperation than in technology—the Eurocheque system. This system allows the 20 million holders of the Eurocheque card to write a check in any European currency at any of the 15,000 participating banks.

Canada

The Canadian Bank Act of 1980 opened the way for a limited extension of competition among Canada's financial institutions—an already competitive arena relative to most of the world. Like the United Kingdom (which the Canadian financial system resembles in many ways), Canada has a highly concentrated commercial banking system—five "chartered banks" (operating more than 7,000 branches nationwide) dominate this sector. (There are six other banks—all regional.) As is the case with their U.K. counterparts, the chartered

banks must compete with building societies, mortgage loan compa
nies, trustee savings banks, and other financial institutions (see Figure 3-1). Canada's unique "trust companies"—which exist largely
because no other financial institutions are allowed to act in a fidu-
ciary capacity—are highly significant depository institutions. Still
another similarity between Britain and Canada holds in the relative
decline in the commercial banking sector's share of financial assets.
Major dissimilarities lie in the importance of provincial regulation in
Canada's federal system and the existence of a deposit insurance
system.[16]

Much of Canadian financial competition is of recent vintage, stemming from the Canadian Bank Act of 1967,[17] The 1967 act eliminated deposit rate ceilings and broadened the allowed lending purview of depository institutions. The chartered banks were thus en-
abled to compete more aggressively for time and savings deposits and
to move vigorously into mortgage lending (hitherto proscribed to
chartered banks) and consumer credit (previously unattractive be-

Figure 3-1. Canada's Major Financial Intermediaries (*based on total
assets as of December 31, 1979*).

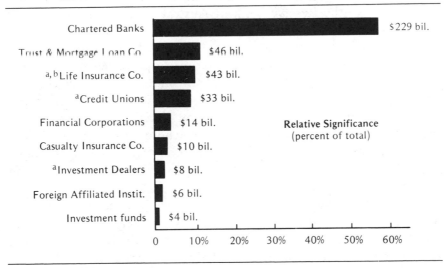

a. As of September 30, 1979.

b. Excludes segregated funds, and accident and sickness branches of federally registered
life insurance companies.

Source: Thomas W. Thompson and Raoul D. Edwards, eds., *The Changing World of
Banking*, United States Banker Series (Richmond, Va.: Robert F. Dame, Inc., 1982), p. 236.
(Originally published as "The Canadian Banking System," *U. S. Banker* (October 1980).)

cause of a loan rate ceiling of 6 percent). As the trust companies, savings banks, and credit unions retaliated, the Canadian financial system became increasingly competitive. Consumers benefited from the widespread introduction of ATMs, interest-bearing checking accounts, and a wider range of conveniently accessible services. The chartered banks are also pressing for an expanded role in securities brokerage. As in many other nations, past specialization of depository institutions is increasingly giving way to diversification and pluralistic approaches to the provision of financial services.

Australia and New Zealand

The financial systems of Australia and New Zealand—the structures of which are shown in Table 3-1—are highly regulated.[18] Such regulation, much of it aimed at attaining macroeconomic goals, is facilitated by the high degree of concentration of the commercial and savings banks systems. Both nations virtually exclude any significant foreign presence in their banking markets.

Most financial regulation in both nations is administered by their central banks—the Reserve Bank of Australia and the Reserve Bank of New Zealand. In addition to the usual "safety, soundness, and stability" objectives of regulation, the Reserve Banks use regulatory controls for purposes of credit allocation to preferred sectors (government, housing, agriculture, and export industries). These controls consist primarily of interest rate controls, restrictions on the assets and liabilities of financial institutions, and direct credit controls. Further, as in the United States, mortgage-lending institutions (savings banks and building societies) have been constrained (by a combination of balance sheet restrictions and tax incentives) to focus on housing finance.

Australia's savings banks and building societies account for about 85 percent of all mortgage lending. The six privately owned (by commercial banks) national savings banks are heavily regulated by the federal government and a seventh is federally owned. Until 1982, savings banks could accept deposits only from individuals and nonprofit organizations, and such deposits were limited to demand deposits (seldom offered in practice) and savings accounts subject to thirty-day notification requirements for withdrawal. Deposit rates were subject to prescribed ceilings until December, 1980, when they were

Table 3–1. Structure of the Financial Systems in Australia and New Zealand.

	Australia	New Zealand
A) Deposit-Taking Institutions		
Commercial banks	7 nationwide (1 government) 4 regional (3 government) 2 small foreign	5 nationwide (1 government, 3 foreign)
Savings banks	7 nationwide (1 government) 5 regional (3 government) 120 building societies	5 nationwide (1 government) 12 regional 1 Postal savings (government) 44 building societies
Credit unions	700 credit cooperatives	950 credit cooperatives
B) Specialized Lending Institutions	4 development banks (3 government) 1 export refinance 50 merchant banks 33 finance companies	1 housing (government) 1 rural (government) merchant banks (no data) 436 finance companies 20 rural agencies solicitor's nominee cos. (no data)
C) Others	9 security dealers 46 life insurance cos. 200 general insurance pension funds (no data)	4 security dealers 31 life insurance general insurance (no data) 213 pension funds

Source: Hang-Sheng Cheng, "Financial Reform in Australia and New Zealand," Federal Reserve Bank of San Francisco, *Economic Review* (Winter 1983), p. 11.

removed for all depository institutions. Assets of savings banks consist almost entirely of liquid assets, government securities, and housing loans. Housing loans could not exceed 60 percent of savings bank assets. The interest rate on housing loans (virtually all of which are variable-rate mortgages) is subject to a prescribed ceiling rate (raised from 12.5 percent to 13.5 percent in 1982), which is usually below a market rate. The mandated underpricing of housing loans has obliged savings banks to ration such credit by means of compensating savings account balance requirements and conservative loan-to-value ratios.[19] New Zealand has a similar structure of institutions and regulations for its nonbank depository institutions.

Australia's building societies and the smaller savings banks are regulated by the state governments and are free of federal controls, although federal-state cooperation generally assured regulatory consistency. The building societies are mutual in nature and are exempt from taxation if at least 90 percent of their loans are for housing finance.

Deregulation in New Zealand, 1976–80. The rate of inflation in New Zealand rose from 7 percent in 1972 to 17 percent in 1976, playing havoc with the nation's tightly regulated financial system. Financial disintermediation boomed and yield-regulated funds uses (such as housing finance) began to dry up. In response, a wave of deregulation was begun in 1976. Ceilings on bank-lending rates and deposit rates on large, long-term bank deposits were removed. Ceiling rates on other bank deposit types were raised. All interest rate controls on nonbank financial institutions were removed in the 1976 program. In 1977, all remaining interest rate controls on banks were removed except the prohibition of interest payments on demand deposits and the ceiling rate on passbook savings accounts. During the period from 1976 to 1980 a number of activity and investment restrictions on depository institutions were removed, leaving New Zealand financial institutions largely unregulated. In 1981, however, interest rate controls were reimposed.

Deregulation in Australia, 1979–81. In 1979, the Australian government established a study commission to review the country's financial system and recommend changes. The Campbell Committee, as it was called, submitted its final report in December, 1981. The committee recommended abolishing interest rate controls and credit controls and the instituting of a revised system of reserve requirements. It proposed a restructuring of the regulatory and supervisory framework for Australian depository institutions. The committee's restructuring proposal urged dismantling of the separate regulation of the different types of institutions in favor of unified, national regulation and supervision along functional lines. The study group also recommended relaxation of restrictions on entry by both foreign and domestic financial institutions in order to promote competition in financial markets.

Financial deregulation in Australia was proceeding concomitant with the Campbell Committee's deliberations. Relaxation of interest rate controls began in 1979, and total removal of bank deposit rate ceilings came the next year.

Japan

As in Australia and New Zealand, the financial system of Japan is subject to extensive government control.[20] The structure of the Japanese banking system has been shaped by regulations that separate short-term and long-term financing and force institutional specialization along functional and economic-sector lines. Government financial intermediaries play a major role in the allocation of credit in the Japanese economy. The allocation and cost of credit is further influenced by interest rate controls, financing-source restrictions on financial institutions, and various activity and portfolio constraints on the country's financial entities. Until the late 1970s virtually all interest rates were controlled to some degree by the government. Deposit rate ceilings were set at artificially low levels, and after 1970, lending rates were tied to the central bank discount rate. Banks were limited to deposit funding (and loans from the central bank) by limitation on their access to money and capital markets (via proscription of the issuance of negotiable certificates of deposits, debentures, and the like). Still, other traditional restrictions fettered the entire financial system, embracing even the funding avenues open to nonfinancial firms.

There are seventy-six commercial banks in Japan, of which thirteen are large (the "city banks") and sixty-three are regional. The assets of these banks are primarily short- and medium-term business loans and government securities. Funds sources are principally time and demand deposits and loans from the bank of Japan.[21] Financing for small business, agriculture, housing, and foreign trade is provided primarily by government financial institutions, which in turn are funded by the government postal savings system. (Japan has no major group of private-sector institutions supplying mortgage financing.)

Commercial banks and other private financial institutions are regulated by the Ministry of Finance, which has extensive explicit powers to direct their activities. The ministry sets the level of regulated rates and ceilings and reviews applications by banks for approval of numerous domestic and foreign activities. Further, the ministry has a great deal of implicit, informal regulatory power over bank portfolios and activities. The Bank of Japan generally limits its role to monetary policy and foreign exchange market operations.

A degree of liberalization in both the domestic and foreign dimensions of the Japanese financial system has been accomplished in recent years. In 1978–79, most restrictions on commercial bank access to the money market were removed. Banks were authorized to issue negotiable certificates of deposit, albeit with high minimum denominations (about $2 million). In 1982, changes in the country's fundamental banking law authorized banks to purchase, sell, and underwrite government securities. Restrictions on the access of foreign banks to Japan's financial markets have been greatly eased. But bank deposit rate ceilings and other interest rate controls remained intact.

Implications

It is apparent that the winds of financial change are presently at gale force in many nations other than the United States. It is a time of uncertainty for financial institutions around the world, as international economic trends force adaptation and innovation in the financial system at a faster and faster pace. Economic and financial change have, in turn, led to reexamination of existing regulatory frameworks. Such assessments have led to a significant movement toward deregulation and greater reliance on competitive market forces in a number of nations. Whether this trend continues depends largely on future economic events, as well as the perceived degree of success of the deregulatory measures already taken.

The U.S. banking system differs markedly from other nations in its lack of concentration in the number of institutions (see Table 3–2).

Table 3-2. Deposit Concentration in Selected Countries.

Share of Total Deposits at the Five Largest Banks	
Canada (1981)	77.7%
France (1981)	76.1
West Germany (1980)	61.8
United Kingdom (1979)	56.8
Japan (1981)	34.5
United States (1981)	19.2

Sources: *American Banker*, July 28, 1982; *OECD Financial Statistics*, 1981.

An assessment of comparative financial systems around the world also serves as a reminder of the *relative* freedom of the financial system of the United States. Only in its geographic restrictions on depository institutions has this country been significantly more restrictive than other economically advanced nations. And no other nation has posed fewer controls and restrictions on international capital flows and international banking than the United States. In turn, both international activities of U.S. banks and the operation of foreign banks in the United States have served to further liberalize the U.S. financial structure.

OVERSEAS BANKING AND THE U.S. FINANCIAL SYSTEM

The size and strength of the U.S. banking system have caused major U.S. banks to become significantly involved in overseas banking and foreign banks to seek a share of the U.S. banking market. Both the international operations of U.S. banks and the activities of foreign banks in the United States have had major impacts on the regulatory structure of the banking system.

Scope of Overseas Operations of U.S. Banks

During the past two decades, international banking operations have grown at a phenomenal rate. The highest rate of growth has been in multinational activities of U.S. banks.[22] The United States, particularly as compared to European nations like Great Britain, is very much a newcomer to international banking. Only since World War II, as U.S. corporations began their great wave of overseas expansion, have U.S. banks moved abroad in a significant fashion. In a sense, U.S. banks were following their largest customers abroad—customers they wished to retain. Overseas branching was also encouraged by various tax advantages and by the foreign lending constraints of the 1960s that could be avoided by foreign branches. By 1981, more than 150 U.S. banks had foreign branches (of which there were more than 750) with total assets amounting to more than $400 billion.

Some of the most significant expansion in U.S. banks' international activities is under the purview of legislation passed early in this century.[23] The 1919 Edge Act (an amendment to the Federal Reserve Act) authorized the Fed's Board of Governors to permit banks to establish corporations for the purpose of engaging in international or foreign banking, either directly or through the acquisition of local institutions in foreign countries. U.S. banks were thus allowed to engage in international banking activities and to acquire foreign banks by the establishment of subsidiary "Edge Act Corporations" (EACs). The latter proved not only to be a means of entry into overseas banking but also a means (albeit limited) of achieving an interstate banking presence in the domestic market.

The Edge Act permitted U.S. banks to indirectly own foreign bank subsidiaries, which they had long been prohibited from doing directly. Further, the Edge Act permitted EACs to have U.S. offices throughout the entire nation (often located in Chicago, Los Angeles, Miami, San Francisco, and Houston) to service their multinational customers, accept deposits related to foreign transactions, and refer potential new customers to the parent bank. Such offices have permitted large U.S. banks to develop an interstate network of banking services, despite the federal prohibition of interstate branching. This development was expedited when, in 1979, the Federal Reserve System excluded EACs from the interstate branching rule. Edge Act corporations may now, subject to approval by the Fed, establish and operate branches in other states. The Fed took this action under the mandate of the International Banking Act of 1978, which includes a directive to the Fed for relaxation of restrictions on EACs in order to allow them to compete more effectively with foreign banks operating in the United States (which are allowed interstate branches at home and abroad). Edge Act overseas subsidiaries are generally allowed to engage in activities common to foreign banking practice in the host county, even though such activities may be prohibited in the United States (or even to the country's own resident banks). EACs are regulated by the Federal Reserve System; the Fed governs the scope of operations of both the domestic and foreign offices and must approve all equity participations in foreign institutions.

Overseas operations of U.S. banks are notable in aggregate impact, but only a relatively small proportion of this country's banking institutions (the largest banks) are involved. Only about 1 percent of U.S. banks (approximately 140 of 14,500 banks) have overseas branches or affiliates. Many of these 140 banks have only a few relatively small branches abroad or have only "shell" branches (essentially a set of accounts in a Caribbean-area or other such offshore office, where international transactions originating in the United States are recorded). Ownership of more than 80 percent of overseas branches and affiliates and 90 percent of all overseas banking assets is held by only twenty U.S. banks. As might be expected, these same banks also dominate domestic banking, holding more than 30 percent of U.S. bank assets.

Overseas branches and affiliates of U.S. banks are located throughout the world. Of the total, 30 percent are located in Latin America, 20 percent in Europe, and 20 percent in Asia. Most of the others are shell branches located in the Bahamas and the Cayman Islands. Because of London's special significance in international finance, U.S. banks are heavily represented in the city, with more than fifty branches and affiliates located in London.

Overseas operations have provided U.S. banks with both the means and the incentive to deepen and broaden significantly their international lending. In addition to traditional export and import financing and lending to U.S. multinational firms and their foreign affiliates, the foreign lending of U.S. banks now includes extensive amounts of loans to foreign local firms, foreign banks, and foreign governments and their entities. Much of the banking regulatory change in Europe that occurred in the late 1960s and 1970s (such as Britain's 1971 move to stimulate and restructure competition) is attributable, at least in part, to U.S. overseas bank competition.[24]

Along with increased amounts of overseas lending, a number of U.S. banks have undertaken extensive diversification programs abroad. To a large degree such diversification was necessary for U.S. banks to compete effectively with their European counterparts, which have traditionally offered their customers a full range of financial services. A domestic base for worldwide diversification was provided in the late 1960s as one-bank holding companies provided a means for involvement in such activities as leasing, factoring, cash management, and mortgage banking. The Federal Reserve Board has generally permitted such "finance related" activities of Edge Act subsidiaries abroad. (Foreign branches are limited to the same activities permitted to their U.S. parent banks.) Such large U.S. banks as Bank of America, First National Bank of Chicago, and Manufacturers Hanover Trust have investment banking subsidiaries in Europe.

U.S. Overseas Banking and Domestic Regulation

Foreign operations of U.S. banks have significantly affected domestic regulatory trends, mostly in the direction of liberalization. Edge Act Corporations have allowed banks to establish an interstate presence, with a subsequent eroding effect on geographic restrictions. As U.S. banks have expanded the scope of their activities via foreign branches and subsidiaries into areas proscribed to them in their domestic markets, they have become increasingly impatient with various U.S. constraints and have pressed for their relaxation. The use of foreign branches to circumvent Regulations Q and D (often successful) was one reason for the DIDMCA provisions phasing out deposit rate ceilings and overhauling reserve requirements.

One aspect of U.S. banks' international activities—lending to less developed countries (LDCs)—may result in new regulatory restrictions, however. The international debt crisis that surfaced in 1982 has already triggered new disclosure requirements and may lead to still more such mandated disclosures, and has resulted in more stringent capital adequacy standards for U.S. multinational banking organizations.

Between 1977 and 1982, as indicated by data from the Federal Reserve Board's June, 1982, Country Exposure Lending Survey, foreign loans to LDCs by U.S. banks grew from about $47 billion in 1977 to almost $100 billion (see Tables 3-3 and 3-4). More than half of the total amount of these loans were to Mexico, Brazil, and Argentina. It is estimated that creditor U.S. banks would presently lose $14 billion in interest and principal due if these three nations failed to meet their scheduled payments for a single year. Unfortunately, the ability of these and other LDCs to service their foreign

Table 3-3.   U.S. Bank Claims on Non-OPEC Developing Countries.

End of Period	On All Countries			On Argentina, Brazil, and Mexico	
	In Billions of Dollars	As Percent of		In Billions of Dollars	As Percent of Total Bank Capital
		Total Bank Assets	Total Bank Capital		
1977	46.9	6.5	115	25.8	63
1978	52.2	6.3	116	26.8	59
1979	61.8	6.6	124	29.9	60
1980	75.4	7.1	132	37.0	65
1981	92.8	8.0	148	46.7	78
June 1982	98.6	8.3	149	52.4	84

Note: Data are for domestic and foreign offices of U.S. banking organizations with significant foreign banking operations. Data cover only cross-border and nonlocal currency lending.

Source: Board of Governors of the Federal Reserve System.

debt to U.S. and European banks is very much in doubt. And widespread default by LDCs could seriously endanger the viability of these banks, almost certainly necessitating government financial support. At present, a series of restructuring of loan repayments, "bridge" loans, and an increase in International Monetary Fund (IMF) lending has served to avert defaults.[25]

Congressional and regulatory response to these developments has been a series of proposals to further regulate and supervise foreign lending by U.S. banks. It is recognized, however, that a curtailment of lending to LDCs could precipitate the feared defaults. Acknowledgment of this fact served to cool the early fervor of some lawmakers for prescribed lending limits. Instead, banks will have to make public in the future a great deal more information about foreign lending, increase loan-loss reserves for problem foreign loans, and be subjected to increased regulatory scrutiny of their overseas lending practices. It is also likely that accounting changes may be mandated that will reduce reported income from problem foreign loans. In particular, fees charged for rescheduling loan payments would no longer be credited to current income.

At the present time, it is quite apparent that the international debt crisis is not over. The ultimate effect on U.S. banks remains unclear.

Table 3-4. Claims of Nine Largest U.S. Banks on Non-OPEC Developing Countries.

End of Period	On All Countries			On Argentina, Brazil and Mexico		
	In Billions of Dollars	As Percent of		In Billions of Dollars	As Percent of	
		Total Bank Assets	Total Bank Capital		Total Bank Assets	Total Bank Capital
1977	30.0	8.1	163	15.6	4.2	85
1978	33.4	7.9	176	16.4	3.9	82
1979	39.9	8.2	182	18.2	3.7	83
1980	47.9	9.0	199	22.7	4.3	95
1981	57.6	10.2	220	27.4	4.9	105
June 1982	60.3	10.6	222	30.5	5.4	113

Note: Data are for domestic and foreign offices of the nine banking organizations and cover only cross-border and nonlocal currency lending.

Source: Board of Governors of the Federal Reserve System.

International Banking Facilities

A more salutary recent development in U.S. international banking is worthy of note. Since 1981, International Banking Facilities (IBFs) have been allowed to be established by any U.S. depository institution, Edge Act Corporation, or U.S. office of a foreign bank.[26] IBFs are a structure banks can use to conduct international banking business exempt (for the most part) from domestic regulation and reserve requirements. An IBF can accept foreign-source deposits and make overseas loans with essentially the same degree of freedom as an overseas branch. Indeed, one of the purposes of IBFs was to "bring offshore banking home." There is a great deal of irony in the need for IBFs. As expressed by one author, the "crazy quilt of U.S. banking regulation" put this country in the "extraordinary position of having to create special banking facilities to repatriate to the United States a gigantic financial market whose principal commodity is none other than our own currency."[27]

The appeal of IBFs lies in their ability to combine the attractive features of offshore deposits and lending operations with only U.S. sovereign risk. They serve to free U.S. banks of the burden of establishing and operating offshore branches and subsidiaries. The IBF structure is relatively simple -a set of asset and liability accounts segregated on the books of a banking organization from its other assets and liabilities. IBFs are not separate legal entities. U.S. banks can now use IBFs as a base to compete in the international market for deposits and loans.

By 1983, there were about 400 IBFs in the United States, with total assets of almost $160 billion. Continued growth of IBFs hinge on domestic regulatory developments, corresponding regulatory and political developments in offshore banking sites, perceptions of U.S. bankers regarding the long-run viability of the IBF structure, and the degree of interest of banks lacking overseas branches in using IBFs to gain an international market presence.

Export Trading Companies

The Export Trading Company (ETC) Act, signed into law by President Reagan on October 8, 1982, allowed banks to own and finance export trading companies upon approval by the Fed of their formal application to do so. Bank-owned ETCs are permitted to engage in all aspects of international trade—financing, marketing, taking title to goods, processing orders, warehousing, documentation, and managing transport. The services offered by ETCs facilitate the development of export markets by small- and medium-size firms by providing them with a one-step package of financing, paperwork, shipping, selling, and collection services.

In May, 1983, Security Pacific Corporation became the first bank holding company to gain Fed approval for an ETC. Approval of applications of Bank of America, Citicorp, First Interstate Bank Corporation, and other major banking organizations followed soon thereafter. The potential for bank-owned ETCs is considerable. Attractive features of ETCs include their potential for enhancing and protecting middle market business by providing international services to firms in this market and their possible use as a means of entry to restricted foreign markets. Relative to nonbank competitors, banks have the advantage of an established customer base, access to capital, financing expertise, and a framework of international contacts.

It is too soon to assess the extent to which depository institutions will choose to establish export trading companies. Certainly, it is premature to assert that ETCs will become a significant arena of activity by banking organizations. But if this were to transpire, U.S. banks would be conducting merchant banking operations in an unprecedented fashion. One can speculate that major involvement in merchant banking under the ETC rubric would soon lead to intensified lobbying for regulatory change conducive to *domestic* merchant banking activities.

THE SCOPE AND IMPACT OF FOREIGN BANKING IN THE UNITED STATES

The level of foreign banking operations in the United States increased dramatically in the 1960s and 1970s.[28] Foreign bank assets in the United States grew from about $7 billion in 1965 to almost $300 billion in 1983. Foreign bank deposit holdings in this country exceed $150 billion. About 300 foreign banks have offices in this country. These offices, which include foreign investment companies, representative offices, and agencies, as well as subsidiary and branch banks, total more than 600. Foreign bank operations are now being carried on in only twelve states and are concentrated in the cities of New York, Los Angeles, San Francisco, Chicago, and Houston, with New York being the major center. (In 1983 foreign banks had 141 branches, 81 subsidiaries, 56 agencies, and 103 representative offices in New York City.)[29]

The reasons for the rapid growth of foreign bank operations in the United States are similar to those accounting for the expanded overseas operations of U.S. banks. Just as U.S. banks followed multinational U.S. firms abroad, foreign banks have followed their customers into U.S. operations. Investment in the United States by foreign firms has grown enormously in recent years as a consequence of both periodic declines in the value of the U.S. dollar (when U.S. assets become relatively cheaper in terms of many foreign currencies) and a higher rate of economic growth in this country as compared to most European countries. The latter factor also serves to make the United States an attractive arena for foreign banks to pursue new lending business. In addition to these factors, foreign banks have initiated or expanded U.S. operations in order to operate outside their home country's restrictions and regulatory constraints, to improve their access to U.S. money and capital markets, and to obtain a new source of dollars by competing for deposits. Foreign banking operations in the United States have focused primarily on the wholesale market, with most retail banking activity stemming from acquisitions of U.S. banks.

Regulation of Foreign Banks Before 1978

Prior to the International Banking Act of 1978, foreign banks in the United States were regulated primarily by the states in which they were chartered.[30] Almost all foreign banks received state rather than national charters because of the requirement that all directors of national banks be U.S. citizens. Federal regulatory authority over foreign banks was essentially limited to that of the Federal Reserve Board purview over foreign bank subsidiaries under the 1970 Bank Holding Company Act. Also, foreign bank branches were not eligible for FDIC deposit insurance.

There was (and still is) a great deal of variation among the states regarding the nature and extent of regulation of foreign banking activities. As of 1978, sixteen states explicitly prohibited entry of foreign banks in any form (other than representative offices). Eighteen permitted some form of foreign activity, while the rest had no laws regarding foreign banks. The states that issued foreign licenses or charters processed them in the same manner as for domestic banks. Foreign banking corporations usually entered U.S. markets through New York or California, simply because a significant proportion of the U.S. commercial and international financial transactions occur in these states. These states and certain others were receptive to foreign banks because of their interest in becoming international financial centers and their concern about reciprocity for their domestic bank's foreign operations.

Foreign bank branches, agencies, and other offices were thus entirely free of federal examination and supervision and largely outside the purview of federal regulation as well. Of particular importance was foreign bank exemption from federal prohibition of interstate banking and investment banking activities. Congressional concern about the lack of federal jurisdiction over foreign banks operating in this country led to passage of the International Banking Act of 1978.

The International Banking Act of 1978

The purpose of the International Banking Act (IBA) of 1978 was to establish a framework for Federal Reserve supervision and regulation of foreign banking and to put foreign banks operating in this country on the same footing as domestic banks, insofar as governmental restrictions are concerned.[31] The IBA made all branches, agencies, and commercial lending companies of foreign banks subject to the Bank Holding Company Act and thus to Fed regulation and supervision. A "grandfather" clause, however, protected *existing* activities prohibited by this law and its amendments.

The IBA permitted the Comptroller of the Currency to grant a national charter to a subsidiary or affiliate of a foreign bank if a majority of the directors are U.S. citizens. (Prior to the act, all directors had to be U.S. citizens). Federally chartered foreign banks can now operate in all states where permitted by state law, subject to the rules and regulations of the National Bank Act. State branches and agencies may be converted to federally chartered institutions with approval of the Comptroller of the Currency.

Foreign banks engaged in retail deposit-taking were made eligible for deposit insurance and, indeed, are required to have it if chartered in states requiring deposit insurance of domestic banks. Foreign banks were allowed to form Edge Act Corporations, the regulation of which was liberalized for both foreign and domestic varieties. Foreign banks were made subject to the McFadden Act and Douglas Amendment regarding interstate branching, but existing interstate operations were "grandfathered" under the act. (A foreign bank operating in more than one state was required to declare a "home state.") Foreign banks were brought under the same restrictions as U.S. banks regarding the nonbanking activities of their affiliates. Foreign branches and agencies were required to submit federal quarterly report-of-condition reports.

Other provisions of the IBA authorized the federal regulatory authorities to issue rules and regulations necessary to carry out the act, provided for studies of foreign treatment of U.S. banks and of the interstate banking issue, and authorized the Fed to impose reserve requirements on agencies and branches of foreign banks with worldwide assets of more than $1 billion.

The IBA served to establish a competitive balance between foreign and domestic banks, although many U.S. bankers grumbled about the "grandfather" clauses in the act and various exemptions from disclosure requirements. Of equal importance, the IBA constituted a step toward liberalization of geographic restrictions on all banks operating in the United States. Indeed, the study of interstate branching restrictions that was authorized by the act called for their elimination. It is fair to say that foreign banking in the United States has served to focus public and political attention not only on geographic restrictions in the U.S. banking system, but on other questionable regulatory characteristics as well. The influence of foreign banks on domestic regulation was not ended by the IBA. The act, by bringing foreign banks into the U.S. regulatory framework, gave these banks the incentive to seek to affect the course of changes in this framework through the Institute of Foreign Bankers and otherwise.[32]

CONCLUSIONS AND IMPLICATIONS

This chapter surveys international trends in financial innovations and regulation and reviews the effects of the internationalization of banking on the U.S. financial system. It is apparent that economic, technological, and social changes of recent years have resulted in a worldwide climate for financial change. Most Western nations, even though their individual banking structures all display unique characteristics, are exhibiting strong tendencies to unfetter their financial systems and allow competition to play a greater role.

The U.S. banking system has been significantly affected by the internationalization of banking. While there have been important legislative and regulatory developments that can be traced, directly or indirectly, to U.S. overseas banking or foreign banking in this country, the changes in *attitudes* stemming from international developments is equally notable.[33] International banking trends and influences have clearly provided a strong push toward the rationalization of the U.S. regulatory framework for depository institutions. In succeeding chapters, the nature and extent of this effort is described and assessed and the implications for the future of U.S. depository institutions are explored.

NOTES TO CHAPTER 3

1. Leon Holleman, "Japan's New Banking Laws," *The Banker* (January 1982), pp. 37–39.

2. This trend is not universal, however. In New Zealand, for example, interest rate controls were *reimposed* in late 1981 after more than five years of gradual decontrol. The new rate ceilings applied not only to financial institutions but to all suppliers of credit and purchasers of financial assets. See Hang-Sheng Cheng, "Financial Reform in Australia and New Zealand," Federal Reserve Bank of San Francisco, *Economic Review* (Winter 1983), pp. 9–24.

3. So-called "liquidity banks" were established in West Germany and Luxembourg to provide facilities for banks buffeted with liquidity drains, thus reducing the likelihood that the problems of such banks could spread to other institutions. In Britain, the Bank of England organized a "lifeboat committee" of emergency lenders to perform a similar function.

4. Jack Revell, *The British Financial System* (London: Macmillan, 1973).

5. A. R. Prest and P. J. Coppock, *The U.K. Economy* (London: Weidenfeld and Nicholson, 1978), pp. 67–72.

6. The August, 1981, issue of *The Banker* (pp. 41–58) features a number of short articles concerning London's merchant banks.

7. George Blunden, "The Supervision of the U.K. Banking System," *Bank of England Quarterly Bulletin* (June 1975), pp. 188–189.

8. James C. Baker, *International Bank Regulation* (New York: Praeger Publishers, 1978).

9. Stuart W. Robinson, Jr., *Multinational Banking* (Leiden, Holland: A. W. Sizthof, 1972), p. 67.

10. E. Victor Morgan, Richard Harrington, and George Zio, *Banking Systems and Monetary Policy in the EEC* (London: *Financial Times*, 1974).

11. Diether H. Hoffman, "German Banks as Financial Department Stores," Federal Reserve Bank of St. Louis, *Review* (November 1971), pp. 8-13.

12. Baker, *International Bank Regulation*, pp. 161-163.

13. Salvatore Mastropasqua, *The Banking System in the Countries of the EEC* (Germantown, Md.: Sizthoff & Noordhof, 1978).

14. "New Life in Italian Banking," *Euromoney* (August 1983), pp. 90-131.

15. W. J. Luetkens, "Austrian Banks Temper Their Steel," *The Banker* (January 1982), pp. 109-110.

16. B. V. Gestrim, "Understanding Banking in Canada," *Bankers Magazine* (Winter 1976), pp. 50-56.

17. H. H. Binhammer and Jane Williams, *Deposit-Taking Institutions: Innovation and the Process of Change* (Ottawa, Canada: Economic Council of Canada, 1976),

18. Hang-Sheng Cheng, "Financial Reform in Australia and New Zealand," pp. 9-24.

19. Warwick Temby and John L. Goodman, Sr., "Coping with Volatile Financial Markets: Australia's Experience," *Federal Home Loan Bank Board Journal* (March 1983), pp. 2-5.

20. Charles Pigott, "Financial Reform in Japan," Federal Reserve Bank of San Francisco, *Economic Review* (Winter 1983), pp. 25-45.

21. In Japan, bank lending to commercial banks is more akin to, in this country, FHLBB advances to its members than to Federal Reserve Bank lending to banks; such lending by the Bank of Japan is a significant source of "permanent" funding for Japanese banks.

22. Sarkis J. Khoury, *Dynamics of International Banking* (New York: Praeger, 1980), pp. 38-85.

23. James C. Baker and M. Gerald Bradford, *American Banks Abroad: Edge Act Companies and Multinational Banking* (New York: Praeger, 1974).

24. Robinson, *Multinational Banking*, p. 286.

25. For an excellent assessment of the debt problem, its causes, and means of coping with it, see Norman S. Fieleke, "International Lending on Trial," Federal Reserve Bank of Boston, *New England Economic Review* (May-June 1983), pp. 5-13.

26. Julian Walmsley, "International Banking Facilities—We Have Lift Off," *The Banker* (February 1982), pp. 91-96.

27. Franklin R. Edwards, "The New International Banking Facility: A Study in Regulatory Frustration," *Columbia Journal of World Business* (Winter 1981), p. 6.

28. Khoury, *Dynamics of International Banking*, pp. 86–134.
29. "Foreign Banks in America," *Euromoney* (August 1983) Supplement, p. 6.
30. Baker, *International Bank Regulation*, pp. 43–72.
31. *International Banking Act of 1978*, Report of the Committee on Banking, Housing, and Urban Affairs, U.S. Senate (Washington, D.C.: U.S. Government Printing Office, 1978).
32. Nigel Ogilvie, "Foreign Banks in the U.S. and Geographic Restrictions on Banking," *Journal of Bank Research* (Summer 1980), pp. 72–79.
33. H. Patrick Kennedy, "The Role of Foreign Banks in a Changing U.S. Banking System," *The Banker* (February 1982), pp. 101–103.

4 THE DEPOSITORY INSTITUTIONS DEREGULATION AND MONETARY CONTROL ACT OF 1980

The three previous chapters have examined the evolution of depository institutions and some of the more important developments in competing nondepository financial institutions. We have also discussed the rationale and record of depository institutions regulation from both domestic and international vantage points. In this and the following chapter, attention is turned to two pieces of legislation that have recently been enacted to alter the functions of depository institutions: the Depository Institutions Deregulation and Monetary Control Act of 1980 and the Garn-St Germain Depository Institutions Act of 1982. While overall changes in the financial system are certainly broader than the features of this legislation, there is little question about the major importance of both bills.

Initial attempts by Congress to deal legislatively with the rapidly evolving financial system were made in 1979 and culminated in early 1980 with the passage of the Depository Institutions Deregulation and Monetary Control Act of 1980 (DIDMCA), also variously known as the Monetary Control Act of 1980 and the Omnibus Banking Act. This bill represented the first major legislative restructuring of the financial system since the passage of the Banking Act (Glass-Steagall) of 1933. As Kaufman has pointed out, the Banking Act of 1933 resembles the DIDMCA in at least four ways:

1. Both acts were passed in an environment of financial crisis. Whether either or both would have been passed in an atmosphere of financial stability is, of course, subject to conjecture.

2. Both pieces of legislation are quite long and highly complex, treating the functions of financial institutions in a highly detailed manner.

3. Both acts substantially increased the powers of the Federal Reserve.

4. Both acts represented political compromises in which the final bills worked up by the House-Senate Conference Committees differed considerably from bills originally passed by the House and the Senate.[1]

Given the great significance of DIDMCA in affecting the functions of financial institutions, the present chapter explores the origins and provisions of the legislation in considerable detail. The reforms implemented by the legislation alter greatly the structure of the U.S. financial system and change both the cost of financial services and the array of services available. Yet the legislation is perhaps as important for what it did not do as for what it did.

We will begin by reviewing the historical background of the legislation, including numerous previous proposals that incorporated the principal reforms later included in DIDMCA. After a description of the major provisions of the bill, the chapter closes with a discussion of some important reform proposals that were omitted from the legislation.

THE ORIGINS OF DIDMCA

The lineage of the DIDMCA can be traced to the reports of a number of blue ribbon commissions that were created to study the financial system and make recommendations for appropriate structural and policy changes. (See Tables 4-1 and 4-2 for further information on the evolution of financial reform.) In fact, there is little in the act that does not correspond to recommendations made by one or more of these commissions. For example, the Hunt Commission[2] recommended in late 1971 that savings and loan associations be allowed to invest a substantial fraction of their assets in consumer loans and that savings and loan associations, credit unions, and mutual savings banks be authorized to offer third-party payment devices, including, in some instances, demand deposits. Under the Hunt Commission proposals, the traditional monopoly by commercial banks over transactions accounts would be eliminated. Moreover, the Hunt Commission recommended that Regulation Q ceilings on deposit accounts be eliminated gradually and retained only on a standby basis. Many of these same recommendations had been made a decade earlier by the Commission on Money and Credit. Furthermore, the Omnibus Banking Act incorporated many of the recommendations of the Financial Institutions and the Nation's Economy (FINE) study performed by the House Banking Committee in 1975.

The fact that these proposals, based on studies done years before, were enacted into law in 1980 reflects, to some extent, the pressure of events and economic conditions—a not uncommon phenomenon. Recall that the Federal Reserve Act was passed following a series of money "panics" in the early 1900s. Similarly, the basic regulatory environment that existed in the post–World War II era developed in the wake of a massive number of bank failures in the early 1930s. It is thus not surprising that the Omnibus Banking Act was also passed in a time of perceived crisis. In early 1980, interest rates reached historic highs, many savings institutions were on the verge of bankruptcy, the Federal Reserve was engaged in the use of selective credit controls on an unprecedented scale, and the rate at which member banks were withdrawing from the Federal Reserve System was accelerating. Banks withdrawing from Fed membership generally did so in order to avail themselves of lower state reserve requirements or the opportunity to hold reserves in interest-earning form. In effect, the cost of Fed membership rose as interest rates rose. Moreover, many of the innovations authorized by the federal regulatory authorities, including various types of interest-bearing checking accounts, had been challenged by a court decision. The need for fundamental legislative and regulatory changes became apparent to Congress at last. Thus the apparent financial crisis of 1980 gave the necessary impetus to enactment of various legislative changes previously recommended by study groups and other informed observers.

Table 4-1. Alternate Proposals for Change at the Congressional Level.

	Hunt Commission	FIA (Senate)	FRA-Fine (House)	Consumer Checking Account Equity Act (House)	Deposit Institution Deregulation Act (Senate)	House/Senate Compromise Regarding 1979 Court Decision	Depository Institutions Deregulation and Monetary Control Act of 1980
Broaden deposit liability powers	X	X	X	X[c]	X	X[f]	X
Broaden invest-ment-asset powers	X	X	X		X		X
Expand the number of alter-native mortgage instruments	X				X[d]		X[d]
Remove deposit rate ceilings	X	X	X[a]		X		X[h]
Tax credit and other housing incentives	X	X	X[b]		X[e]	X[g]	X[i]

Results						
Basis for discussion, but many reforms have not been enacted.	Passed Senate Dec., 1975, but never considered in House.	Split into three separate bills, but none passed	Passed House Sept., 1979; stalemate conference with Senate.	Passed Senate Nov., 1979; stalemate conference with House.	Authorized court banned items, but only until March 31, 1980.	Passed by the House and Senate and signed into law at the end of March 1980.

a. Called for flexibility in deposit rate ceilings, but tied the ceiling to the amount of assets in housing.
b. Included special tax and other financial institutions to invest in low- and moderate-income housing.
c. Broadened powers somewhat but only NOW accounts, share drafts, remote service units, and automatic transfers.
d. Includes same mortgage-lending powers for S&Ls as for commercial banks. Would therefore legalize a full range of alternative mortgage instruments; regulatory action would also be necessary to authorize such new mortgages.
e. No mortgage instrument tax credit, but preempts state usury ceilings.
f. Only authorizes share drafts, RSUs, and automatic transfer.
g. Preempts state usury ceilings, but only until March 31, 1980.
h. Phases out Regulation Q rate ceilings over six years, subject to the actions of a Depository Institutions Deregulation Committee.
i. Preempts state usury ceilings, but provides affected states the right to override the preemption.

Table 4-2.   Milestones in Deregulation.

May 1978	Federal regulatory agencies authorized commercial banks and thrift institutions to issue Money Market Certificates, effective June 1.
	These certificates have a 26-week maturity, a minimum denomination of $10,000 and interest ceilings indexed to the 26-week Treasury bill rate, with a differential between commercial banks and thrift institutions.
September 1978	The International Banking Act of 1978 was enacted.
	This legislation aimed at leveling the playing field between U.S. banks and branches and agencies of foreign banks.
December 1979	Federal regulatory agencies authorized commercial banks and thrift institutions to issue Small Saver Certificates, effective January 1, 1980.
	These certificates have a 30 to 48-month maturity, no minimum denomination and interest ceilings indexed to the average 2½-year yield for U.S. Treasury securities. Thrift institutions enjoy a ceiling differential.
March 1980	The Depository Institutions Deregulation and Monetary Control Act was enacted.
	This legislation authorized NOW accounts nationwide, extended reserve requirements to nonmember banks and other depository institutions, expanded the powers of thrift institutions, and created the Depository Institutions Deregulation Committee (DIDC). The DIDC was charged with gradual elimination of Regulation Q ceilings.
October 1980	The DIDC authorized a new category of 14 to 90-day time deposit.
	It established the ceiling on that account and NOW accounts at 5¼ percent, with no differential between commercial banks and thrift institutions. At the same meeting, the DIDC issued final rules governing premiums, finders fees and prepayment of interest on regulated deposits.
June 1981	The DIDC adopted a schedule for gradual phase-out of interest ceilings, beginning with longer term accounts.
July 1981	The U.S. District Court of the District of Columbia invalidated the phase-out schedule which the DIDC had adopted.

(*Table 4-2. continued next page*)

Table 4-2. continued

August 1981	The Economic Recovery Tax Act of 1981 was passed.

This act authorized depository institutions to issue All Savers Certificates, effective October 1, with interest paid exempt from Federal Income Taxes and broadened eligibility for IRA and Keogh Accounts, effective January 1, 1982.

September 1981 The DIDC increased interest ceilings on passbook and statement savings accounts by 50 basis points, effective November 1.

At the same meeting, it authorized a ceilingless instrument for IRA and Keogh Accounts.

October 1981 The DIDC postponed indefinitely the scheduled increase in passbook and statement savings account interest ceilings.

March 1982 The DIDC adopted a new schedule for gradual phase-out of interest ceilings, beginning with accounts with maturity of 3½ years or longer.

At the same meeting, it authorized a new 91-day savings certificate with a $7,500 minimum denomination and interest ceilings tied to the 13-week Treasury bill rate. The ceilings give thrift institutions a one-quarter point differential.

Source. Federal Reserve Bank of Minneapolis *Annual Report* 1981.

The Hunt Commission

The Hunt Commission was officially labeled as the President's Commission on Financial Structure and Regulation. In its 1971 report, the Hunt Commission proposed sweeping legislative changes in the financial regulatory framework. These proposals included:

1. Removal of deposit rate ceilings.
2. Allowing nonbank depository institutions to offer transactions accounts.
3. Broadening the loan and investment authority of depository institutions.
4. Imposition of uniform federal income tax provisions for depository institutions.

5. Transferral of the examination and supervisory functions of the Fed, FDIC, and Comptroller of the Currency to two new agencies — one for federally chartered and one for state chartered institutions.
6. Creation of a single deposit insurance agency for all depository institutions.
7. Elimination of differential reserve requirements via mandatory Fed membership.
8. Urging states to allow statewide branching.

The FINE Report

The congressional FINE report (Financial Institutions and the Nation's Economy) reiterated many of the Hunt Commission proposals and added some of its own. The FINE report urged repeal of the statutory prohibition of interest payment on demand deposits. It recommended easing entry and branching restrictions for financial institutions, as had the Hunt Commission. Broader powers for thrift institutions (consumer loans, credit card issuance, trust powers, transactions accounts), equal tax treatment, uniform reserve requirements, and elimination of deposit rate ceilings were proposed. Also in harmony with Hunt Commission recommendations were proposals to consolidate regulatory, supervisory, and deposit insurance functions in a new agency.

Also in 1975, a U.S. Senate report offered similar recommendations. Like the Hunt Commission and FINE reports, continuing tax and other subsidy programs were recommended to support the mortgage market.

These proposals by the Hunt Commission and the FINE study represented the most important review and assessment of the financial system in many years. This similarity in philosophy and recommendation was perhaps remarkable. While neither set of recommendations was enacted into law, these studies obviously set the stage for the reform of the financial structure that began with DIDMCA.

Economic Events

We have seen how virtually all of the legislative changes embodied in DIDMCA had been proposed in earlier efforts aimed at the study and reform of the financial system. These previous attempts over a considerable time span reflected the pressures that had been building for a restructuring of depository financial institutions in the United States.

The increased volatility and high levels of interest rates that characterized the 1970s made it difficult for specialized financial institutions to fulfill their basic functions. The impact of high and volatile interest rates coupled with an inverted yield curve had been especially pronounced on the savings and loan industry. Indeed, the existence of the industry itself had been brought into question. Equally important, though, in forcing change had been the spread of electronic means of communication. A strong argument could be made that changing economic and financial conditions along with advances in technology had already produced structural changes in the nature of financial institutions and that Congress, with its passage of DIDMCA, was merely legitimizing many of these changes.[3]

As previously noted, many of the recommendations of the Hunt Commission were subsequently incorporated into the FINE Discussion Principles prepared by the House Banking Committee in 1975. Hearings were also held in 1975 on proposals to reform the financial structure, and the Financial Reform Act of 1976 was introduced into the House. The bill incorporated a variety of diverse recommendations and was, apparently, too broad to receive serious consideration. Further, there was only limited external economic and financial pressure for reform at this time.

External pressures for financial reform were increased when the U.S. Court of Appeals for the District of Columbia Circuit ruled that the financial institution regulatory agencies—the Federal Reserve Board, the Federal Home Loan Bank Board, and the National Credit Union Administration—had exceeded their authority in allowing depository financial institutions to offer interest-bearing transactions accounts such as automatic transfer from savings to checking for commercial banks, share drafts for credit unions, and remote service units for savings and loans. The court allowed Congress until January 1, 1980, to pass legislation that would give the financial regulatory agencies appropriate authority. If not authorized by this date, the activities would be prohibited.

Responding to the pressure of this court ruling, the House passed on September 11, 1979, the Consumer Checking Account Equity Act. This proposed legislation expressly gave authority to the financial regulatory agencies to authorize various forms of interest-bearing transactions accounts. It also extended NOW accounts to all depository financial institutions nationwide. The Senate then passed on November 1, 1979, the Depository Institutions Deregulation Act. This more comprehensive act included the following terms: (1) authorization of those practices banned by the Court of Appeals; (2) authorization of NOW accounts nationwide; (3) approval for savings and loans to invest up to 10 percent of their assets in unsecured consumer loans, commercial paper, and corporate debt securities; (4) authority for savings and loans to invest in real estate on the same terms as national banks; (5) the phase-out of Regulation Q ceilings over a ten-year period; and (6) the preemption of state usury ceilings on mortgage interest rates.

The two bills were sent to a conference committee. However, unable to agree on a compromise prior to adjournment, Congress authorized the courtbanned practices until March 31, 1980. Finally, just prior to this deadline Congress passed the Depository Institutions Deregulation and Monetary Control Act. It is important to note that the final bill that emerged from the conference committee was quite different from either bill that had been sent to the committee. In fact, some of the provisions of the bill reported out of the conference committee had never been discussed by either the House or Senate.

In many respects, the legislation from the U.S. Congress in reforming the financial system was reactive rather than proactive. Congress responded to enormous changes in the financial system that had made the old rules obsolete. These changes and innovations included the following: (1) the development of money market certificates of deposit; (2) the development of NOW accounts and other forms of interest-bearing transactions accounts; (3) development of adjustable rate mortgages; and (4) enormous technological changes. Table 4-2 provides a chronology of some of these developments both before and after DIDMCA. The implications of these developments are significant for all financial institutions.

First authorized on June 1, 1978, money market certificates profoundly changed the balance sheet of the savings and loan industry. By the end of 1979, almost 30 percent of the total deposits at savings and loans were accounted for by these variable rate deposit instruments. The growth in these certificates has dramatically shortened the liability structure of savings and loans and made their sources of funds much more sensitive to interest rates. A similar effect has been produced by the development and growth of NOW accounts in New England and with their spread nationwide. In addition, as sources of funds have become more sensitive to interest rates and as interest rates have become high and volatile, it is even more important to emphasize variable rate lending.

More fundamentally, however, passage of DIDMCA was facilitated by the reinterpretation that was made by academics and others of the economic and financial collapse of the 1930s.[4] For many years, it had been thought that the distress conditions in the economy of the 1930s generally reflected the inability of monetary policy to counter an economic decline, while the banking collapse of that period was attributed to excess competition. More recent research, however, suggests that the economic conditions of the period had been accentuated (if not caused) by incorrectly applied monetary policy and that excessive competition was not associated with the failure of individual financial institutions. As a result, legislation that improved the functioning of monetary policy became more important, and there appeared to be little objection from a social perspective to greater competition among depository institutions.

DESCRIPTION OF DIDMCA

DIDMCA contained nine titles, each dealing with an aspect of reform of the financial system.[5] Taken together, these provisions were intended to improve both the implementation of monetary policy and the equity in financial regulation. Basic to the legislation, of course, was the desire to increase the degree of competition in the financial system. *Title I* addressed the problem of declining membership by commercial banks in the Federal Reserve System and the range of reserve requirements among the different types of depository financial institutions. *Title II* dealt with Regulation Q, which limits the rates depository institutions may pay for time and savings deposits and provides for the gradual elimination of such limitations. *Title III* granted to all depository financial institutions nationwide the right to offer to individuals some form of interest-bearing checking accounts. *Title IV* increased the lending powers of thrift institutions, primarily by giving savings and loan associations the legal right to increase the proportion of consumer loans in their portfolios. *Title V*

Table 4-3. Ten Major Provisions of DIDMCA.

1. Established uniform reserve requirements for all depository financial institutions (transition period March 31, 1980, to March 31, 1988).

2. Instructed the Federal Reserve System to provide services, including access to the discount window, to all depository institutions.

3. Instructed the Federal Reserve to publish a price schedule for services and to charge all users of Fed services on the basis of the established price schedule.

4. Consolidated the power to set interest rate ceilings (Regulation Q) in the Deregulation Committee and instructs that committee to eliminate the ceilings gradually. Interest rate ceilings are to be eliminated by March, 1986.

5. Authorized all depository institutions nationwide to provide, in effect, checking account services.

6. Empowered all depository institutions, in effect, to pay interest on demand (checkable) deposits.

7. Raised the federal deposit insurance coverage on individual accounts from $40,000 to $100,000 (for all insured depository institutions).

8. Authorized savings and loan associations to expand greatly their consumer loan business, to issue credit cards, and to offer trust services.

9. Authorized mutual savings banks to make business loans and to accept demand deposits from business customers.

10. Eliminated the effects of state usury laws on certain types of loans (mortgage, business, and agricultural).

sharply reduced the applicability of state usury laws. The remaining four titles covered some narrow, although important, issues concerning the regulation of financial institutions. Table 4-3 lists ten major provisions of the act; a brief summary of the provisions of each of the first five titles to the act follows.

Title I—The Monetary Control Act of 1980. This title established new reserve requirements and extended their applicability to all depository institutions, including those not members of the Federal Reserve System (Fed). Specifically, this title provided for identical reserve requirements for member and nonmember commercial banks, thereby sharply reducing any incentive to withdraw from the Fed. It further established the same reserve requirements for commercial

Table 4 4. Depository Institutions Reserve Requirements After Implementation of the Monetary Control Act.

Type of Deposit and Deposit Interval	Percent
Net transactions accounts	
$0–$26.3 million	3%
Over $26.3 million	12
Nonpersonal time deposits	
by original maturity	
Less than 2.5 years	3
2.5 years or more	0
Eurocurrency liabilities	3

Notes: Transactions accounts include all deposits on which the account holder is permitted to make withdrawals by negotiable or transferable instruments, payment orders of withdrawal, and telephone and preauthorized transfer (in excess of three per month) for the purpose of making payment to a third person or others

Nonpersonal time deposits are time deposits, including savings deposits, that are not transactions accounts and in which the beneficial interest is held by a depositor that is not a natural person.

Source: *Federal Reserve Bulletin*, May 1983, Statistical Section, p. A8.

banks as for savings and loan associations, mutual savings banks, and credit unions. Prior to passage of the act, reserve requirements for these groups differed, as did reserve requirements for commercial banks that are members of the Federal Reserve system (all national banks and some state chartered banks) relative to "nonmember" banks. After 1988, the year in which full implementation of the act will be complete, Federal Reserve discretionary changes in reserve requirements will affect the levels of required and excess reserves at all depository institutions simultaneously and to the same degree. (Table 4–4 provides information on reserve requirements after implementation of DIDMCA).

An important section included in Title I instructed the Federal Reserve Board to publish, not later than September 1, 1980, a set of pricing principles and a schedule of fees for services performed by the Federal Reserve banks for depository institutions.[6] Prior to the passage of this act, Federal Reserve services to member banks generally had been furnished without charge. The act extended availability of the Fed's services to *all* depository institutions, but at a fee. The purpose in requiring the publication of the pricing principles and fee schedule was to provide an opportunity for public comment. Having allowed a full year for comments and debate, the act then required the Federal Reserve Board to implement the system of service fees.

Title II — Depository Institutions Deregulation. This title provided for the gradual elimination of the limitations on interest rates payable on accounts in depository institutions covered by the act. These Regulation Q ceilings had been criticized as discriminating against small savers and also as producing disintermediation during periods of high interest rates, when funds tend to flow into high-yielding, open-market instruments such as money market funds and "away from" financial intermediaries. The phasing out of interest rate controls was to occur over a six-year period and was to have been completed by or before March 31, 1986 (this timetable was subsequently accelerated in 1982).

The act established the Depository Institutions Deregulation Committee (DIDC) to implement the phased elimination of deposit rate ceilings. The voting membership of the DIDC are the Secretary of the Treasury, and the chairs of the Federal Reserve, the Federal Deposit Insurance Corporation, the Federal Home Loan Bank Board, and the National Credit Union Administration. (The Comptroller of the Currency is a nonvoting member.)

This committee was instructed to eliminate the interest rate ceilings while observing the effects upon the housing market and small savers, as well as the viability of depository institutions in general. Special note was to be taken of the effects, if any, upon thrift institutions of eliminating the interest rate differential they had been allowed to pay in excess of those paid by commercial banks.

Title III — Consumer Checking Account Equity Act of 1980. Title III authorized all depository institutions, in effect, to provide checking account services. It also authorized Automatic Transfer Systems (ATSs) accounts, which provide for automatic funds transfer from interest-bearing to demand accounts, and negotiable order of withdrawal (NOW) accounts and share drafts for individual depositors and religious, charitable, and philanthropic organizations. ("Share drafts" refer to checks drawn on account that are technically "share deposits" in depositor-owned institutions.) These accounts, while not legally checking accounts, are functionally the equivalent of demand deposits, although paying interest. Prior to this act, depository institutions in only a few states (primarily in New England) offered these services. This title also raised federal deposit insurance coverage for individual accounts in all insured depository institutions from $40,000 to $100,000.

Title IV — Power of Thrift Institutions and Miscellaneous Provisions. Prior to passage of the act, consumers of financial services faced a number of specialized kinds of depository institutions. For checking privileges, commercial banks were the main supplier. Similarly, if a consumer needed the services of a trust department, a commercial bank was the only feasible source. Credit cards and consumer loans were generally unavailable at savings and loans associations and mutual savings banks. To obtain the maximum yield on savings deposits, consumers had to deal with savings and loan associations, mutual savings banks, and credit unions rather than commercial banks. For home mortgage loans, the sources of available funds were principally the nonbank thrift institutions.

The 1980 legislation not only eliminated many of the regulatory differences between depository institutions but also reduced the effects of many of the remaining restrictions. Savings and loan associations, for example, were empowered to issue credit cards and to expand greatly their consumer loan business. Mutual savings banks were allowed to make business loans and accept demand deposits from their business customers. The act had the effect of enabling depository institutions to become "financial supermarkets" at which consumers could shop for checking accounts, trust administration, mortgage loans, credit accounts, and other services.

Title V — State Usury Laws. The act effectively exempted several kinds of loans from state usury laws (e.g., mortgage, business, and agricultural loans). These provisions became essential parts of the act because, at the time of its passage, the inflation rate was approximately 18 percent, and the prime interest rate was approaching 20 percent. This high level of interest rates was causing usury laws to become especially troublesome, producing severe distortions in the flow of credit. With a state-mandated maximum interest rate of 10 percent and a market rate of 9 percent, a usury ceiling would have no effect. But with the same 10 percent usury limitation and a market rate of, say, 20 percent, borrowers would want to borrow more funds (at the maximum legal rate) than creditors would be willing to lend. The ensuing shortage of funds would cause home building, farm production, and small business activity to suffer. Further, lenders have an incentive to lend outside the state to escape usury ceilings, thus reducing available funds in states with usury laws.

Usury laws are generally enacted with the intention of protecting low-income individuals from excessive rates of interest. The real effect, however, is to reduce loan availability during periods of inflation when creditors add an inflation premium to their interest charges. If the inflation rate is high, as it was in the spring of 1980, the market interest rate is likely to rise above the maximum rates allowed under usury laws. When it does, small businesses, farmers, and home builders are often forced out of the market as lenders "ration" credit at the ceiling rate of interest. The 1980 legislation dealt directly with these problems, and, in effect, eliminated usury ceilings on many types of loans.[7]

WHAT WAS LEFT OUT?

Although the Omnibus Banking Act of 1980 was grounded in the earlier recommendations of the Hunt Commission and the Discussion Principles of the FINE study, only selected portions were incorporated into the legislation.[8] Indeed, in hindsight, the act may be judged more important for what it did not do than for what it did. Some of these omissions—intentional or not—are noted below.

Equality of Regulation.   Both the Hunt Commission and the FINE study dealt with the functions of depository institutions and the need for equality of regulation. The FINE study, perhaps the most far-reaching in its recommended changes, favored creation of a set of depository institutions that were virtually indistinguishable in function. Yet, such equality of function requires equality of taxation, equality of capital adequacy guidelines, and so forth. The Omnibus Banking Act of 1980 attempted to bring greater similarity of function to the nation's depository institutions, but did not deal with equality of taxation or other such matters of law and regulation. This omission may prove important, as the act may have inadvertently given some financial institutions a regulatory advantage over others.

If so, the inequality may create substantial problems for the financial system.

Availability of Mortgage Credit. To a considerable extent, passage of the Omnibus Banking Act in early 1980 involved the intent to save the thrift industry and the mortgage market. Yet, when the Hunt Commission and the FINE study approached the same problems, they recognized that broadening the power of the thrifts might reduce the flow of credit to the mortgage market. They, therefore, proposed a mortgage subsidy. Since no such subsidy was incorporated into the Omnibus Banking Act, the effect of the reforms on the availability of mortgage credit remains an open issue.

The Regulatory Framework. The Hunt Commission and the FINE study recognized that it was illogical to have similar types of depository financial institutions regulated by different agencies. Both proposed consolidating the overlapping and complex system of financial regulation. The FINE study went furthest by proposing that regulation, supervision, and examination of all federally chartered depository institutions be handled by a single commission. This would merge into one agency the functions of the Comptroller of the Currency, the Federal Deposit Insurance Corporation, the regulatory and supervising function of the Federal Reserve, the Federal Home Loan Bank Board, and the National Credit Union Administration. Despite the apparent logic of such a reform, the Omnibus Banking Act made no changes in the structure of the regulatory agencies. This omission may cause serious problems if individual agencies attempt to gain a competitive edge.

Branching. The Hunt Commission and the FINE study recommended increased branching powers for commercial banks. In fact, it would seem that expanded branching powers for financial institutions would be an integral part of any attempt to reduce regulation. Less regulation and more competition are likely to push more institutions into financial distress. As alternatives to closings, it would be more reasonable to allow acquisition by a holding company or absorption into a branch system. Indeed, there have been a number of forecasts that the Omnibus Banking Act will lead to consolidation of depository financial institutions. Such a consolidation would be much easier with expanded branching. In fact, such potential failures seem increasingly likely to produce changes in the financial system that will force consideration at the federal level of interstate branching.

Provision of Banking-Type Services by Nondepository Institutions. The DIDMCA of 1980 also did not deal directly with the growing number of nondepository institutions providing banking-type services, but without the regulation applicable to depository institutions. It is true that the provision to phase-out Regulation Q interest rate ceilings did deal indirectly with the competition that was posed by money market funds. But it was not until 1982, when the Garn–St Germain Act was passed, that legislation specifically authorized depository institutions to offer a deposit vehicle fully competitive with money market funds.

CONCLUSIONS AND IMPLICATIONS

The DIDMCA made a number of major changes in the allowable functions of depository institutions and in the regulation of these institutions (summarized in Table 4–5). The new ability of nonbank depository institutions to offer transactions accounts and the provision for gradual elimination of Regulation Q interest rate ceilings certainly provide for enormous changes in the operations of depository institutions. Important also are the broadened lending powers of the thrift institutions. From a monetary policy perspective (as well as a regulatory view), the authority granted to the Federal Reserve to set reserve requirements for all depository institutions may have especially long-lasting consequences. While the general thrust of the legislation was toward reducing regulatory limitations on the borrowing and lending powers of individual depository institutions, major changes (often referred to as reregulation) in the nature of existing regulation and the powers of different regulatory authorities were an important part of the legislation.

That DIDMCA was a response to a real or perceived financial crisis is not surprising given the history of enacted and failed financial reform proposals. It must be recalled that there was an intervening period of almost fifty years between the financial reform legislation of the 1930s and the passage of DIDMCA. Yet what may be surprising is the short period of time between passage of DIDMCA and the

Table 4-5. A Before and After Comparison of the Principal Features of DIDMCA.

Before	After
No uniform reserve requirements for depository financial institutions. No uniform reserve requirements even for commercial banks. No reserve requirements at all for credit unions.	Reserve requirements for all depository financial institutions established at uniform levels by the Federal Reserve.
Federal Reserve provided services only to member commercial banks and generally without charge (excepting interest on borrowing).	Federal Reserve provides services, including access to the discount window, to all depository institutions, although on an explicit fee basis.
Interest rate ceilings established separately by each regulatory agency, although with mutual consultation and coordination.	Power to control interest rate ceilings transferred to deregulation committee with instructions to eliminate ceilings gradually, completely by 1986.
Interest-bearing transactions accounts (NOW accounts, share drafts, and so forth) generally available at all depository institutions only in the northeastern United States.	All depository institutions nationwide allowed to offer interest-bearing transactions accounts.
Transactions accounts generally available at all depository institutions only in the northeastern United States.	All depository institutions nationwide allowed to offer transactions accounts.
Savings and loans generally not allowed to make consumer loans, except those related to housing and not allowed to offer trust services. Mutual savings banks not allowed to make business loans or accept demand deposits.	Savings and loans allowed to make large amounts of consumer loans and to offer trust services. Mutual savings banks allowed to make business loans and to accept demand deposits from their business customers.
State usury laws had substantial effect on flow of credit in different states.	Application of state usury laws virtually eliminated.

Source: Donald R. Fraser and Gene C. Uselton, "The Omnibus Banking Act," *MSU Business Topics*, Autumn 1980.

enactment of another financial reform bill. Clearly, DIDMCA did not achieve all its objectives of salvaging the financial system from financial crisis. It was a short two years later when—in 1982—Congress again considered and passed additional major financial reform legislation in the Garn-St Germain Depository Institutions Act of 1982, which is the subject of the next chapter.

NOTES TO CHAPTER 4

1. George Kaufman, "The Depository Institutions Deregulation and Monetary Control Act of 1980: What Has Congress Wrought," *Journal of the Midwest Finance Association* (1981), pp. 20–35. Also, Cargill and Garcia point out the following similarities and differences between DIDMCA and the financial reform legislation of the 1930s. The similarities include the following: (1) both represent response to a crisis; (2) both deal with financial reform and monetary policy; (3) both concentrate on the soundness of depository institutions. The principal difference in the two sets of legislation focuses on different interpretations of soundness. In the 1930s, soundness was interpreted to mean the reduction of competition and the protection of depository institutions against failure. By 1980, soundness of the financial system was interpreted to mean an increase in competition and management flexibility at depository institutions and was thought to be consistent with the failure of some individual institutions. See: Thomas Cargill and Gillian Garcia, *Financial Deregulation and Monetary Control*, (Stanford, Ca.: Hoover Institution Press, 1982).

2. The Hunt Commission is more properly called the "President's Commission on Financial Structure and Regulation." The less formal designation is an acknowledgment of the committee chairman, Reed O. Hunt, then Chairman of the Board, Crown Zellerbach Corporation. As Cargill and Garcia (*Financial Deregulation and Monetary Control*) point out, the DIDMCA of 1980 reflects both the philosophy and many of the specific proposals of the Hunt Commission.

3. Rapid technological change, particularly the development of electronic funds transfer systems, should also contribute to the consolidation of the financial system by increasing the extent of economies of scale. In the past, economies of scale have been limited in the financial services industry.

4. Cargill and Garcia, *Financial Deregulation and Monetary Control*, pp. 31–33.

5. For additional information on the legislation, see Charles R. McNeill, "The Depository Institutions Deregulation and Monetary Control Act of 1980," *Federal Reserve Bulletin* 66 (June 1980), pp. 444–453; and Thomas McCord, "The Depository Institutions Deregulation and Monetary Control Act of 1980," *Issues in Bank Regulation* 3 (Spring 1980), pp. 3–7.

6. The specific services to be covered by the fee schedule were (1) currency and coin services; (2) check clearing and collection services; (3) wire transfer services; (4) automated clearinghouse services; (5) settlement services; (6) securities safekeeping services; (7) Federal Reserve float; and (8) any new services that the Federal Reserve System offers, including but not limited to payment services to effectuate the electronic transfer of funds.

7. In the case of mortgage credit, a state could reinstate usury law limitations prior to March 31, 1983. Moreover, business and agricultural loans of $25,000 or more are exempted from state usury laws. This blanket exemption was replaced on April 1, 1983, by a rate ceiling rule that provides for a maximum rate on loans of these kinds of 5 percent more than the prevailing Federal Reserve discount rate. Again, this provision can be overridden by the state legislatures.

8. A number of the proposals of previous study groups were omitted from DIDMCA. These included the previous proposals to allow all depository institutions to offer demand deposits (as contrasted to NOW accounts), and the proposals to create equality of taxation for all depository institutions.

5 THE GARN-ST GERMAIN DEPOSITORY INSTITUTIONS ACT OF 1982

The Depository Institutions Deregulation and Monetary Control Act of 1980 that was discussed in the previous chapter was passed, at least partially, to deal with the thrift institutions problem. But by 1982 the thrift problem had become the thrift crisis. Many savings and loans that were financially distressed in 1980 were bankrupt by 1982, principally reflecting the extraordinarily high interest rates in 1981 and 1982. In addition, the pace of technological change was clearly accelerating while the innovations in the financial services industry, particularly from nonbank institutions, were continuing at a rapid rate. The net effect of these developments, as well as other pressures for financial reform, was passage in October 1982 of the Garn-St Germain Depository Institutions Act of 1982.

Garn-St Germain has been called the most significant piece of banking legislation to pass Congress in fifty years (such a claim was also made about DIDMCA). In fact, in most respects the legislation was quite narrow in scope. While there were a number of parts to the legislation that dealt with specific (and principally technical) details of the operations and regulation of depository institutions, the major focus of the legislation was on preventing the collapse of the thrift industry. This rescue legislation encompassed both short- and long-run dimensions. The short-run component of Garn-St Germain sought to prop up the industry until fundamental changes incorpo-

127

rated into the legislation (as well as changes in functions authorized by previous legislation) could make the industry viable. The long-run component sought to transform radically the nature of the industry so that the basic financial problems that affected thrifts in the late 1970s and early 1980s would never occur again. Related to this long-run component, Garn-St Germain also provided for the more rapid elimination of Regulation Q and for the introduction of a deposit account (the money market deposit account) that was competitive with money market mutual funds.

This chapter summarizes the major provisions of the Garn-St Germain Depository Institutions Act of 1982, but concentrates primarily on those features of the legislation affecting the functions of depository institutions. Technical features of the legislation are covered either in a cursory fashion or not at all. In addition, the chapter discusses some of the effects of the legislation from the time of its passage and implementation until late 1983, roughly one year later. Important issues left unaddressed by the legislation are dealt with at the closing of the chapter.

MOTIVATION FOR THE PASSAGE OF GARN-ST GERMAIN

To a considerable extent the principal motivation for passage of the Garn-St Germain Act was fear. Managers of savings and loan associations and other thrifts feared that their institutions would collapse as the high interest rates they were having to pay to attract funds exceeded in many instances the rates they were earning on their portfolios. The result was a decline in traditional capital ratios to levels below those acceptable to regulators and, in some cases, to negative levels. The regulators themselves also feared the collapse of the industry they were charged with regulating and fostering. Finally, Congress feared the potential spread of these problems into the entire financial system and particularly the possibility of a run on the commercial banking industry should savings and loans fail in large numbers. Congress was also concerned over the potential effects of a thrift industry collapse on the availability and cost of mortgage credit.

A related factor in producing Garn-St Germain was the realization that the deregulation of deposit rate ceilings and lending powers at savings and loans and other thrifts (that had been contained in DIDMCA in 1980) had not gone far enough. That legislation had allowed thrift institutions to enter the competition for transactions accounts by offering interest-bearing negotiable order of withdrawal (NOW) accounts. Yet these transactions accounts were limited to individuals and nonprofit organizations, a provision of the legislation that continued to screen the thrifts out of the market for business accounts. The DIDMCA had also provided for gradual phasing out of Regulation Q. However, thrifts (as well as commercial banks) continued to operate at a disadvantage as compared to money market funds in attracting deposits. On the asset side of the balance sheet, while the 1980 legislation had broadened the lending powers of thrifts, it did not appear that the changes had been extensive enough to allow the thrift institutions to balance effectively the interest sensitivity of their assets and liabilities.

A need to enact a number of technical changes into the banking laws also motivated the proponents of the 1982 legislation. Some of these technical changes were of interest and concern only to a few managers in the banking industry. Others were of great concern to all participants in the financial system. An example of the latter case was the controversy over due-on-sale provisions of mortgage contracts (which serve to block mortgage assumptions by purchasers of residential properties). Court decisions in California had effectively blocked enforcement of the due-on-sale clause of mortgage contracts and substantially reduced the flow of mortgage credit in that state. Garn-St Germain specifically provided for override of state-imposed restrictions on the due-on-sale clause of mortgage contracts.

PRINCIPAL FEATURES OF GARN-ST GERMAIN

As already stated, the 1982 legislation may be viewed in either the short or long run. Within a short-run context, the legislation sought to rescue and support the thrifts until more far-reaching reforms could become effective. The legislation ultimately sought to reform the basic functions of the thrift institutions so that they would be viable and competitive regardless of interest rate levels.

Exhibit 5–1.   Rescue Powers of the Regulators.

The FDIC (or the Federal Savings and Loan Insurance Corporation) can make a loan to, deposit in, purchase assets of, purchase securities issued by, assume liabilities of, or make contributions to any insured institution to prevent closing, to restore normal operations, or, if severe financial conditions threaten the stability of a number of insured institutions or of insured institutions possessing significant financial resources, to lessen the risk to the FDIC (or FSLIC) posed by that insured institution.

When an insured institution is closed or is about to close, or the stability of a number of insured institutions is threatened, the FDIC or FSLIC may, to facilitate a merger or consolidation, purchase assets or assume liabilities of the insured institution; make loans or contributions to, or deposits in; or purchase securities of the purchasing or merging insured rescuing institution or the company controlling the rescuing institution; and/or guarantee the insured rescuing institution or company controlling it, against loss.

However, assistance may not be provided in excess of that determined to be reasonably necessary to save the cost of liquidation, unless the FDIC or FSLIC determines the continued operation of the insured bank is essential to the community.

Any institution receiving assistance under this provision may defer payment of state and local taxes based on deposits or interest paid until the assistance isn't any longer outstanding. After the assistance is repaid, the institution must pay the deferred taxes.

Source: Federal Reserve Bank of New York, *Capsule* (January 1983), pp. 4–5.

Rescue of the Thrifts

In Titles I and II of the act, both of which are effective until 1985, regulatory agencies are given a number of broadened powers to deal with troubled banks and thrifts. These broadened powers are summarized in Exhibits 5–1 and 5–2. Exhibit 5–1 relates to the so-called net-worth certificate program that was designed to improve the book net-worth position of floundering institutions.[1] Exhibit 5–2 describes the major changes in the ability of the regulatory authorities to deal with closed institutions.

Prior to passage of this legislation, the regulatory authorities' ability to deal with floundering or failing institutions was limited to the following actions: (1) payoff of insured depositors and liquidation of

---

Exhibit 5-2. Sale of Closed Institution.

- When a closed FDIC-insured commercial or savings banks has assets of $500 million or more, the FDIC, as receiver, may, with any necessary approval of any court or supervisory agency, sell the closed bank to an in-state insured depository institution owned by an out-of-state bank or bank holding company.

- When a failing FDIC-insured mutual savings bank has assets of $500 million or more, and the FDIC determines the savings bank is in danger of closing, the bank may, with regulatory approval, merge with or sell its assets and transfer its liabilities to an in-state insured depository institution owned by an out-of-state bank or bank holding company.

- The FDIC may solicit offers from any prospective purchaser it determines qualified, including out-of-state banks and bank holding companies. If the lowest acceptable offer isn't from an existing in-state bank of the same type, the FDIC is required to solicit reoffers from original bidders if their offers were within 15 percent or $15 million, whichever is less, of the lowest acceptable offer.

  Priority must be given in the following order: institutions of the same type in the same state; institutions of the same type in different states; institutions of different types in the same state; and institutions of different types in different states. In considering interstate offers, the FDIC is required to give priority to those located in adjoining states.

- In acting to permit an out-of-state acquisition, the FDIC can't approve an acquisition which doesn't meet the anti-trust provisions of the Sherman Act or the Clayton Act, unless the FDIC finds the anticompetitive effects of the transaction are clearly outweighed by the public interest.

Source: Federal Reserve Bank of New York, *Capsule* (January 1983), p. 6.

---

the bank by a receiver; (2) the sale of the institution to another institution of the same type in the same state; or (3) if it were determined that continued operation of the institution was essential to the local community, the regulators could provide a loan or other form of assistance. Given the general unwillingness of the regulators to liquidate a failing institution, the sale of the institution or assistance to it often was perceived as the desirable alternative, especially if the problem institution was a large one. Yet the sale of a large institution to another large institution of the same type within the same state was often difficult, given a small number of potential acquiring institutions and the constraints imposed by the antitrust statute. Also, the ability of the regulators to provide assistance was highly limited, for only in a small number of situations could it be argued that the survival of the institution was essential to the community.[2]

The 1982 legislation allows the regulators to make a loan to, deposit in, purchase assets of, purchase securities issued by, and assume liabilities of a failing institution. As a part of this portion of the act, the FSLIC and FDIC are authorized to purchase net-worth certificates from floundering thrifts and real estate oriented banks.[3] For regulatory purposes these certificates issued by the floundering organizations are treated as capital and thereby boost the capital position of the troubled institutions that have been eroded by losses.[4] As pointed out by Garcia et al.,[5] the net-worth certificate program has a number of potential benefits. It contributes to the maintenance of a competitive financial institutions system, it reduces the risk of failure for floundering institutions, it allows regulators to "gamble" that falling interest rates will allow their rescue efforts to succeed without any cash outlay, and it assists in the early identification of nonviable institutions.

The Garn-St Germain Act also alleviated the problems faced by the regulatory authorities in finding acquiring firms for failing institutions by expanding the geographic and institutional barriers constraining such mergers. Under the new legislation, the FDIC may allow the acquisition of a large commercial bank or mutual savings bank (over $500 million in total assets) by another federally insured institution whether the institution is in-state or out-of-state. The FSLIC may arrange a merger of a failing savings and loan on similar terms, except that its new powers may be used without regard for the size of the institution. For a failing savings and loan, any qualified purchaser (including a nonfinancial organization) may offer a bid. For a failing bank, bids may be taken only from federally insured depository institutions. If the lowest bid comes from either an out-of-state institution or from an institution of a type different from the failing one, then bids may be taken again. The following priorities guide the regulatory authorities in minimizing their loss from the sale:

1. same type, in-state institutions;
2. same type, out-of-state institutions;

3. different type, in-state institutions,
4. different type, out-of-state institutions;
5. among out-of-state bidders, priority is to be given to adjacent state institutions;
6. the FSLIC, but not the FDIC, is to give priority to minority-controlled bidders when a minority-controlled thrift fails.

Fundamental Reforms

The act also provided for fundamental changes in the *role* of depository institutions. These changes were most pronounced at savings and loans and mutual savings banks, though they also affected directly and indirectly the commercial banking industry and other financial institutions. Without question, these reforms in the functions of financial institutions will in the long run prove to be the most significant aspects of the legislation. By markedly changing the possible sources and uses of funds at thrift institutions (and to a lesser extent at commercial banks), the legislation will fundamentally affect the roles of depository institutions in the nation's financial system. In particular, the authority to offer money market deposit accounts with no interest rate ceiling represents a fundamental change in the ability of depository institutions to compete for funds. This aspect of the legislation, as well as other important features, are discussed below.

Deposit Powers. Examining first the effects of the legislation on the means by which depository institutions raise funds, the authorization of money market deposit accounts (MMDA) represents a remarkable and revolutionary development. For the first time the nation's depository institutions were given the power to offer a deposit account that was comparable to and fully competitive with shares offered by money market funds. The Depository Institutions Deregulation Committee authorized, effective December 14, 1982, the offering of the MMDA with a minimum balance of $2,500 (subsequently changed to $1,000 after January 1, 1985, and zero after January 1, 1986) and with no interest rate ceiling.[6] The account allows six transfers per month—three by check and three by preauthorized, automatic, or telephonic means. Unlike most money market mutual funds that have a rather high minimum denomination

---

Exhibit 5-3. Principal Changes in Sources of Funds under Garn-St Germain.

- Money Market Deposit Account with no interest rate ceiling permitted for all depository institutions.
- Federal, state, and local governments authorized to hold NOW accounts.
- Federally chartered savings and loans authorized to offer demand deposits to persons or organizations that have a business loan relationship with the association or that wish to receive payment due from nonbusiness customers.
- Depository Institutions Deregulation Committee instructed to eliminate by the beginning of 1984 any Regulation Q rate differentials between banks and thrifts.

---

per check ($500 has been quite common), there is no legislative or regulatory minimum for the checks written against the money market deposit accounts. In order to make the accounts more competitive with the money market funds, no reserve requirements were imposed on personal accounts, though a 3 percent reserve requirement was imposed on nonpersonal MMDAs.

The Depository Institutions Deregulation Committee quickly followed up the MMDA with the "Super-NOW account." Effective January 5, 1983, depository institutions were allowed to offer an account (commonly referred to as the Super-NOW) that had unregulated interest rates *and* also allowed unlimited checking. This account carried an initial $2,500 minimum, as did the MMDA. In contrast to the MMDA, which is treated as a savings account for reserve requirement purposes, the Super-NOW was, quite properly, treated as a transactions account and carried a 12 percent reserve requirement.

Another aspect of the 1982 act that substantially affected the competitive position of depository institutions—banks and thrifts alike—was a broadening of the groups permitted to hold interest-bearing transactions accounts at depository institutions (see Exhibit 5-3). In particular, federal, state, and local governments were permitted to hold NOW accounts. Federally chartered savings and loans were allowed to offer demand deposits to persons or organizations that have a business relationship with the association or that wish to receive payments due from nonbusiness customers. And, though of diminishing importance as Regulation Q ceilings are phased out, the

> **Exhibit 5-4.** Principal Changes in Uses of Funds under Garn-St Germain.
>
> - Savings and loans are allowed to invest up to 55 percent of their assets in three varieties of commercial loans: (1) loans secured by commercial real estate up to 40 percent of assets; (2) secured or unsecured commercial loans up to 5 percent of assets; (3) leasing, up to 10 percent of assets.
> - Savings and loans are allowed to invest in consumer loans up to 30 percent of assets. The DIDMCA of 1980 had allowed savings and loans to invest up to 20 percent of their assets in consumer loans. In addition, the types of consumer loans that savings and loans could make was broadened to include inventory and floor-planning loans.
> - Savings and loans are also allowed to invest in state and local government revenue bonds.

DIDC was required to remove—no later than the beginning of 1984—any remaining differences in the maximum rates that may be paid by banks and thrifts on deposit accounts.

These changes in the deposit account powers of depository institutions are remarkable. They virtually eliminate the possibility of disintermediation at these institutions in future years since they make it possible for depository institutions to bid for funds at market rates regardless of the level of interest rates. Yet it is also important to note that the 1982 legislation did not, in this regard at least, reduce the mismatch of interest-sensitive assets and liabilities at thrifts. In fact, it could be argued that since by their very nature MMDAs are highly interest-rate sensitive, the 1982 legislation may have increased the gap between rate-sensitive assets and rate-sensitive liabilities.[7] It was the changes in the asset powers of thrifts that were designed to close this rate sensitivity gap, a topic to which we now turn.

Asset Powers. The 1982 Garn-St Germain Act also made some fundamental changes in the asset allocation powers of depository institutions, especially at thrift institutions. Taken together, the purpose of these changes was to broaden and diversify the assets held by thrifts and to increase the proportion of those assets that were held in rate-sensitive form. The specific changes (summarized in Exhibit 5-4) include the following points.

Thrift institutions are allowed much greater access to the commercial loan market than had been provided for by DIDMCA in 1980. That legislation had allowed savings and loans to make loans secured by commercial real estate for up to 20 percent of their assets (the thrifts, though, would have to hold a first mortgage on the property). Under the 1982 legislation, the savings and loans are allowed to invest up to 55 percent of their assets in the following varieties of commercial loans: (1) loans secured by commercial real estate up to 40 percent of assets; (2) secured or unsecured commercial loans up to 5 percent of assets; and (3) leasing, up to 10 percent of assets. In addition, the 1982 legislation substantially broadened the consumer lending powers of the thrifts. The power of savings and loans to invest in consumer loans was increased from 20 percent (as provided in the DIDMCA of 1980) to 30 percent of assets. Perhaps more important, the types of consumer loans that savings and loans may make was broadened considerably, and now includes inventory and floor-planning loans. Finally, the 1982 legislation increased the ability of savings and loans to invest in government securities, by giving them the power to invest in state and local government revenue bonds (the 1980 legislation had allowed savings and loans to invest an unlimited amount in federal, state, and local government general obligation securities).

These broadened asset powers should alter the revenue mix of savings and loans, though considerable risk also exists as the associations enter lending areas in which they lack experience. The broadened asset powers coupled with the broadened deposit powers may also contribute to a reduced cost of funds. In past years, savings and loans were allowed to offer a higher deposit rate than commercial banks in order to compensate for their inabilities to provide the wide range of financial services offered by banks, including transactions accounts. As savings and loans begin to offer a competing range of financial services, including transactions accounts, such deposit rate premiums should not be necessary.

OTHER FEATURES OF THE ACT

The 1982 legislation contained a number of other significant features beyond those discussed above. These include a due-on-sale provision, a re-examination of deposit insurance, and various changes in regulations applying to national banks and bank holding companies.

Due-on-Sale Clauses

Garn-St Germain through its Title III–Part C, put an end to the extensive legal controversy over the enforcement of due-on-sale features of many mortgage contracts. Under these contract provisions, the lender has the authority to make the full amount of the loan due at the time of sale of the property that secures the loans. For long-term, fixed-rate lenders (such as thrifts) in a rising interest rate environment the ability to enforce the due-on-sale feature of the mortgage contract is vital in reducing the interest sensitivity gap (the difference between interest rate sensitive assets and interest rate sensitive liabilities). Given the speed with which much residential property turns over, an effective due-on-sale feature in a mortgage contract effectively shortens the life of a long-term, fixed-rate mortgage and allows the lender to benefit. In a period of rising interest rates, of course, the gain to the lender from the due on-sale feature is the loss to the borrower. The existing borrower could sell the property at a higher price if the existing low-rate mortgage could be transferred to a purchaser.

The due-on-sale provision of mortgage contracts became a policy issue when, in 1978, the California Supreme Court ruled that enforcement of the contract was unreasonable and when, later, California court decisions extended the prohibition of enforcement of this provision of the loan contract to *both* state and federally chartered institutions that operated in California. The United States Supreme Court subsequently (in 1982) ruled that, with regard to federally chartered institutions, the due-on-sale contract could be enforced regardless of the decision of California state courts. This action was subsequently broadened and strengthened by provisions of the Garn-St Germain legislation that allow federal override of state restrictions on due-on-sale clauses for a large number of lenders on real property.[8]

Deposit Insurance

While Garn-St Germain itself made no change in the nation's deposit insurance system, it did set in motion the process for potentially significant reform in that system. In particular, the legislation required the three deposit insurance agencies—the Federal Deposit Insurance Corporation for commercial banks and mutual savings banks, the Federal Savings and Loan Insurance Corporation for savings and loan associations and the National Credit Union Administration for credit unions—to engage in studies of the entire deposit insurance system. These studies were to be conducted with regard to a number of issues, including how deposit insurance, as currently constituted, affects the operation of depository institutions and assessment of possible alternatives to (and changes in) the current system. The deposit insurance system and potential changes in that system are discussed in the next chapter.

National Banks and Bank Holding Companies

A number of changes were made by Garn-St Germain in the powers of national banks and bank holding companies. The regulatory changes applicable to national banks generally resulted in an increase in their operating flexibility. In contrast, some of the regulations governing bank holding companies were tightened.

Perhaps the most significant change in the operating powers of national banks relates to their lending authority. Prior to Garn-St Germain, national banks could lend no more than 10 percent of their capital to any one borrower. This limitation was relaxed substantially, so that the percentage is now 15 percent plus an additional 10 percent for loans secured by readily marketable collateral. In addition, the legislation allowed national banks to form bank service companies and to invest in export trading companies. Both of these devices allow national banks considerably more flexibility. Banks may also form banker's banks as a means of providing services to groups of banks in competition with the existing correspondent banking system. The banker's bank authority, as well as the bank service corporation, are especially relevant to smaller banks.

Many of the provisions of Garn-St Germain already discussed also relate to bank holding companies. For example, the emergency provisions of the legislation governing the priorities that must be established in the acquisition of failing banks or savings and loans relate as well to bank holding companies. Bank service corporation functions—that were in fact broadened by Garn-St Germain—also relate to bank holding companies. Of particular importance, though, and not yet discussed, are the provisions of the act that affect financial transactions among affiliates of bank holding companies and that relate to the insurance activities of bank holding companies. The 1982 legislation allowed—with the exception of low-quality assets—almost unrestrained transfer of assets between affiliated banks in a multibank holding company. It also substantially liberalized the collateral requirements for bank loans to affiliated companies. In contrast to this liberalization of powers, the legislation prevents, with some exceptions, bank holding companies from providing insurance as principals, agents, or brokers.

WHAT WAS LEFT OUT?

Just as the DIDMCA of 1980 made fundamental but incomplete changes in the nation's financial system, so too did the Garn-St Germain Act. Indeed, since much of what Garn-St Germain did was to extend further the deregulation provisions of the 1980 legislation, much of what was left undone by Garn-St Germain is essentially identical with what was left undone by DIDMCA. These include the following points:

Equality of Regulation. Both the 1980 and 1982 legislative actions substantially reduced the regulatory differences among the nation's various depository institutions. Substantial differences in legally permitted functions, however, remain among banks, savings and loans, mutual savings banks, and credit unions. Differences in capital requirements and taxation, to name only two, remain as very important regulatory differences among the depository institutions. The 1982 legislation also did not deal with the entry of nonbank firms into the financial services industry.[9]

Branching and Chartering. Neither DIDMCA nor Garn-St Germain dealt with the restrictions on branching and chartering that have traditionally limited the extent of competition between banks and other depository institutions. The prohibition of banking organization expansion through interstate branching as specified in the McFadden Act, as well as the restrictions on interstate expansion of bank holding companies as given in the Douglas Amendment to the Bank Holding Company Act, were not changed by DIDMCA or Garn-St Germain. However, Garn-St Germain did, as discussed above, provide a priority system for interstate acquisition of failing banks and savings and loans. With regard to chartering, both the 1980 and 1982 legislations were silent, though deregulation would seem to encompass a policy of freedom of entry into the industry.

Product Offerings. The Garn-St Germain legislation also provided for very limited changes in the types of products that could be offered by depository institutions. While savings and loans were given broader authority, the services they were allowed to offer were those traditionally provided by depository institutions. The divisions between the functions of commercial banks and investment banks were retained, despite the growing overlap of function between the securities industry and the banking industry. In particular, the prohibition of commercial bank underwriting of municipal revenue bonds was not changed by Garn-St Germain.

SOME EARLY EVIDENCE ON THE EFFECTS OF GARN-ST GERMAIN

One of the principal purposes of Garn-St Germain was to rescue the thrifts. This rescue did have, as pointed out above, both short-run and long-run dimensions. From a short-run perspective, the net-worth provisions of the legislation and the emergency rescue sections of the bill were meant to solve the immediate and pressing problem of large numbers of failing institutions. From a longer viewpoint, the reforms in the deposit-taking and lending powers of the thrifts were designed to make the institutions viable under any interest rate level.

It is interesting to note that the thrift problem receded rapidly after passage of Garn-St Germain. Indeed, the industry as a whole turned from negative to positive profitability shortly after passage of the legislation. Yet the legislation itself had little or nothing to do with the changes in the fortunes of the industry. That reversal in fortunes was principally the result of a fortuitous decline in interest rates that began in August 1982 and continued irregularly through late 1983. For the liability-sensitive thrifts, the declining rates achieved a turnaround in profitability that more fundamental reforms would have taken years to achieve. Yet whether this restoration to profitability of the thrifts is permanent or not depends upon the continuation of lower interest rates.

The MMDAs that were introduced as a result of Garn-St Germain proved, in their first years, to be a great success. The amount of funds raised by depository institutions well exceeded early expectations, so that by the end of 1983 total MMDA deposits exceeded $370 billion. To some extent these funds came from money market mutual funds, with the result that assets of money market mutual funds fell by almost $100 billion in the year after creation of the MMDA. Most of the funds that went into MMDAs, however, issued from transfer from other bank and thrift deposits, thereby really raising the cost of funds to these institutions.

CONCLUSIONS AND IMPLICATIONS

The Garn-St Germain Depository Institutions Act of 1982 represented the second major legislative initiative to deregulate depository institutions within a two-year period, a remarkable development after a period of almost fifty years of limited legislation in this area. While the bill can quite properly be viewed as a rescue effort for thrifts it also may be viewed within a broader context. Together with DIDMCA, Garn-St Germain granted extensive freedom for depository institutions to innovate within the financial marketplace. Pricing restrictions on deposits were almost completely removed, though restrictions on product offerings and other operations of depository institutions were retained.

NOTES TO CHAPTER 5

1. The insolvency of savings and loans may be viewed either from an accounting or an economic perspective. From an accounting perspective, the losses incurred at many savings and loans in the late 1970s and early 1980s had eroded the net-worth position of many organizations to the point where the ratio of equity capital to total assets was below accepted regulatory minimums or, in some cases, below zero. In contrast, from an economic perspective, if the assets of savings and loans were valued at market rather than cost, *most* savings and loans would have had negative net-worth positions.

2. For an extensive review of these powers and the problems caused by them for the regulatory authorities, see Paul Horvitz, "Failure of Large Banks: Implications For Banking Supervision and Deposit Insurance," *Journal of Financial and Quantitative Analysis* (November 1975), pp. 589–600.

3. The net-worth certificates had no effect on the income position of savings and loans since the interest rates on the promissory notes issued by the regulatory agencies and the net-worth certificates issued by the depository institutions were the same.

4. The amount of net-worth certificates that a troubled institution may issue is limited. Institutions with net worth from 0 to 1 percent of assets could issue net-worth certificates for up to 70 percent of the previous year's losses. Institutions with net worth from 1 to 3 percent may issue a smaller quantity of net-worth certificates. Limitations on the amount of net-worth certificates are also imposed on institutions that have excessive operating expenses.

5. Gillian Garcia et al., "The Garn-St Germain Depository Institutions Act of 1982," Federal Reserve Bank of Chicago *Economic Perspectives* (March/April 1983), pp. 3–31.

6. The NOW account interest rate ceiling is applicable to those MMDAs whose balance falls below the minimum requirement.

7. An extensive discussion of the effects of the money market deposit accounts on the asset/liability position of savings and loans and the possible responses by savings and loan management is provided by Donald J. Puglisi and Anthony J. Vignola,"Funds Deployment and Money Market Deposit Accounts," *Federal Home Loan Bank Board Journal* (September 1983), pp. 9–15.

8. The override by federal law of state restrictions on the enforceability of the due-on-sale clause by Garn-St Germain included two exceptions: (1) The law allows a "window period" such that mortgages created during this period remain subject to the state laws for three years. The window period is the period from the date the state prohibited the due-on-sale clause until passage of the Garn-St Germain Act in October, 1982. (2) The legislation prohibits enforcement of the due-on-sale clause if the property is transferred to close family members.

9. For more information see Harvey Rosenblum and Diane Siegal, *Competition in Financial Services: The Impact of Nonbank Entry*, Federal Reserve Bank of Chicago, Staff Study 83–1.

6 THE RISK OF DEPOSITORY INSTITUTION FAILURE AND THE ROLE OF DEPOSIT INSURANCE

The Garn-St Germain Depository Institutions Act of 1982 included a provision requiring each of the federal deposit insurance agencies to conduct a study of the current system of federal deposit insurance and transmit a report to Congress within six months of the date of the legislation's enactment. The agencies were asked to address the following issues:

1. The current system of deposit insurance and its impact on the structure and operations of depository institutions;

2. The feasibility of providing depositors the option to purchase additional deposit insurance covering deposits in excess of the general limit provided by law and the capabilities of the private insurance system, either directly or through reinsurance, to provide risk coverage in excess of the general statutory limit;

3. The feasibility of basing deposit insurance premiums on the risk posed by either the insured institution or the category or size of the depository institution rather than the present flat-rate system;

4. The impact of expanding coverage of insured deposits upon the operations of insurance funds, including the possibility of increased or undue risk to the funds;

5. The feasibility of revising the deposit insurance system to provide even greater protection for smaller depositors while fostering a greater degree of discipline with respect to large depositors;

6. The adequacy of existing public disclosure regarding the condition and business practices of insured depository institutions, and providing an assessment of changes which may be needed to assure adequate disclosure;

7. The feasibility of consolidating the three separate insurance funds.[1]

The reemergence of deposit insurance as a major public policy issue was perhaps an inevitable result of the wave of changes in the U.S. financial system of the past decade. The U.S. deposit insurance system had been the attention of quiet academic inquiry for decades. But it was not until the various economic developments, financial innovations, increased incidence of depository institution difficulty, and the legislative and deregulatory actions of the late 1970s and early 1980s that the prospect for substantive alteration of the structure of deposit insurance became at all likely. As stated in the FDIC study report, *Deposit Insurance in a Changing Environment*:

> Deposit insurance has been an integral part of the financial system for almost a half century, responsible in considerable part for the depository institution structure that has evolved and the nature of the supervision and regulation of depository institutions. It is, therefore, impossible to consider any government action taken in connection with the changing financial structure without addressing the role of the insuring agencies.[2]

This chapter describes the deposit insurance structure and the administrative aspects of the system, discusses the special significance of deposit insurance for the regulation of depository institutions, and describes and assesses various proposals for reform. Since, as discussed in Chapter 2, deposit insurance is specifically designed to prevent banking market failure, the issue of failure risk is also addressed.

THE STRUCTURE OF THE DEPOSIT INSURANCE SYSTEM

The adoption of a deposit insurance system for the United States in 1933 was a bold measure. Only one other nation (Czechoslovakia, in 1924) had established such a national system. In this country, a number of state deposit insurance schemes—New York (1828), Vermont (1831), Indiana (1834), Ohio (1845), Iowa (1855), Oklahoma (1908), Nebraska (1909), Texas (1910), Mississippi (1915), South Dakota (1916), and Washington (1917)—had all failed.[3] But the failure of more than 9,000 commercial banks in the period from 1930 to 1933 prompted Congress to act.

Motives for the Establishment of Deposit Insurance

The establishment of federal deposit insurance stemmed from a mixture of economic concerns and political considerations. The foremost concern was a desire to reestablish confidence in banks and end bank runs. But there was a further desire to protect small depositors (the original ceiling for deposit insurance of $2,500 was raised to $5,000 a year later, where it remained until 1950) who were least expected to be able to discriminate among sound and unsound banks. The support of small banks for deposit insurance largely reflected concerns that small depositors would seek safety in *size*—that fears of bank failure would result in a flow of deposits to larger banks in the absence of the security provided by deposit insurance. Further, smaller banks, insofar as they were unit banks opposed to liberalization of branching laws, saw deposit insurance as a bulwark against proponents of branching as a means of increasing safety and soundness of banks.[4] Large banks were less supportive of (and many were even opposed to) deposit insurance, partly because large banks were less prone to failure stemming from loss of depositor confidence. Further, since deposit insurance premiums were to be assessed as a percentage of total deposits, and since only a portion of deposits were to be insured, large banks were to pay more under the system. This is true because larger banks are likely to have more (and larger) deposit accounts that exceed the ceiling amount of insurance per account and thus a larger ratio of uninsured deposits to total deposits. Larger banks, therefore, generally receive less deposit insurance protection per premium dollar and (unless they constitute a riskier case than smaller banks) in this sense subsidize smaller banks.

It is likely, given the banking crisis of the day, that a more extensive regulatory and examination system would have been set in place even if deposit insurance had not been enacted. But the latter pro-

Table 6–1. Number and Deposits of Banks Closed Because of Financial Difficulties, 1934–1982.

Year	Total	Non-insured[a]	Total	Without Disbursements by FDIC[b]	With Disbursements by FDIC[c]
			Number		
				Insured	
Total	*764*	*136*	*628*	*8*	*620*
1934	61	52	9	—	9
1935	32	6	26	1	25
1936	72	3	69	—	69
1937	84	7	77	2	75
1938	81	7	74	—	74
1939	72	12	60	—	60
1940	48	5	43	—	43
1941	17	2	15	—	15
1942	23	3	20	—	20
1943	5	—	5	—	5
1944	2	—	2	—	2
1945	1	—	1	—	1
1946	2	1	1	—	1
1947	6	1	5	—	5
1948	3	—	3	—	3
1949	9	4	5	1	4
1950	5	1	4	—	4
1951	5	3	2	—	2
1952	4	1	3	—	3
1953	5	1	4	2	2
1954	4	2	2	—	2
1955	5	—	5	—	5
1956	3	1	2	—	2
1957	3	1	2	1	1
1958	9	5	4	—	4
1959	3	—	3	—	3
1960	2	1	1	—	1
1961	9	4	5	—	5
1962	3	2	1	1	—
1963	2	—	2	—	2

Table 6-1. continued

Deposits (in thousands of dollars)				
		Insured		
Total	Non-insured[a]	Total	Without Disbursements by FDIC[b]	With Disbursements by FDIC[c]
20,143,213	143,500	19,999,713	41,147	19,958,566
37,332	35,365	1,968	—	1,968
13,988	583	13,405	85	13,320
28,100	592	27,508	—	27,508
34,205	528	33,677	328	33,349
60,722	1,038	59,684	—	59,684
160,211	2,439	157,772	—	157,772
142,788	358	142,430	—	142,430
29,796	79	29,717	—	29,717
19,540	355	19,185	—	19,185
12,525	—	12,525	—	12,525
1,915	—	1,915	—	1,915
5,695	—	5,695	—	5,695
494	147	347		347
7,207	167	7,040	—	7,040
10,674	—	10,674	—	10,674
9,217	2,552	6,665	1,190	5,475
5,555	42	5,513	—	5,513
6,464	3,056	3,408	—	3,408
3,313	143	3,170	—	3,170
45,101	390	44,711	26,449	18,262
2,948	1,950	998	—	998
11,953	—	11,953	—	11,953
11,690	360	11,330	—	11,330
12,502	1,255	11,247	10,084	1,163
10,413	1,173	8,240	—	8,240
2,593	—	2,593	—	2,593
7,965	1,035	6,930	—	6,930
10,611	1,675	8,936	—	8,936
4,231	1,220	3,011	3,011	—
23,444	—	23,444	—	23,444

(*Table 6-1. continued overleaf*)

Table 6-1. continued

| | | | Number | | |
| | | | | Insured | |
Year	Total	Non-insured[a]	Total	Without Disbursements by FDIC[b]	With Disbursements by FDIC[c]
1964	8	1	7	—	7
1965	9	4	5	—	5
1966	8	1	7	—	7
1967	4	—	4	—	4
1968	3	—	3	—	3
1969	9	—	9	—	9
1970	8	1	7	—	7
1971	6	—	6	—	6
1972	3	2	1	—	1
1973	6	—	6	—	6
1974	4	—	4	—	4
1975	14	1	13	—	13
1976	17	1	16	—	16
1977	6	—	6	—	6
1978	7	—	7	—	7
1979	10	—	10	—	10
1980	10	—	10	—	10
1981	10	—	10	—	10
1982	42	—	42	—	42

a. For information regarding each of these banks, see table 22 in the 1963 *Annual Report* (1963 and prior years), and explanatory notes to tables regarding banks closed because of financial difficulties in subsequent annual reports. One noninsured bank placed in receivership in 1934, with no deposits at time of closing, is omitted (see table 22, note 9). Deposits are unavailable for seven banks.

b. For information regarding these cases, see table 23 of the *Annual Report* for 1963.

c. For information regarding each bank, see the *Annual Report* for 1958, pp. 48–83 and pp. 98–127, and tables regarding deposit insurance disbursements in subsequent annual reports. Deposits are adjusted as of December 31, 1982.

Source: *Annual Report of the Federal Deposit Insurance Corporation*, Washington, D.C.: FDIC, 1982.

Table 6-1. continued

		Deposits (in thousands of dollars)		
			Insured	
Total	Non-insured[a]	Total	Without Disbursements by FDIC[b]	With Disbursements by FDIC[c]
23,867	429	23,438	—	23,438
45,256	1,395	43,861	—	43,861
106,171	2,648	103,523	—	103,523
10,878	—	10,878	—	10,878
22,524	—	22,524	—	22,524
40,134	—	40,134	—	40,134
55,229	423	54,806	—	54,806
132,058	—	132,058	—	132,058
99,784	79,304	20,480	—	20,480
971,296	—	971,296	—	971,296
1,575,832	—	1,575,832	—	1,575,832
340,574	1,000	339,574	—	339,574
865,659	800	864,859	—	864,859
205,208	—	205,208	—	205,208
854,154	—	854,154	—	854,154
110,696	—	110,696	—	110,696
216,300	—	216,300	—	216,300
3,826,022	—	3,826,022	—	3,826,022
9,908,379	—	9,908,379	—	9,908,379

vided a new regulatory rationale, and the FDIC constituted a new means of regulating and supervising banks. Thus, the FDIC joined the Comptroller of the Currency, the Federal Reserve Board, and the various state agencies in the task of regulating and monitoring the sprawling U.S. banking system. Further, the FDIC also took on the task of dealing with failed and failing banks whose numbers the agency's very existence was meant to shrink.

Table 6-1 indicates the statistical record of bank failure since 1934, and reveals that, until quite recently, failures were almost entirely limited to small banks. Certainly, this record is one of vast improvement over the pre-1934 record, as Figure 6-1 makes clear. Most observers credit deposit insurance as the primary reason for the relatively low rate of bank failure since 1934 (see Figure 6-2). Since its establishment, the FDIC has handled more than 620 insured bank failures, and, as indicated in Figure 6-3, almost 99 percent of deposits in these institutions have been protected for depositors.

Nature of the Deposit Insurance System

The deposit insurance program established by the Banking Act of 1933 was not intended to cope with another crisis like that of the preceding three years, but rather was meant to help *avert* such crises in the future. It was believed that the existence of deposit insurance, coupled with a more extensive supervisory and regulatory system, would limit bank failures to a manageable number. More specifically, the financial demands on the system were projected to be within the capabilities of the deposit insurance fund that was accumulated from premium contributions of participating banks. (In addition to the insurance fund, the FDIC is authorized to borrow up to $3 billion from the Treasury, if necessary, to pay deposit claims.)

The FDIC was established to provide deposit insurance for commercial banks. Soon thereafter, legislation established the Federal Savings and Loan Insurance Corporation to insure deposit insurance for S&Ls. The FSLIC, unlike the FDIC, was not made an independent agency, but was instead housed in the Federal Home Loan Bank System and administered by the Federal Home Loan Bank Board (FHLBB). The FDIC and FSLIC have very similar functions and powers, although administrative procedures and organizational form differ. For example, the FSLIC relies on the FHLBB for the services

Figure 6-1. Number of Bank Failures, 1920–1982.

Year	Total Bank Suspensions	Year	Total Bank Suspensions
1920	168	1952	4
1921	505	1953	5
1922	367	1954	4
1923	646	1955	5
1924	775	1956	3
1925	618	1957	3
1926	976	1958	9
1927	669	1959	3
1928	499	1960	2
1929	659	1961	9
1930	1,352	1962	3
1931	2,294	1963	2
1932	1,456	1964	8
1933	4,004	1965	9
1934	61	1966	8
1935	32	1967	4
1936	72	1968	3
1937	84	1969	9
1938	81	1970	8
1939	72	1971	6
1940	48	1972	3
1941	17	1973	6
1942	23	1974	4
1943	5	1975	14
1944	2	1976	17
1945	1	1977	6
1946	2	1978	7
1947	6	1979	10
1948	3	1980	10
1949	9	1981	10
1950	5	1982	42
1951	5		

Source: Adapted from, *Annual Report of the Comptroller of the Currency*, Washington, D.C.: Office of the Comptroller of the Currency, Department of the Treasury.

Figure 6-2. Deposits and Losses in All Insured Banks Requiring Disbursements by FDIC, 1934–1982.

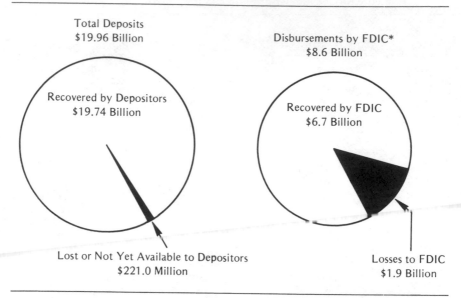

Total Deposits
$19.96 Billion

Recovered by Depositors
$19.74 Billion

Disbursements by FDIC*
$8.6 Billion

Recovered by FDIC
$6.7 Billion

Lost or Not Yet Available to Depositors
$221.0 Million

Losses to FDIC
$1.9 Billion

*Includes collections and disbursements by liquidators in the field ($1.5 billion) which were previously excluded from this chart.

Source: *Annual Report of the Federal Deposit Insurance Corporation, 1982.*

of examiners and other staff personnel. Also, the FSLIC's status as a part of the Federal Home Loan Bank system serves to consolidate the supervisory, regulatory, and insurance function in a single agency for all federally chartered S&Ls—unlike the multi-agency system for national banks.

The third deposit insurance fund—the National Credit Union Insurance Fund (NCUIF)—was established in 1970. The NCUIF, which is administered by the National Credit Union Administration or NCUA (also established in 1970), insures deposits in credit unions in a fashion similar to the FDIC and FSLIC. (The NCUA charters, supervises, and regulates federally chartered credit unions.)

Pricing

The 1933 Banking Act set FDIC premiums at one-twelfth of 1 percent of the deposits (less certain adjustments) of insured banks.

Figure 6-3.   Insured Bank Failures, 1934–1982.

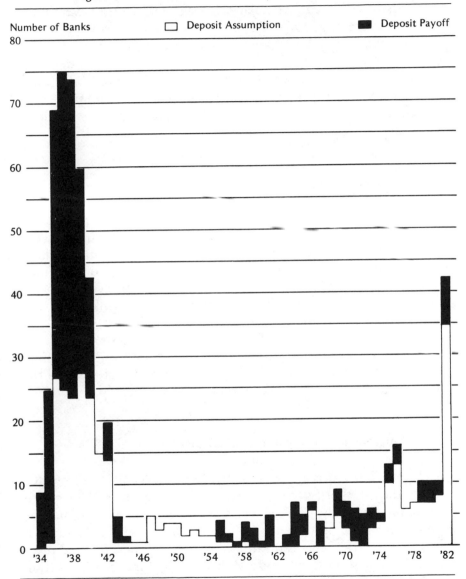

Source: *Annual Report of the Federal Deposit Insurance Corporation, 1982.*

These assessments, to be remitted semi-annually, were to provide funds for operating costs as well as maintenance of an insurance fund. Beginning in 1962, annual rebates to insured institutions of two-thirds of collected assessments, less agency expenses, were mandated by Congress. In 1981, this mandated rebate level was trimmed to 60 percent, with lesser or greater amounts being permitted according to the amount of the reserve fund relative to insured deposits. In 1982, the effective assessment rate to FDIC-insured banks was one-thirteenth of 1 percent of assessable deposits, up from one-fourteenth of 1 percent in 1981. FSLIC premiums are similarly structured.

Covered Deposits

The deposit insurance plan focused on the amount, not the type, of deposit. The ceiling amount was raised periodically, the most recent hike being to $100,000 in the DIDMCA of 1980. Demand, savings, and time deposits in commercial banks were covered up to the ceiling amount, with savings and loan association shares and deposits being similarly covered. Nondeposit liabilities of insured banks were not covered. The distinction in favor of amount of deposit, rather than type of deposit, is significant in the sense that it suggests that protection of depositors is a primary purpose, prevention of bank failure (due to depositor runs) is a secondary purpose, and protection of the money supply (transactions accounts) is at best a tertiary objective.

Surveillance of Insured Institutions

The deposit insurance agencies (FDIC, FSLIC, NCUIF) are obliged to share their authority to supervise and examine insured banks with the Comptroller of the Currency, the Federal Reserve System, and the various state banking commissions. Procedures for federal examinations are currently being standardized by the Federal Financial Institutions Examination Council established by the Financial Institution and Interest Rate Control Act of 1978. Deposit insurance agency examiners constantly monitor insured institutions for signs of trouble. Call reports and other data are periodically scrutinized. Loan portfolios and management practices are assessed during on-site ex-

Table 6-2. Number of Problem Banks Listed by FDIC, 1968-1983.

1968	240	1976	385
1969	216	1977	368
1970	251	1978	342
1971	239	1979	287
1972	190	1980	217
1973	155	1981	223
1974	181	1982	369
1975	347	1983[a]	620

a. As of November, 1983.

Note: FDIC classification procedures were revised in 1980.

Sources: 1968-1976, compiled by Joseph F. Sinkey from fourth-quarter Problem-Bank Lists prepared by the FDIC's Division of Bank Supervision. See Joseph F. Sinkey, Jr., *Problem and Failed Institutions in the Commercial Banking Industry* (Greenwich, Conn.: Jai Press, 1979), p. 59. 1977-1982: year-end figures cited in FDIC *Annual Reports*.

aminations with an eye to any evidence of questionable loans and dubious management actions. "Problem" institutions are pinpointed as those having high potential asset losses relative to capital. In the case of banks, the number of problem banks is usually small as a percentage of all insured banks. At year-end 1983, more than 600 FDIC-insured banks were so classified, as shown in Table 6-2.

The traditional secrecy concerning the identity of perceived "problem" institutions (and the nature of their problems) was long viewed as necessary to protect the institutions from a rush of withdrawals by uninsured depositors. Until recently, public policy generally permitted and encouraged agencies to be highly secretive about information developed from the surveillance process.

Financial Disclosure by Depository Institutions

Full disclosure of relevant financial information to the public by business corporations is the core concept for regulation of the securities markets in this country. The Securities Act of 1933 mandated numerous financial disclosures pertaining to new securities issues and established the Securities and Exchange Commission (SEC). The Securities Exchange Act of 1934 required periodic reporting to stockholders and the SEC of the operating results and financial position of publicly held companies, independent of any new security issues. Banks, however, were largely excluded from the purview of these acts and of the SEC. The reason for these general exemptions from financial disclosure requirements lay in concerns about public confidence in the banking system. Further, it was argued that the existence of government regulation and deposit insurance obviated the need for mandated financial disclosure.[5]

Deposit institutions are, of course, obliged to generate a great deal of financial information for supervisory authorities. The issue was the degree of confidentiality with which regulators were to treat such financial disclosures, particularly those of an adverse nature. Until recent years, the rule was to treat adverse information as highly confidential.

In 1964, disclosure requirements were extended to banks by amendments to the Securities Exchange Act of 1934, with the various banking supervisory agencies being given responsibility for their administration. Also, as more banks adopted the holding company form of organization, they became subject to the 1930s securities acts. (The 1933 and 1934 acts exempted banks, but not bank holding companies.) The eventual effect was to bring most large banks under the disclosure requirement framework. As for smaller banks outside this net, the supervisory agencies began moving toward policies of increased disclosure in the 1970s.

The increase in the number of problem depository institutions in the 1970s brought new demands for more public disclosure of the financial position of these institutions. The SEC instituted a series of new disclosure requirements concerning loan portfolio composition, problem loans, and other sensitive subjects. The FDIC (for $25) began offering reports on the earnings, assets, liabilities, and financial structure of every FDIC-insured bank. These reports also offer comparisons of each bank with other banks in its home state in terms of its financial profile and performance. In 1984, the FDIC will begin including information on problem loans and interest rate risk of the banks. The FDIC and comptroller of the currency are currently considering requiring public audits of financial statements of national banks, public announcements of disciplinary actions taken against (named) banks, and disclosing bank weaknesses uncovered by examination.[6]

It is clear, insofar as the policy ever existed, that protecting depository institutions from adverse information disclosure is a dead letter. Any future changes in the deposit insurance system or the regulatory structure must be couched in terms of full disclosure.

Treatment of Failed Institutions

Deposit insurance agencies can carry out their mission of protecting depositors of failed or failing insured institutions by any of five approaches. In the case of an FDIC- or FSLIC-insured institution failure, the agencies may choose to:

1. Close and liquidate the institution and pay depositors the full value of their insured deposits up to the maximum amount (sharing any losses due to an excess of the amount of insured deposits over the proceeds of liquidated assets with uninsured depositors and creditors); or

2. Assist in the process of the failed institution being absorbed by another (new or existing) institution (called a *purchase-and-assumption* transaction); or

3. Provide resources to keep the failing institution afloat; or

4. Reorganize the troubled institution (which would ordinarily require nondeposit creditor cooperation and concessions); or

5. Temporarily (a maximum of two years is allowed) take over operations of the failed institution.

The agencies generally employ either the liquidation or purchase-and-assumption method, with the FSLIC being much more apt to attempt to keep failing S&Ls viable (via FHLB advances and other efforts) than the FDIC in the case of its insured institutions that flounder.[7] While both the FDIC and FSLIC employ the purchase-and-assumption approach in the great majority of insured institution failures, the FDIC has been much more willing to liquidate failed institutions and pay off insured depositors than has the FSLIC (since 1945, about 74 deposit payoffs versus 148 assumption cases.) The FSLIC has experienced only one deposit payoff in the last decade.[8] And, for the FDIC, prior to the 1982 Penn Square Bank failure, all deposit payoffs since 1960 involved banks having average deposits of less than $8 million. Since 1934, the FDIC has handled 319 payoff cases involving deposits of $1.1 billion and 301 assumption cases involving $18.9 billion of deposits.

The 1933 legislation that created the deposit insurance system for commercial banks provided only for liquidation and deposit payoffs. A 1935 amendment provided that the FDIC could use its funds to arrange a purchase-and-assumption (rather than proceed with liqui-dation) if the agency regards this measure as serving to "reduce the risk or avert a threatened loss to the corporation." Purchase-and-assumption is often less costly to the FDIC than a deposit payoff, and the larger the failed bank, the more likely this will be the case. Further, finding a merger partner for larger banks tends to be easier than for smaller banks. However, the primary reason for the FDIC and FSLIC desire to avoid deposit payoffs, particularly for larger institutions, is concern for the effect that liquidations have on pub-lic confidence in depository institutions generally and their effect on uninsured depositors specifically. When insured institutions are liqui-dated and deposit payoff proceeds, uninsured depositors are likely to experience losses and, in any event, must await sale of assets and settling of claims before receiving even partial restitution. In a pur-chase-and-assumption case, all depositors and general creditors are fully protected against loss irrespective of the size of their deposit accounts (although stockholders and any subordinated creditors are likely to sustain losses). Thus, uninsured depositors have an incentive to place funds in larger institutions, since such institutions are less likely to be liquidated in the event of failure. It also follows that the greater the likelihood that failure of an institution will be handled via a purchase-and-assumption, the less motivation uninsured depositors have to scrutinize and monitor the failure risk of institutions in which they hold deposits.

In purchase-and-assumption transactions, the failed institution's assets and its deposits and nonsubordinated liabilities are assumed by the merger partner. (Recently, the FDIC has also provided financial assistance to facilitate "open-bank mergers" of failing savings banks.) The financial assistance provided the acquiring institution by the FDIC is intended to cover, in whole or in part, the shortfall between the amount of liabilities assumed by the latter firm and the value of assets being obtained. Such agency assistance may be cash or, in recent years, promissory notes on which the magnitude of interest payments are linked to performance of transferred assets.[9]

Payments and commitments necessary to effect purchase-and-assumption transactions ballooned for both the FDIC and FSLIC in 1981 and 1982, raising concerns about the insurance funds of the agencies (see Table 6-3). The FSLIC spent almost a billion dollars in 1981 managing thirty assisted mergers of savings and loan asso-ciations. The FDIC provided almost $1.8 billion in assistance arrang-

Table 6-3. Size of the Respective Funds (in millions) and Ratio to Insured Deposits.

	FDIC Fund Balance	FDIC Fund/ Insured Deposits	FSLIC Fund Balance	FSLIC Fund/ Insured Deposits
1982	$13,771	1.21%	$6,418	1.16%
1981	12,246	1.24	6,301	1.23
1980	11,019	1.16	6,462	1.29
1979	9,792	1.21	5,848	1.27
1978	8,795	1.16	5,328	1.26
1977	7,992	1.15	4,873	1.29
1976	7,268	1.16	4,480	1.37
1975	6,716	1.18	4,120	1.48
1974	6,124	1.18	3,791	1.60

Source: *Deposit Insurance in a Changing Environment*, Federal Deposit Insurance Corporation, 1983.

ing the mergers of eleven mutual savings banks in 1981 and 1982. To protect their cash and the book value of their insurance funds, the agencies made increased use of noncash assistance arranging mergers—promissory notes, contingent payment schemes, and various forms of "regulatory forgiveness" (such as relaxation of geographic and accounting restrictions). These measures, along with an increase in effective deposit insurance premiums, served (as of 1983) to result in a slight increase in the FSLIC insurance fund to about $7 billion and to increase significantly the FDIC fund to more than $14 billion. Nonetheless, concern about the viability of the deposit insurance system was sufficiently acute to result in a number of significant legislative changes in 1982 and to prompt Congress to approve a resolution declaring that the full faith and credit of the government stands behind insured bank deposits.

Increased Deposit Insurer Flexibility

Title I of the Garn-St Germain Depository Institutions Act of 1982, the Deposit Insurance Flexibility Act, broadened the scope of deposit insurance agency powers to cope with failing and failed institutions. Although the agencies are directed not to expend funds in excess of the alternative cost of liquidation (unless continued operation of the institution is deemed essential to the community), the FDIC and the FSLIC are now permitted to:

> make a loan to, deposit in, purchase assets of, purchase securities issued by, assume liabilities of, or make contributions to any insured institution, to prevent closing, to restore normal operations, or, if severe financial conditions threaten the stability of a number of insured institutions possessing significant financial resources, to lessen the risk to the FDIC (or FSLIC) posed by that insured institution.

Furthermore,

> when an insured institution is closed or is about to close, or the stability of a number of insured institutions is threatened, the FDIC or FSLIC may, to facilitate a merger or consolidation, purchase assets or assume liabilities of the insured institution; make loans or contributions to, or deposits in; or purchase securities of the purchasing or merging insured rescuing institution or the company controlling the rescuing institution; and/or guarantee the insured rescuing institution or company controlling it against loss.[10]

In addition to expanding the circumstances and forms by which the FDIC and the FSLIC can provide capital assistance to troubled, insured institutions and use its funds to facilitate mergers with rescuing institutions, the 1982 act allowed out-of-state acquisitions of failing institutions in certain circumstances. The need for increased flexibility of action on the part of deposit insurance agencies had become apparent as a result of relatively large bank failures of the previous decade and by the very real prospect of a wave of savings and loan association and mutual savings bank failures, but it is not at all clear that the Garn-St Germain Act did enough to facilitate management of future depository institution failures. The main feature of the capital-assistance program enacted by the legislation—issuance of "net-worth certificates" by the FDIC and FSLIC to troubled institutions—is limited to three years and is essentially only an accounting fix. Since the promissory notes issued by the deposit insurance agencies for the net-worth certificates carry the same yield as the latter, this program amounts only to an artificial expansion of the capital account. Thus, the agencies must still rely primarily on the deposit payoff and purchase-and-assumption approaches, both of which have problems in implementation.

Various proposals for reform of the deposit insurance system are assessed in a later section of this chapter. We turn now to a discussion of the relationship between deposit insurance and the regulatory framework for depository institutions.

DEPOSIT INSURANCE AS A BARRIER TO DEREGULATION

The special significance of asymmetric information relative to transactions account contracts between depositors and depository institutions was described in Chapter 2. The fact that, for most depositors, withdrawal of deposits is less costly (and more certain) than monitoring the financial soundness of depository institutions makes the latter subject to "runs" whenever safety concerns arise. Such runs may result in failure of affected institutions, even if they were otherwise financially sound.

The Value of Deposit Insurance

Deposit insurance addresses directly this market failure characteristic of banking.[11] Insured depositors need concern themselves only with one item of information bearing on the safety of any depository institution—whether or not it is insured. Insured depositors have no incentive to join in "runs" on institutions in which they have deposits. Deposit insurance agencies, in effect, monitor information for depositors via their role as supervisors and examinors. This monitoring function is perhaps performed more efficiently and effectively by these agencies since duplication of effort is avoided while scale economies are exploited, and examination by the agencies narrows the inherent information asymmetry and alleviates possible moral problems.

The most important perceived contribution of the deposit insurance system, however, is the contribution it makes to public confidence in the nation's banks. Rightly or wrongly, deposit insurance is frequently credited with having stabilized the U.S. banking system in the wake of crises in the 1930s. An average of only 48 banks per year failed in the first five years after establishment of the FDIC (1934–1939). In 1933, 4,000 banks had failed, following 1,453 failures in 1932, 2,293 in 1931, and 1,350 in 1930. After the disastrous record of these four years, the post-FDIC era looked halcyon, indeed! Even compared to the generally prosperous period from 1923 to 1929, when an average of 692 banks failed each year, the banking reforms of the 1930s appeared to be working well. During the postwar period, bank failures became relatively rare, and in the period from 1960 to 1974, an annual average of less than 6 banks failed. And while appropriately a matter for concerned attention, the increased number of failures since 1974—116 between 1975 and 1982 (42 in 1982)— clearly remains a manageable phenomenon.

It is possible, however, that the role that deposit insurance has played relative to the stability of the U.S. banking system since 1933 has been overstated. Certainly, other changes in the depository institution regulatory system (particularly increased restrictions on entry) have contributed to the sharp decrease in the rate of bank failure. Also, the purging of the weakest institutions in the period from 1930 to 1933 left the strongest banks to share the market. More importantly, the general stability of the overall economy in the postwar period has been a vital element of financial stability. While there have been periods of economic recession, these dips in the economy have not even approached the level of severity of 1930 to 1933.

It is likely that the most significant contribution of deposit insurance to preventing a crisis of confidence in depository institutions has been made in recent years—and not in the case of commercial banks but in the case of beleaguered savings and loan associations and mutual savings banks. The problems of these institutions in the 1970s and early 1980s were widely publicized and generally recognized by depositors. The fact that virtually all deposits in savings and loans are insured (unlike commercial banks) almost certainly kept the so-called "quiet run" on S&L deposits stemming from safety concerns from becoming a stampede.[12]

The Cost of Deposit Insurance

The contribution of deposit insurance to the averting of banking market failure is apparent. But what is the price paid for these benefits? The premiums paid by insured institutions, of course, are one cost aspect. These premiums have risen in recent years, and now average about one-fourteenth of 1 percent of assessable deposits. The burden of the premium is surely shared by depository institution stockholders (lower returns on equity), depositors (lower deposit yields), customers (higher loan rates and fewer services), and employees (lower wages). But there are other costs as well.

The existence of deposit insurance affects the behavior of depository institutions, the regulation of these institutions, and the financial markets in interconnected ways that impose costs on society.[13] Deposit insurance also dramatically affects the behavior of managers of depository institutions toward risk. Insured institutions escape the concerned scrutiny of insured depositors, and the risk of bankruptcy (and its resulting costs to management and stockholders) is greatly reduced at all levels of risk-taking. (Not only does deposit insurance eliminate the possibility of solvency losses for insured depositors, in its applied form deposit insuring also reduces risk of liquidation by making assistance by deposit insurance agencies probable.) Thus, depository institution managers have a strong incentive to increase leverage (reduce capital relative to assets) and undertake increased asset risk in quest of higher returns. Since (at the present time) deposit insurance premiums are levied on a flat-fee basis, increased portfolio risk will not result in higher deposit insurance costs. The deposit insurance system has the effect of distorting risk-return preferences of depository institution managers.

But, of course, deposit insurance agencies only sell a joint product—deposit insurance *and* regulation; depository institutions cannot have the former without the latter. (However, they cannot totally avoid regulation, supervision, and examination by foregoing deposit insurance—a fact that lowers the *incremental* cost of deposit insurance to insured institutions.) Deposit insurance agencies seek to safeguard their resources by forestalling failures. The system of regulation, supervision, and examination is intended to accomplish this objective. Resources consumed by the agencies form a directly observable cost of this process. Less observable is the *compliance cost* of the regulated institutions. The latter includes the *incremental* time and funds requirements imposed on insured institutions (recognizing again that much of these requirements may exist even without deposit insurance). In this process, the deposit insurance agencies' natural tendency is to over-supervise; their incentive framework is the negative one of avoiding failures. To the extent that the component of the regulatory process that is an outgrowth of deposit insurance is excessive and otherwise inefficient, both agency funding and compliance costs include elements of wasted resources. Further, the actions of deposit insurance agencies can impose costs on society by distorting the capital allocation process. The latter can result not only from portfolio effects, but also from agency decisions relating to management of failed (or failing) institutions.

The greatest potential cost of deposit insurance, however, stems from the role it plays as a barrier to deregulation and rationalization of the U.S. banking system. The existence of deposit guarantees by the federal government sets in place a powerful incentive for federal regulation of the institutions that hold these deposits. The relationship includes elements of economic efficiency, equity, and political reality. From the perspective of economic efficiency, the negation of much of the market discipline over risk-bearing that deposit insurance entails requires government intervention. From an equity standpoint, it is unfair that depository institution managers and stockholders reap rewards of risk-taking without bearing its costs. It would be inequitable (in the eyes of most observers) to allow free entry of new depository institutions when deposit insurance stands ready to secure their liabilities (and provides an exit "safety net"). And the political aspects of the linkage between regulation and deposit insurance are obvious. Thus, to the extent that deregulation of depository institutions would create benefits in excess of ensuing costs, and to the degree that the deposit insurance system retards or prevents such deregulation, society bears the opportunity loss.

Deposit insurance also acts as an institutional arrangement that makes possible the existence of the very large number of small depository institutions in this country (relative to other nations). While geographical and merger restrictions doubtless bear a greater responsibility for this aspect of the U.S. banking structure, deposit insurance still plays a major role. Almost certainly, deposit insurance makes many small institutions viable that would otherwise fold (or never come into being) for lack of depositor confidence. The considerable consolidation of the savings and loan industry in recent years would surely have been much more pronounced (and bloody) had FSLIC deposit guarantees not existed. If allocation and operational efficiency would be better served by a smaller number of depository institutions in this country, the costs of the superfluous institutions are in large measure the fault of deposit insurance.

Deregulation has already proceeded to the point where many observers express concern over the implications for deposit guarantees of the deregulation-induced increase in scope for risk-bearing on the part of depository institutions. However, identifying means of reforming the deposit insurance system so as to make it more compatible with a freer banking system is made difficult by the very nature of deposit guarantees and inherent contradictions in the deposit insurance structure. Deposit insurance is intended to negate a natural market phenomenon—a preference by depositors for expeditious withdrawal of deposits as compared to monitoring the financial condition of depository institutions. The fact that U.S. deposit insurance is only partial (about 70 percent of commercial bank deposits are insured) is justified as a means of limiting that negation. It is hoped that uninsured depositors will provide a source of market scrutiny. But this means of market discipline requires full information disclosure, which can spark "runs" by uninsured depositors. Further, it requires a willingness of the deposit insurance agencies (as in the Penn Square liquidation) to let uninsured depositors take losses. More generally, a greater reliance on the market mechanism for assuring proper functioning of depository institutions in the U.S. financial system may require an increased willingness to allow depository institutions to fail.

Failure Risk

The FDIC has categorized the causes of commercial bank failures of the past decade as shown in Table 6-4.[14] Loan losses are shown as accounting for most failures, and certainly *credit risk* is one of the major risks confronting depository institution management. *Interest rate risk*, which stems from significant differences in maturity of assets and liabilities, has become more significant due to increased interest rate volatility. Related to both credit and liquidity risk is *diversification risk*, the concentration of assets and liabilities in particular types of investments, industries, locations, or other specialized avenues of investment or funding. (The recent problems of S&Ls and MSBs is an example of how lack of diversification in lending creates interest rate risk; the recent difficulties of some banks due to large amounts of energy-related loans is illustrative of the link to credit risk.) *Moral hazard risk* is the danger of fraud, embezzlement, or losses stemming from self-dealing and other insider abuses. Of less significance are *liquidity risk* (related to potential insolvency due to lack of liquidity), *capital adequacy risk* (inability to absorb losses due to lack of a capital "cushion"), and *operational inefficiency risk*

Table 6-4. Causes of Commercial Bank Failures 1971–1982: Causes as a Percent of Number of Failures.

Causes of Failure	1971–1982		1980–1982		1982	
	Major	Primary	Major	Primary	Major	Primary
Credit Quality Losses						
Loans	77.4%	61.3%	82.7%	67.3%	76.5%	55.9%
Insider loan	36.3%	14.5%	26.9%	9.6%	26.5%	14.7%
Poor Funds Management						
Interest rate risk	20.2%	4.8%	19.2%	5.8%	17.6%	8.8%
Liquidity	36.3%	2.4%	30.8%	1.9%	17.6%	2.9%
Fraud and Embezzlement						
Internal	13.7%	11.3%	15.4%	11.5%	17.6%	14.7%
External	7.3%	5.6%	5.8%	3.8%	5.9%	2.9%
Number of cases (including assistance cases)	124		52		34	

Note: This table includes 124 commercial banks and 11 mutual savings banks. The commercial banks include four assistance transactions. One bank that failed eleven years after receiving assistance was counted twice. Of the remaining commercial bank cases, only thirty-one were depositor payoffs, and the rest were closed bank purchase and assumption transactions or open-bank assisted merger transactions. There were no payoffs of mutual savings banks.

Source: *Deposit Insurance in a Changing Environment*, Federal Deposit Insurance Corporation, 1983.

(threat to solvency stemming from unduly high interest operating costs).

Bank failures have been categorized by one observer according to the dichotomy of *normal failure* and *crisis failure*.[15] Normal failures stem from the fact that there is no inherent reason why bank managers should be any more honest, competent, or lucky than managers of other types of business enterprises. Normal failures will occur in good to moderate overall economic conditions as the result of mismanagement, fraud, or simple misfortune. Such failures are independent events and need not significantly affect the viability of other institutions. Crisis failures occur in poor economic conditions (such as the Great Depression) and tend to spread to other institutions.

Failures of commercial banks in the U.S. since World War II have been of the normal failure type. Most failures of savings and loan associations and mutual savings banks have also been "normal," but some failures of these institutions specializing in mortgages in recent years have been the result of a new kind of crisis—a mismatch of assets and liabilities induced by regulation during a period of unforeseen interest rate behavior.

While this rough dichotomy has a degree of usefulness, it is far too simple a description of the risk of failure in depository institutions in the complex U.S. economy. Developments in recent years have made the incidence of isolated, self-contained normal failure unlikely, as more and more institutions have sought brokered deposits, participated in loan syndications and sales, and otherwise linked their destinies with other institutions. Economic change (particularly the emergence of a high and volatile interest rate structure) has broadened the scope of potential mismanagement to such avenues as mismatching asset and liability terms. Such economic events, coupled with increased interdependence among depository institutions and increased international operations of many institutions, have expanded the possibility of crisis failure well beyond that of a severe downturn in the business cycle. Salient examples are the international lending crisis and the interest rate level and structure problems of S&Ls and MSBs.

The impact of regulation (and deregulation) on the risk of failure of depository institutions in an economic environment that has clearly heightened this risk is difficult to assess. Some aspects of regulation, in conjunction with economic change, have actually served to increase failure risk. Regulatory barriers to S&L diversification is an obvious example.[16] Less obvious is the type of regulation-induced, risk-seeking behavior of depository institutions in pursuing unregulated risk "loopholes." Professor Edward Kane indentifies three recent examples of the latter as "financial-technology risk," "interest rate risk," and "sovereign risk."[17] Kane asserts that lack of a regulatory response encouraged depository institutions to expand retail-oriented, "bricks-and-mortar" branch networks even as technological advances threatened the viability of such expansion. Further, many institutions maintained or increased imbalances between asset and liability maturities even as interest rates became increasingly volatile. Finally, some institutions accepted greatly increased sovereign-risk exposure by large increases in lending to foreign borrowers despite evident deterioration (due to international economic developments) in the ability of such debtors to service loans.

In any event, the framework of regulation intended to minimize bank failure has been contracted and may contract further. The removal of deposit rate ceilings, for example, increases potential interest rate risk and also provides an incentive for depository institutions to undertake more credit risk. Relaxation of asset and activity restrictions serves to give institutions more scope to diminish diversification risk, but otherwise increases operating risk. The increased level of competition among depository institutions and between the latter group and other suppliers of financial services is likely to bode well for consumers, but may bode ill for a number of individual institutions.

Deregulation of depository institutions apparently entails, on balance, increased risk of failure for these institutions. This degree of risk clearly has highly significant implications for the deposit insurance system, a view shared by many observers, including the deposit insurance agencies themselves.

PROPOSED CHANGES IN THE DEPOSIT INSURANCE SYSTEM

There is no serious discussion of rescinding deposit insurance in this country. While most other major industrialized nations do not have deposit insurance, their banking systems differ considerably from the United States. In particular, the level of government involvement (degree of central bank control and government ownership) in many nations amounts to an implicit government guarantee of deposits. Further, highly concentrated banking structures have little need for deposit insurance protection. In this country, both the structure of banking and the public policy goal of preserving private ownership of banks and some measure of market competition make deposit insurance an efficient means of avoiding banking market failure.

However, there are a number of proposed changes in the deposit insurance system that have received serious attention. The most important proposals include changes in the coverage of deposit insurance, replacing the present flat-rate premium for deposit insurance with variable rate premiums (based on risk), and altering purchase-and-assumption transactions in a way that would expose uninsured depositors to more risk. Consolidation of the three separate deposit insurance agencies and funds is one recommended administrative change. Provision of deposit insurance by the private insurance industry is another suggestion.

One Hundred Percent Deposit Insurance

Full deposit coverage is urged on the grounds of greater efficiency and equity.[18] The efficiency argument is based on the generally accepted concept of failure in that segment of the financial information market bearing on the financial condition of depository institutions and stemming from the liquidity of deposit claims. But limited deposit insurance leaves depository institutions unprotected against runs by uninsured depositors. And the greater the degree of public disclosure of the problems of problem banks, the more likely such runs are. The failure of Franklin National Bank is often cited as an example. After its problems became known, funds withdrawals by uninsured depositors made Fed loans of $1.7 billion necessary to keep the bank solvent until a purchase-and-assumption could be arranged.[19]

The equity argument for 100 percent deposit insurance is based on the evident preference of the deposit insurance agencies to employ the purchase-and-assumption method, rather than deposit payoff, whenever possible in the case of failures of large institutions. Only very unlucky, uninsured depositors (such as in the Penn Square Bank case) or the relatively few uninsured depositors in small banks ever sustain deposit losses as the result of institution failures. The impact of this alleged inequity is heightened in the competition among depository institutions for large deposits. Since the likelihood of a deposit payoff (and losses for uninsured depositors) is inversely related to institution size, larger institutions have an unfair advantage in competing for uninsured deposits.[20]

The principal argument against 100 percent deposit insurance is its negation of whatever degree of constraint on depository institution risk-taking is exercised by uninsured depositors. Since depositors needn't fear losses in the event of institution failure, their criteria for selection of an institution in which to deposit funds need not include the safety and soundness of the institution. Selection based purely on the drive toward greater yields would surely provide depository institutions with yet another incentive to undertake larger risks. Another argument against 100 percent deposit insurance centers on the increase in risk to insurance funds (since almost 30 percent of U.S. domestic deposits are uninsured). But what such expanded coverage would most likely mean is virtual termination of deposit payoffs in favor of other approaches (and such necessary legislation as to protect the agencies from unknown, contingent liabilities of failed institutions). More importantly, expanded coverage may have the effect of retarding (if not reversing) the pace of deregulation due to the increased risk to the deposit insurance agencies.[21]

Other Proposed Changes in Coverage

Other proposals include 100 percent insurance of demand deposits but limited (or no) insurance of time deposits.[22] The argument here is that public policy requires compulsory insurance only for transactions accounts, that is, money. Runs on other accounts can be avoided by proper maturity management of time deposits and sufficiently stringent early withdrawal provisions (including prohibition thereof). The argument has considerable appeal. Uninsured demand deposits amount to about $125 billion, but the bulk of these funds is in business accounts (with much of the balances being of the compensating balance variety) and is about three-fourths offset by loans.[23] Thus, the increase in exposure to the FDIC insurance fund would be only about $50 billion while eliminating the risk of runs from the type of account most subject to run-type withdrawals.

The major flaw in any proposal hinging on a distinction between transactions and nontransactions accounts is the increasing difficulty of doing so. Such differentiation is now limited to a designated number of permissible monthly withdrawals—hardly a sturdy peg on which to hang eligibility for deposit insurance.

Introducing an element of voluntarism in the amount of deposit insurance obtained has also been proposed. One of the charges of Congress in the mandated study of deposit insurance prescribed by the Garn-St Germain Act was an investigation of the feasibility of providing depositors the option to purchase additional deposit insurance covering deposits in excess of the general limit of $100,000. A variant of this proposal to provide *depositors* with an avenue of obtaining additional insurance protection is to provide *depository insti-*

tutions with the option of securing such protection for their depositors.[24] A more radical variation is to shift all premium payments for deposit insurance to depositors and allow them to purchase whatever amount of protection they select. But all these proposals are fraught with practical difficulties. The basic problem is the nature of deposit insurance as a "public good" and the "free rider" problem inherent in such cases. All depository institutions and depositors benefit from the existence of deposit insurance because it reduces the risk of failure. But because this risk is low, no *individual* institution or depositor has a strong incentive to purchase deposit insurance.

As a practical matter, 100 percent deposit insurance is virtually already in effect due mainly to the dominance of the purchase-and-assumption approach to handling bank failures. The elevation of the deposit insurance ceiling to $100,000 in 1980, though, has also played a significant role. This latter development had repercussions beyond simply expanding the proportion of total deposits covered by insurance. By bringing large certificates of deposit into the protected fold, various means of obtaining insurance protection for large sums came into being with the emergence of deposit brokering perhaps being the most significant. The present problem is thus not one of inadequate deposit protection, but rather one of reconciling such protection with an increasingly deregulated and risky banking environment. Certainly, this is the view of the FDIC, and this agency has proposed a change in its powers and procedures that, in the agency's view, would restore a proper measure of uninsured depositor vigilance.

Modification of Payoff and Purchase-And-Assumption Procedures

The FDIC could frighten uninsured depositors into increased scrutiny of banks with more deposit payoffs in large bank failures, as in the Penn Square case. But this approach is very costly to the agency as well as to uninsured depositors. Part of the cost to the latter in a deposit payoff is the long lag between the closing of an institution and distribution of assets from liquidation. The FDIC has proposed a plan that, in effect, combines some of the elements of a deposit payoff and a purchase-and-assumption.

Under the FDIC proposal, the agency could take two immediate actions following closing of a bank and the agency's establishment of a receivership. First, insured depositor claims would be quickly paid. Second, uninsured creditors would be paid an "advance" based on the FDIC's estimate of bank assets to be recovered in liquidation. Both these steps could likely be accomplished in most cases by a transfer of liabilities in the sum of the insured deposits and the "advance" (and corresponding assets) to an existing or newly chartered bank. (In the latter case, the FDIC proposal is more aptly termed a modified purchase-and-assumption than a modified payoff.)

An alternative variation of this approach would be a legislatively mandated *co-insurance* provision. Deposit balances would be fully insured up to some maximum amount (say, $100,000), with deposit balances above this amount subject to a reduced level of coverage (say, 75%); depositors of amounts exceeding the fully insured amount would "co-insure" the excess. In this case, nondeposit creditors would not be covered. Uninsured depositors would know exactly their potential losses in the event of failure. The potential controversy concerning determination of the amount of the "advance" (in the modified purchase-and-assumption proposal) would be avoided.

This proposal has considerable potential for enhancing or restoring the market discipline on depository institution behavior that uninsured depositors can provide. But such market discipline is gained by putting uninsured depositors at risk. The decision calculus of the latter group would determine whether the former potential benefits or the former potential costs were greater. The elements of this calculus are the costs to uninsured depositors of analyzing and monitoring banks, the magnitude of their potential losses from a bank failure, and the costs of expeditious withdrawal of funds at the first sign of trouble. The fact that the last of these three categories of costs is likely to be the lowest is the source of the potential danger of this approach.

It is also possible that the FDIC proposal would have little impact. At present, most thrift institutions and small banks hold almost totally insured deposits. Brokering of certificates of deposit—a new activity burgeoning in the wake of the Penn Square Bank liquidation—would likely expand further in significance. (Indeed, some measure or measures to control money brokering might be necessary—the most draconian of which could be partial or complete denial of deposit insurance for brokered deposits.) Further innovations to secure deposit insurance coverage for funds would almost certainly emerge.

The FDIC also proposes a change in the pricing of deposit insurance, albeit a rather modest one. While a system of risk-related insurance premiums is consistent with the FDIC's focus on market discipline, the agency supports the change primarily on the basis of equity.

Risk-Related Deposit Insurance Premiums

The current fixed-rate system of deposit insurance premiums has been a target of criticism for many years. All depository institutions pay the same rate, independent of their risk profiles. Risk-taking is controlled by supervision and regulation, not by higher insurance premiums. This system is thus certainly contrary to private insurance principles and is perceived by critics as both inequitable and inefficient. Past resistance to variable insurance rates by the deposit insurance agencies and other regulators has been justified primarily on the basis of practical difficulties of implementation. It is also argued that, since differences in deposit insurance premium rates would become public knowledge, high premium (riskier) banks could suffer unduly from withdrawals by concerned, uninsured depositors. Given the level of disclosure that now exists, this concern is perhaps presently superfluous. The operational problems of risk-based deposit insurance pricing remain.

In concept, risk-related deposit insurance pricing is difficult to fault. Each insured bank would pay a total premium equivalent to the product of the probability of its failure and the cost to the insurance fund of such failure. If premiums thus fully reflected risk (the ideal), and if there were no other constraints on depository institution use of deposit funds, each institution could then accept risk until the corresponding increment in the insurance premium was just *equal* to incremental returns.[25] In this "ideal" case, marginal costs and marginal benefits of risk would be equal, and the optimum degree of risk-taking would result. In addition to being efficient, the system would be equitable in the sense that each insured institution would pay a premium commensurate with its potential cost to the insurance fund. Much of the administrative and compliance costs of regulation and capital adequacy standards would be eliminated, although costs of deposit insurance agencies monitoring and examining insured depository institutions would continue and almost certainly increase. (The examining function would be necessary as part of the rate-setting process.)

When the problem of implementing the operation of a variable deposit insurance rate system is considered, the strength of the foregoing argument ebbs. On page II–I of its study, *Deposit Insurance in a Changing Environment*, the FDIC states flatly that:

> The "ideal system" with premiums tied closely to risk is simply not feasible. Such a system would require the FDIC to be given an extreme amount of authority. Moreover, it would entail unrealistic data requirements and much more advanced risk quantification techniques than are currently imaginable.

The agency report adds quickly, however, that:

> Even though the "ideal" is not feasible, the FDIC believes that a lesser system based on reasonably sound measures of risk has merit. Relating premiums to risk would reduce the inequity in the current system whereby low-risk banks subsidize the activities of high-risk banks and [would] discourage excessive risk taking in an environment that is likely to encourage it.

The FDIC proposes, as a first step, a system of only three risk classes: normal, high, and very high. The maximum premium differential would be the assessment credit (which means the maximum premium would be, at present, one-twelfth of 1 percent of assessable deposits). The FDIC suggests that it might be given authority to vary the assessment credit rate. Risk differentials would be established primarily on the basis of credit risk and interest rate risk as they relate to capital. Credit risk would be measured according to the dollar volume of classified assets. Interest rate risk would be measured by computing the present value of potential changes in future pretax earnings resulting from a sharp shift in interest rates at a point in time. As an addendum to this plan, the FDIC proposes that it be allowed to charge high-risk banks (a composite CAMEL rating of 3 or worse) for the incremental supervisory costs they impose on the agency.

The relative modesty of the FDIC proposal is defensible. The agency's assessment of current abilities to measure risk is accurate. Even if an appropriate scheme of risk measurement existed (and necessary information could be efficiently obtained), barriers would still exist to the optimal resource allocation that an ideal system supposedly could achieve. It would be necessary to dismantle all existing activity, geographical, portfolio, and capital-adequacy restraints on depository institutions, while giving the deposit insurance agencies power to levy premiums up to 100 percent of deposits. Aside from the lack of political feasibility to accomplish such measures, there is very grave doubt that deposit insurance pricing alone could avert the various forces (as discussed in Chapter 2) that tend to drive the banking market to failure. And to the degree that regulatory constraints on depository institutions remain in place, the optimal outcome of a risk-related insurance pricing scheme is compromised.[26]

What the FDIC plan would accomplish is partial alleviation of the clear inequity in which low-risk institutions subsidize high-risk institutions. It may serve also as a further means of imposing market discipline on the risk-taking propensities of institutions if (as is likely) the inclusion of institutions in the "high" and "very high" risk classification is made public. This is particularly true if measures to increase the risk of loss to uninsured depositors (and general creditors)—such as the FDIC's proposal to modify its purchase-and-assumption procedures—are adopted. And, of course, while the proposed additional premium charges for riskier banks are modest, they may be sufficient in some instances to deter banks from undertaking excessive risk. Further, the proposed new system would provide both an incentive and arena for the deposit insurance agencies to develop an improved system of risk measurement.

It is important that development of a credible, generally acceptable, and reasonably "accurate" system of risk measurement precede adoption of a more rigorous (as compared to the modest FDIC initiatives) approach to risk-related deposit insurance pricing.[27] Improper pricing of premiums may result in unintended and injurious behavior on the part of institutions. Premiums that are too high may encourage undue conservatism, and premiums that are too low may motivate excess risk-taking on the part of banks. In either event, neither equity nor efficiency in resource allocation is well served. While it must be recognized that flat-rate insurance premiums are necessarily too high or too low for most institutions, it is also true that their risk behavior cannot presently alter their deposit insurance costs.

If deregulation of depository institutions continues, risk-related deposit insurance pricing is an idea whose time has come. In the past and at the present time, deposit insurance agencies have been able to use the regulatory mechanism to bring insured institution risk-taking behavior in line with the flat-rate premium system. The very prospect of increased surveillance and monitoring by the agencies has served to deter undue risk-bearing. In effect, regulatory intervention has served as a system of implicit (and variable and risk-based) insurance premiums. In effect, the agencies use their regulatory powers to bring client risk positions in line with premiums rather than, as with private insurance, adjusting premiums to correspond to risk. This approach will become increasingly less efficacious if the regulatory structure continues to shrink.

See the appendix for an illustration of the possible effects of pricing deposit insurance according to risk.

Deposit Insurance Agency Merger

The question Congress raised regarding "the feasibility of consolidating the three separate insurance funds" in its study directive to the deposit insurance agencies doubtless reflected congressional concerns over the adequacy of the individual funds. Merger of the FDIC, FSLIC, and NCUSIF funds would swell the resources available to deal with a crisis in the commercial bank, thrift institution, and credit union industry. Certainly a crisis for thrift institutions was perceived in 1982 when the Garn-St Germain Act (of which the deposit insurance study mandate was a part) was passed. But the Garn-St Germain Act itself was also the most significant in a series of developments that made the existence of separate insurance funds seem anachronistic.

The 1983 study by the FDIC strongly urged mergers of the separate funds and other restructuring of the regulatory framework for depository institutions:

> Separate regulatory and insurance systems for savings and loan associations and banks are becoming intolerable from the standpoint of fostering the most effective and efficient regulatory system. . . . Similarities of objectives and functions for the deposit insurance agencies and a growing similarity in banks and thrift institutions all argue that a single fund is a logical alternative to the present framework. The future of the financial services industry will require a larger, better-diversified insurance fund and greater flexibility in dealing with troubled or failed institutions, particularly cross-industry takeovers.

Merging the funds will also provide for less public confusion and greater public confidence in the deposit insurance system, and foster more uniformity of supervision. An additional important reason is that of separating the role of deposit insurance from chartering and regulation.[28]

The FDIC proposes a number of changes that, in the agency's view, would result in "a more rational system which would provide uniformity of deposit insurance, a coordinated system of supervision, and greater flexibility in dealing with troubled or failed banks and thrifts." These suggested changes are:

- Merging the Federal Savings and Loan Insurance Corporation (but not the NCUSIF) into the FDIC;

- Granting the FDIC authority to require reports from, take enforcement actions against, and conduct examinations of all federally insured banks and thrifts and their affiliates;

- Removing the FDIC from the applications process and all other regulatory functions not directly related to safety and soundness; and

- Establishing a separate, single agency for chartering and regulating all federal banks, thrifts, and holding companies.

The FDIC argues for its proposed absorption of the FSLIC on the basis of its greater size, experience, and administrative resources. The agency's argument for restructuring the regulatory and supervisory framework is more complex. A single agency would be created that would combine most of the present regulatory and supervisory functions of the FHLBB, the Federal Reserve Board, and the Comptroller of the Currency. This agency would issue all federal charters for depository institutions and supervise all federally chartered depository institutions and holding companies. The states would continue to charter and supervise state chartered institutions. The FDIC would be authorized to examine insured institutions, require reports, and take enforcement actions as related to its deposit insurance function.

This proposal would remove bank regulatory and supervisory functions from the Federal Reserve Board; the conduct of monetary policy would then be its sole primary mission. This would please those observers who express concern over potential cross-purposes between monetary policy and bank supervision.[29] The FDIC asserts that the overall effect of the proposed restructuring would result in significant operating savings and a more effective, equitable, and uniform framework for supervision and regulation of depository institutions.

The evident sprawling complexity of the depository institution regulatory structure has spawned many reform proposals. The FDIC's present suggestions are similar to a number of these proposals, differentiated primarily by its understandable desire to retain its own identity (and expand). For example, the Hunt Commission recommended a similar restructuring, but with a new agency (the Federal Deposit Guarantee Administration) consolidating the functions of the FDIC, FSLIC, and NCUSIF. Others have proposed consolidating all federal supervisory, regulatory, and deposit insurance functions into a single agency.[30] Some of the reform proposals would maintain the dual banking structure and some would not.

It is likely that the time has come for an overhaul of the regulatory apparatus. Deregulation and the growing similarities of previously specialized institutions have made much of the present structure both superfluous and inefficient. While Congress has shown little interest in administrative restructuring of the regulatory system in the past, this attitude is presently changing. Some of this past congressional lack of concern stems from an "if it ain't broke, don't fix it" attitude. More is due though to a belief that the public interest was served by the existence of specialized agencies for specialized institutions and functions. The latter rationale is apparently fading, and indeed, the present system may be on the way to getting "broke" (and in need of some fixing) under a wave of pressure emanating from the activities of deregulated institutions operating in an altered economic environment.

The FDIC's restructuring proposal has merit. While it clearly serves the FDIC's interest, a merger of the deposit insurance agencies is warranted and the FDIC is obviously the dominant agency. A merger of the insurance funds themselves is also in order, although perhaps a preferable change would be to make deposit guarantees a contingent liability of the U.S. Treasury (which is the *de facto* case) and eliminate the funds. There is, however, no overriding reason to separate the regulatory and deposit insurance functions by agency; supervision, regulation, and deposit insurance are so closely related as to be most efficiently housed in a single agency. Monetary control, however, should be separate from the latter functions and should remain in the province of a Federal Reserve Board relieved (albeit unwilling-ly) of its supervisory and regulatory functions.

CONCLUSIONS AND IMPLICATIONS

This country's system of deposit insurance has well served the eco-nomic objective of a safe, sound, and stable banking system. Milton Friedman, in *A Monetary History of the United States*, cited fed-eral deposit insurance to be " . . . the most significant structural change in the banking system to result from the 1933 panic and, in-deed in our view, the structural change most conducive to monetary stability since state banknote issues were taxed out of existence im-mediately after the Civil War." Deposit insurance has protected de-positors from the financial consequences of bank failure, and, by providing such protection, has played the major role in eliminating the bank runs that periodically plagued the U.S. financial system in the era before deposit insurance. The total number of insured bank failures since 1934 is not much greater than the average annual num-ber of bank failures in the 1920s.

As deregulation and other changes in the financial system con-tinue, the importance and pervasiveness of deposit insurance suggest that it must play a key role in the process of change. Such a role may be one of a barrier against further deregulation or one of accommo-dating (and even helping shape) a freer and more competitive finan-cial system.

Deposit insurance may act to retard or even halt deregulation be-cause of its impact on the risk behavior of depository institutions. The present system of deposit insurance greatly reduces, for deposi-tory institutions, the usual role of the marketplace in providing disci-pline for the managers of other people's money. Depository institu-tions, as financial intermediaries, would be highly levered business enterprises even in the absence of deposit guarantees. But the latter has the effect of augmenting the usual incentives for leverage because of the minimal bankruptcy costs that a system of deposit insurance assures for depository institutions. The effect is a significant reduc-tion, relative to other types of business firms, of stockholder disci-pline. Depository institution creditors are also lulled by deposit insurance. Certainly, insured depositors have no cause for concern.

Uninsured depositors and general creditors are also protected in the great majority of depository institution failures by deposit insurance preference for the purchase-and-assumption technique of dealing with such failures. In most cases, only junior creditors and stockholders of depository institutions are truly at risk as far as the private sector is concerned, and their aggregate stake in these institutions (as a percentage of total assets) is invariably small. Thus, it is the deposit guarantors who bear most of the risk associated with the use of funds by depository institutions.

The governmental system of supervising, examining, and regulating depository institutions is, in large measure, a response to the risk posed by deposit guarantees. In a very real sense, governmental monitoring and controls have served as substitutes for the market discipline displaced by deposit insurance. But as economic forces and changing philosophies lead to progressive dismantling of government restraints on risk-taking by depository institutions, what is to be done to protect deposit insurers? In the absence of deposit insurance reform, the result is likely to be a halt to deregulation.[31]

Change in the nature and structure of deposit insurance must lead to the reinstatement of market forces as a significant source of discipline over the actions of depository institutions. The difficulty in bringing this about is the threat that such measures will also reinstate, after a fifty year absence, the phenomenon of bank runs by uninsured depositors. The FDIC proposal to increase the significant risk to uninsured depositors might, unfortunately, accomplish both the desired and the undesired objective. The proposal to institute risk-related deposit insurance premiums, by itself, poses no threat to uninsured depositor confidence and possesses the laudable elements of equity and efficiency. But, when combined with the threat of significant losses to uninsured depositors that a modified purchase-and-assumption method would pose, the placing of banks in "high" and "very high" risk categories by the FDIC (if such actions became known) would be likely to spark runs of varying scales.

The ease of withdrawal associated with deposit funds continues as a strong reason for prudence in placing uninsured depositors at risk. Actions in this regard would be best implemented with considerable caution and moderation. A less risky course of action in seeking enhanced market discipline for depository institutions is to rely on their stockholders and nondeposit creditors. This is best accomplished via more stringent capital-adequacy requirements. By obliging institutions to go to the nondeposit (and noninsured) market for funds more often and in greater amounts, managers of depository institutions would have to be more careful about the risk profile of their institutions. This effect would be augmented by the significantly more stringent disclosure requirements now imposed on banks and other depository institutions. And the nondeposit funds raised would serve the traditional role of cushioning institution failure.[32]

Administrative and organizational changes related to deposit insurance are also in order. The three separate insurance agencies should be consolidated and their insurance funds replaced by an explicit Treasury guarantee of insured deposits. Action should be taken to halt such abuses of deposit insurance as extending it to municipal bond coverage and using it as a means of brokering deposits. Finally, a strong case can be made for the proposal that, as part of a broader restructuring of the regulatory framework, the deposit insurance function should be combined with consolidated supervisory, examination, and regulatory functions.

NOTES TO CHAPTER 6

1. Federal Deposit Insurance Corporation, *Deposit Insurance in a Changing Environment*, A Study of the Current System of Deposit Insurance Pursuant to Section 712 of the Garn-St Germain Depository Institutions Act of 1982 (Washington, D.C., 1983).
2. *Ibid.*, p. v.
3. George Benston, "Deposit Insurance and Bank Failures," Federal Reserve Bank of Atlanta, *Economic Review* (March 1983), p. 9. Benston notes that Mississippi's program, which included a greater degree of supervision and bank examinations than other state systems, was the most durable and lasted until the 1930 banking crisis—suggesting that such supervision and examination is indeed a necessary condition for a viable deposit insurance system. More recently (1962), Mississippi, like a number of other states, established a share insurance plan for state chartered S&Ls. It collapsed in 1976 after a major failure. See James W. Park, "The Mississippi Deposit Insurance Crisis," *Bankers Magazine* (Summer 1977), pp. 74–80.
4. See Golembe Associates, Inc., "Deposit Insurance—A Sense of History and a Shattered Illusion," *Golembe Reports*, vol. 1982–2. This report also points out the early opposition of the Roosevelt administration to deposit insurance (for which it later took credit) and suggests such opposition stemmed from concerns that deposit insurance would retard reform of the U.S. banking structure.

5. See Paul M. Horvitz, "Commercial Bank Financial Reporting and Disclosure," *Journal of Contemporary Business* (Summer 1977), pp. 59–75.
6. The 1982 failure of Penn Square Bank, which resulted in initial losses to uninsured depositors of almost $200 million, is an example of how lack of such disclosure can lead to losses for the uninformed. Penn Square had been identified as a problem institution by bank examiners for almost two years prior to its failure, but the bank's deficiencies were not disclosed.
7. However, the FDIC has occasionally used direct infusions of funds to avert closure of banks. A notable example is the case of the First Pennsylvania Bank, one of the nation's largest banks. In 1980, the FDIC loaned $325 million to First Pennsylvania while instituting special reporting and supervisory requirements for the troubled bank.
8. In 1982, the FSLIC took action on seventy-eight problem cases. All but one of these failing institution cases was resolved by merger, although fourteen associations (having aggregate deposits of $3.7 billion) were placed in receivership before a viable and willing merger partner was found. In the one nonmerger case, another association assumed the insured deposits of the closed institution (and took over its offices), so that no deposit payoff was necessary.
9. The FDIC often indemnifies takeover banks against potential liabilities of the acquired institution that may surface in the future, such indemnity being supported by the insurance fund. When such an indemnity is both necessary to effect a merger and appears imprudent, the FDIC is likely to opt for liquidation (as in the Penn Square Bank case).
10. "The Depository Institutions Act of 1982," Federal Reserve Bank of New York, *Capsule* no. 27 (January 1983), pp. 4–6.
11. For a rigorous exposition of the benefits of deposit insurance, see Douglas W. Diamond and Philip H. Dybvig, "Bank Runs, Deposit Insurance, and Liquidity," *Journal of Political Economy* (August 1983), pp. 401–419.
12. In 1980, 1981, and 1982, S&Ls lost billions of dollars in deposit withdrawals, with much of these funds being redeposited in corresponding commercial bank accounts. This gradual deposit hemorrhage was labeled the "quiet run" by Andrew S. Carron in *The Plight of the Thrift Institutions*, Studies in the Regulation of Economic Activity (Washington, D.C.: The Brookings Institution, 1982). The major cause of S&L deposit losses in this period was disintermediation—a problem also confronting commercial banks.
13. For discussions of the relationship among deposit insurance, risk behavior, and regulation, see Stephen A. Buser, Andrew H. Chen, and Edward J. Kane, "Federal Deposit Insurance, Regulatory Policy, and Optimal Bank Capital," *Journal of Finance* (March 1981), pp. 51–60; and John H. Kareken and Neil Wallace, "Deposit Insurance and Bank Regulation: A Partial-Equilibrium Exposition," *The Journal of Business* (July 1978), pp. 413–438.

14. See also Peter S. Rose and William L. Scott, "Risk in Commercial Banking: Evidence from Postwar Failures," *Southern Economic Journal* (July 1978), pp. 90–106.

15. William E. Gibson, "Deposit Insurance in the United States: Evaluation and Reform," *Journal of Financial and Quantitative Analysis* (March 1972), pp. 1,575–94.

16. Michael F. Koehn, in *Bankruptcy Risk in Financial Depository Intermediaries: Assessing Regulatory Effects* (Lexington, Mass.: Lexington Books, 1982), asserts that the net effect of depository institution solvency regulations is to *increase* the probability of institution failure.

17. Edward J. Kane, *The Gathering Crisis in Federal Deposit Insurance: Origins, Evolution, and Possible Reforms.* (Forthcoming).

18. For discussions of expanded deposit coverage, see Robert E. Barnett, Paul M. Horvitz, and Stanley C. Silverberg, "Deposit Insurance: The Present System and Some Alternatives," *Banking Law Journal* (April 1977), pp. 304–332; and Gary Leff, "Should Federal Deposit Insurance Be 100 Percent?" *Bankers Magazine* (Summer 1976), pp. 23–30.

19. Uninsured depositors can also protect their deposits in failing institutions by means other than withdrawal—such as securing offsettable loans, pledged assets, or another preferred status for their deposits.

20. The increasing number of deposits being placed by "money brokers" ameliorates this disadvantage for small banks. For a relatively small fee, small banks can "buy" portions (generally $100,000 units—the insured maximum) of large deposit sums.

21. One hundred percent deposit insurance would end the collateralization (pledging of federal or municipal securities) requirement for public deposits and thus would probably adversely affect demand for municipal securities to some (likely slight) degree.

22. See Benston, "Deposit Insurance and Bank Failures," pp. 4–17, and "Federal Regulation of Banking: Analysis and Policy Recommendations," *Journal of Bank Research* (Winter 1983), pp. 216–244, for one variant of this proposal.

23. Federal Deposit Insurance Corporation, *Deposit Insurance in a Changing Environment*, Washington, D.C., 1983, p. F–7.

24. Clifton H. Kreps, Jr. and Richard F. Wacht, "A More Constructive Role for Deposit Insurance," *Journal of Finance* (May 1971), pp. 605–614.

25. Thomas Mayer, "A Graduated Deposit Insurance Plan," *Review of Economics and Statistics* (February 1963), pp. 114–116.

26. A more abstract (and global) issue is that any policy measure aimed at equating marginal costs and benefits in *one* sector of the economy may not improve resource allocation if marginal cost pricing is absent elsewhere in the economy: See R.G. Lipsey and R.K. Lancaster, "The General Theory of Second Best," *Review of Economic Studies* no. 63 (1956–57), pp. 11–32.

27.   The academic literature regarding approaches to implementing (as opposed to literature *recommending*) a risk-related insurance premium system is relatively sparse. This literature, which is reviewed (and cited) in the 1983 FDIC deposit insurance report, includes use of option pricing theory to value deposit insurance, bank failure prediction models, and various other approaches. Two of the more promising approaches are offered by Robert C. Merton, "An Analytical Derivation of the Cost of Deposit Insurance and Loan Guarantees: An Application of Modern Option Pricing Theory," *Journal of Banking and Finance* (June 1977), pp. 3–11; and William F. Sharpe, "Bank Capital Adequacy, Deposit Insurance and Security Values," *Journal of Financial and Quantitative Analysis* (November 1978), pp. 701–718.

28.   FDIC (1983): p. VI-1, VI-2.

29.   An excellent assessment of the reasons to narrow the Federal Reserve Board's responsibilities is offered by Paul M. Horvitz, "Reorganization of the Federal Regulatory Agencies," *Journal of Bank Research* (Winter 1983), pp. 245–263. For an alternative view, see Roger Guffey, "After Deregulation: The Regulatory Role of the Federal Reserve," Federal Reserve Bank of Kansas City, *Economic Review* (June 1983), pp. 3–7.

30.   A cogent argument for this change is made by Professor Horvitz, "Reorganization of the Federal Regulatory Agencies."

31.   For an interesting and cogent argument that Congress must act soon, and for an appraisal of congressional alternatives, see John H. Kareken, "Deposit Insurance Reform, Or Deregulation is the Cart, Not the Horse," Federal Reserve Bank of Minneapolis, *Quarterly Review* (Spring 1983), pp. 1–9.

32.   Given the existence of deposit insurance guarantees, a clear conceptual case can be made for stringent capital requirements as well as for risk-related insurance premiums. The total value of any firm (including banking firms) may be expressed as its value as an all-equity firm plus the value of its debt-secured tax shield minus potential bankruptcy costs (all in present-value terms). Firms not enjoying government guarantees for their debts must rely on equity to balance off the rise in bankruptcy costs that accompanies increased debt issues. In maximizing firm value, banks have no such incentive, since deposit insurance results in near-zero bankruptcy costs. The resulting tendency of depository institutions to use excessive leverage (relative to a market outcome) must be offset with mandated capital requirements if deposit insurance is not priced according to risk.

7 THE CHANGING STRUCTURE OF THE FINANCIAL SERVICES INDUSTRY
Innovation, Deregulation, and the New Competition

The market for financial services in this country has changed dramatically in recent years. Preceding chapters in this book have focused on a salient aspect of such change—depository institution deregulation. In particular, Chapters 4 and 5 described the two statutes, DIDMCA and Garn-St Germain,—both of sufficient importance as to be appropriately labeled "landmark" legislation in the realm of financial regulation—that have significantly reshaped the nature (and narrowed the scope) of the regulatory framework for banks and thrift institutions. Deregulation, however, is only one of the elements of change in the financial services industry, although it is linked (generally as cause or consequence) to other agents of change (see Table 7-1).

Discussion in previous chapters has made the case that deregulation was triggered by economic change, technological advance, and financial and organizational innovation. Even before the major deregulatory actions were in place, the third set of forces just mentioned was acting to reshape the financial services industry. Deregulation wrought by these forces thus became an additional variable in a complex equation of change. To further complicate the already intricate process of financial change, it is now apparent that even that portion of the regulatory framework not touched directly by legislation is steadily eroding.

Table 7–1. Chronologies of Change.

---

1. Banks Fight Back

April 1981. Citibank and Northwestern National Bank allow their customers to borrow money on their six-month market certificates through a checking account.

May 1981. The Bank of California NA, San Francisco, introduces a new account to compete with money market funds. Because the account is housed in the bank's London branch, BanCal says it is not subject to interest rate ceilings and reserve requirements, but the Fed disagrees.

May 1981. J.P. Morgan & Co., forms a subsidiary to trade financial futures for Morgan Guaranty's account. In July 1981, the Federal Reserve Board allows Morgan Guaranty to execute trades for its customers; in December 1982, the Commodity Futures Trading Commission approves.

September 1981. Dreyfus Service Corporation sweeps excess cash from bank accounts into its money market funds, and other firms follow Dreyfus' lead.

November 1981. BankAmerica Corporation plans to acquire Charles Schwab & Company, the nation's largest discount brokerage firm; the Federal Reserve Board approves the acquisition early in 1983.

January 1982. Banks and thrifts collaborate with brokerage firms to offer discount brokerage services to customers of the banks and thrifts.

March 1982. Orbanco Financial Services Corporation, a Portland, Oregon, holding company, proposes a note with a minimum denomination of $15,000, which bears market interest rates, and which has transactions features. The Federal Reserve Board, however, disallows the note.

May 1982. Three S&Ls receive permission to start a joint securities brokerage service that S&Ls nationwide can use to offer investment services to their customers. The service, known as invest, begins operations in November.

June 1982. Citicorp purchases two transponders on the Westar V satellite in preparation for global banking.

July 1982. The Federal Reserve Board allows Citicorp to offer various data processing and data transmission services nationwide through a new subsidiary, Citishare Corporation.

August 1982. The Comptroller of the Currency allows First National Bank of Chicago to form a subsidiary to trade in the futures market for its customers. In January 1983, the Commodity Futures Trading Commission approves.

September 1982. Talman Home Federal Savings and Loan Association introduces its Instant Cash Account to compete with money market funds. The account requires a $5,000 minimum balance and pays the rate of a 6-month CD.

Table 7-1. continued

---

1. Banks Fight Back (continued)

September 1982. North Carolina National Bank's NCNB Futures Corporation receives final approval from the Commodity Futures Trading Commission to act as a futures commission merchant.

September 1982. The Federal Reserve Board allows Bankers Trust New York Corporation to buy and sell futures contracts for its customers through a new subsidiary, BT Capital Markets Corporation. In January 1983, the Commodity Futures Trading Commission approves.

September 1982. Poughkeepsie Savings Bank applies to the FHLBB to acquire Investors Discount Corporation, a Poughkeepsie discount brokerage firm.

October 1982. The Comptroller of the Currency allows Security Pacific, Los Angeles, to acquire Kahn & Co., a Memphis-based discount brokerage firm.

October 1982. The DIDC authorizes an account which federal depository institutions can offer and which is "directly equivalent to and competitive with money market funds."

November 1982. Security Pacific National Bank forms a subsidiary, Security Pacific Brokers Inc., to provide back office support for other banks which offer discount brokerage services.

December 1982. The DIDC authorizes a Super-NOW account which federal depository institutions can offer on January 5, 1983.

2. Interstate Barriers Crumble

March 1980. South Dakota passes legislation which allows out-of-state bank holding companies to move credit card operations to South Dakota. Three years later, the state passes a new bill that allows out-of-state bank holding companies to own state chartered banks which can own insurance companies.

February 1981. Delaware passes an out-of-state banking bill which opens the state to major money center banks.

June 1981. Citibank establishes Citibank (South Dakota) NA in Sioux Falls to handle its credit card operations.

August 1981. Marine Midland Banks, Inc., Buffalo, New York, infuses $25 million into Industrial Valley Bank and Trust Company, Philadelphia, by buying newly issued common stock and nonvoting preferred stock with warrants to buy an additional 20 percent of Industrial Valley's common stock should interstate banking be permitted.

(*Table 7-1. continued overleaf*)

Table 7-1. continued

2. Interstate Barriers Crumble (continued)

September 1981. United Financial Corporation, San Francisco, a subsidiary of National Steel and parent of Citizens Savings and Loan, acquires an S&L in New York and one in Miami Beach. The Combined S&Ls later become First Nationwide Savings.

November 1981. Casco-Northern Corporation, Portland, Maine, parent of Casco Bank and Trust Company, sells First National Boston Corporation 56,250 shares of its convertible preferred stock and warrants to buy additional common shares. In March 1983, First National Bank of Boston Corporation agrees to acquire Casco-Northern.

December 1981. J.P. Morgan & Company establishes Morgan Bank (Delaware), to engage in wholesale commercial banking.

December 1981. Home Savings and Loan Association, Los Angeles, acquires one Florida thrift and two in Missouri. In connection with the acquisitions, Home Savings and Loan becomes Home Savings of America.

January 1982. North Carolina National Bank Corporation acquires First National Bank of Lake City, Florida, by using a legal loophole in a grandfather clause.

January 1982. AmSouth Bancorporation of Alabama, South Carolina National Bank Corporation and Trust Company of Georgia plan to merge into a single holding company if and when interstate banking is permitted. Until then, each is buying $2 million of nonvoting preferred stock in the other two.

January 1982. Home Savings of America, Los Angeles, acquires five Texas savings associations and one in Chicago.

March 1982. Marine Midland Banks, New York, invests $10 million in Centran Corporation, Cleveland, in the form of newly issued nonvoting preferred stock and warrants to buy over 2 million shares of Centran's common stock should interstate banking be permitted.

June 1982. Alaska's new banking law permits out-of-state banks to acquire Alaskan banks without the states of those banks enacting reciprocal legislation.

July 1982. New York legislation amends the state's banking law to allow out-of-state bank holding companies to acquire control of New York banks provided that the states of these banks reciprocate.

August 1982. The Federal Reserve Board and the shareholders of Gulfstream Banks Inc., Boca Raton, Florida, approve the acquisition of Gulfstream Banks by North Carolina National Bank Corporation.

Table 7 1. continued

2. *Interstate Barriers Crumble (continued)*

September 1982. In the first reciprocal interstate bank acquisition between New York and Maine, Key Banks Inc. of Albany agrees to acquire Depositors Corporation of Augusta; the acquisition is expected to be completed by the end of 1983.

December 1982. The Federal Reserve Board allows Exchange Bancorporation, Florida, to merge into North Carolina National Bank Corporation, and the Fed approves the merger of Downtown National Bank of Miami into NCNB/Gulfstream Bank Inc.

December 1982. Both houses of the Massachusetts State legislature pass an interstate banking bill which allows Massachusetts banks to expand into other New England states on a reciprocal basis. The law is effective in 1983.

Source: Harvey Rosenblum, Diane Siegel, and Christine Pavel, "Banks and Nonbanks: A Run for the Money," Federal Reserve Bank of Chicago, *Economic Perspectives* (May-June) 1983, p. 10.

It has become evident that technological and economic forces, in conjunction with deregulatory actions, financial and organizational innovation, and a new pattern of competition have resulted in nothing less than a revolution in the market for financial services. Indeed, it appears that the component of the economic system that has long been called the "banking sector" is being supplanted by a *financial services industry* of which depository institutions are only a segment. We begin our description and assessment of this phenomenon by evaluating recent changes in the demand for and supply of financial services.

THE CHANGING MARKET FOR FINANCIAL SERVICES

Recent significant changes in the market for financial services include the emergence of new kinds of financial services, changes in the mode of delivery for financial services, and a marked increase in the activity of nondepository institutions in this market. Both supply and demand forces have worked to bring forth these changes. On the demand side, higher and more volatile interest rates and the increased sophistication of consumers of financial services have served to heighten greatly the receptiveness of financial service users to new products and new delivery systems. The supply side of the market has been characterized by a myriad of significant influences, the most important of which is perhaps technological developments having a dramatic, salutary effect on the costs of producing financial services. But deregulation, too, has had an enormous impact on the supply function for the financial services industry. We will review and assess these and other "supply side" influences after discussing the "demand side" of the financial services market.

Demand Changes

The demand for financial services by both institutions and individuals is greatly shaped by their need for liquid, readily transferable assets to effect transactions. The traditional dominance of the financial services industry by depository institutions stems from the latter's ability to offer deposit claims to serve this purpose. As the opportunity cost of traditional deposits—offering regulation-suppressed, below-market rates—mounted, both household and institutional consumers sought less costly, alternative means of holding liquid wealth. For individuals, this shift in the nature of demand found expression in the explosive growth of money market mutual funds. For institutional consumers, especially commercial enterprises, the manifestation was one of sharp economizing of cash balances, of the increasing performance of in-house functions previously purchased as bank services (otherwise altering banking relationships), and of widening the scope of their ongoing financial relationships beyond traditional banking links. The traditional dominance of commercial lending by banks is being threatened (see Table 7–2).

Higher interest rates made worthwhile the incurrence of higher search costs in seeking sources of financial services. Higher interest rates made convenience relatively less important in choosing providers of financial services, further acting to break down the local nature of financial services markets. The acceptance of ATMs by retail customers also made location a diminished consideration.

The forays into traditional banking territory by nondepository institutions were not limited to deposit substitutes such as money market mutual funds. Beginning with Merrill Lynch's Cash Manage-

Table 7-2. Business Lending by Selected Nonbanking-Based Firms and Bank Holding Companies at Year-End 1981.

	Commercial and Industrial Loans	Commercial Mortgage Loans	Lease Financing	Total Business Lending
	($ million)			
Fifteen Industrial/ Communications/ Transportation[b]	39,365	1,768	14,417[a]	55,550
Ten Diversified Financial[b]	3,602	3,054	1,581[a]	8,237
Four Insurance-Based	399	35,506	892[a]	36,797
Three Retail-Based	606	—	—	606
Total	43,972	40,328	16,890[a]	101,190
Fifteen Largest BHCs				
Domestic	141,582	19,481	14,279[a]	175,342
International	118,021	5,046	—	123,067
Total	259,603	24,527	14,279	298,409
Domestic Offices, All Insured Commercial Banks	327,101	120,333[c]	13,168	460,602

a. Includes domestic and foreign lending and may include leasing to household or government entities.

b. Financing by banking and savings and loan subsidiaries has been subtracted.

c. Includes all real estate loans except those secured by residential property.

Source: Harvey Rosenblum and Diane Siegel, *Competition in Financial Services: The Impact of Nonbank Entry*, Federal Reserve Bank of Chicago, Staff Study 83-1, Table 10, p. 26.

ment Account, securities firms sought to attract affluent individual financial service consumers with service packages. As the "universal banks" of Europe have long made clear, financial consumers like one-stop financial services arrangements. In this country, regulatory constraints have proscribed universal banking, and consumers seeking such "packaged" services have had to search outside the traditional banking system. Recent deregulatory actions have included numerous provisions to allow depository institutions the flexibility to meet this demand. (New deposit instruments and discount brokerage services are examples.)

While it is important to note these various changes in the nature of retail and wholesale demand for financial services, it is also important to note what has *not* changed. The demand for consumer, residential mortgage, and small business credit, for example, remains largely centered on local institutions. Demand for trust services also remains localized, and for much the same reasons—personal contact needs and local knowledge are of great importance. (The traditional advantage of local depository institutions in this regard is, however, being challenged as nonbank competitors develop means of customer contact.) Further, while customer *acceptance* of ATMs is rapidly evolving into customer *demand* for these facilities, consumers cling to traditional means of payment. The fact that the technological reach of EFTS and ACH (automated clearing houses) so greatly surpasses their grasped implementation is clear testimony to this fact. Institutional means of sharing the cost savings EFTS makes available to financial service providers (and payees) with financial services consumers (and payors) need to be more fully developed.

The Supply Side in the Financial Services Industry

Alfred Marshall's observation that supply and demand are scissor blades remains an apt way of expressing the tandem nature of these economic forces; developments on the supply side generally alter demand, and vice versa. Nonetheless, the supply-demand dichotomy remains useful for analysis.

The supply function for financial services reflects the absolute and relative costs of the factors necessary for production of these services. This function includes, of course, the labor, capital, and other resources necessary to produce and deliver financial services. As for production of any commodity, opportunity costs and taxes impact on supply. As a regulated industry, the cost of regulatory compliance is a highly significant component of a financial services production function. It should be noted further that a large portion of the labor, capital, and resources necessary for the production and distribution of financial services will be devoted to the process of gathering, processing, and transmitting of information—and it is here that we begin our assessment of recent changes on the "supply side."

Technology and the Supply of Financial Services

Revolutionary developments in the electronic computer industry have served to reduce greatly the costs of transmitting, processing, and storing information. The significance for the costs of producing and delivering financial services is enormous. Computing advances have made, for example, so-called "electronic banking" operationally and economically feasible. The latter incorporates automated clearinghouses (ACHs), automated teller machines (ATMs), and point-of-sale terminals (POSTs) into an electronic funds transfer system (EFTS).

The spread of electronic funds transfer systems has been less rapid than many had originally anticipated. The slow development of EFTS has resulted from consumer reluctance to adopt the new technology, various problems of adapting the technology to a system of substantial regulations, and restrictions on the behavior of individual financial institutions. Yet EFTS is now spreading rapidly and promises to become commonplace in the future. The development of EFTS involves the substitution of capital for labor and, to a considerable extent, the substitution of fixed costs for variable costs. The equipment needed to operate an EFTS efficiently involves substantial capital outlays.

Less dramatic applications of electronic data-processing advances than electronic banking have had significant effects in the financial services industry. For example, reduced data-processing costs have made economically feasible the issuance of small-denomination debt instruments, and nonfinancial as well as financial institutions have subsequently moved to offer these deposit-competing securities as a source of funds. More notably, such information-processing cost reductions probably made possible money market mutual funds (at least in terms of the scope of the services they offer). And, more generally, it is now economically feasible for many financial institutions to expand greatly both the scope of their offerings of financial services and the geographic span of their market reach (often across state lines, and frequently nationwide). The new technology also has made feasible the opening of financial service centers in supermarkets and department stores.

Technological advance also raises the intriguing prospect of the delivery of financial services directly into the home via computer terminals or television linkups. This development would pose the same threat of obsolescence to ATMs as the latter currently poses to bricks-and-mortar branches. And home banking combined with nationwide use of debit cards in POST systems could lead to the demise of banking as we presently know it.[1]

There is still another highly significant impact of the new technology that is already jarring the framework of the financial services industry. Both economies of scale and economies of scope (economies of joint production) have become much more important as the production and delivery of financial services has become more capital-intensive due to increasing requirements for computer and related equipment. A great deal of empirical research conducted prior to the "information revolution" indicated a lack of significant economies of scale in banking (beyond a $100 million deposit threshold), but these studies may be obsolete. Certainly, financial institutions are behaving as if they are. In any event, it is obvious that larger institutions have an advantage in being able to muster the large amount of capital resources necessary to meet the equipment requirements mandated by the new technology.

Economies of joint production in the financial services industry, unlike economies of scale, have received little attention from empirical investigators. Such economies pertain to reductions in the cost of producing and delivering each particular type of service as the total number of types of services produced and distributed increases. For example, the production and delivery of virtually all financial services require extensive data-processing and communications capabilities. When such facilities are in place to produce and deliver a single financial service, the incremental cost of producing and delivering second, third, etc. types of financial services are greatly reduced relative to the initial cost of the first product. The behavior of suppliers of financial services in recent years suggests that the existence of significant economies of scope has become well recognized in the marketplace.

In sum, technological changes have dramatically altered the nature of the supply function for financial services in recent years. We consider next how regulatory changes have affected production and delivery functions for financial products.

Deregulation and the Supply of Financial Services

Previous chapters in this book clearly suggest that the most significant financial regulatory change has occurred as a result of congressional legislation—the DIDMCA of 1980 and the Garn-St Germain Act of 1982. But a great deal of change in the financial services industry has occurred in recent years separate and apart from these statutes—regulatory "erosion" has accelerated as the pace of technological, organizational, and financial innovation has quickened.

In Chapter 2, the regulatory structure was characterized as placing the following constraints on banks:

1. Restrictions on pricing of deposits,
2. Restrictions on entry and expansion,
3. Restrictions on scope and nature of activities,
4. Restrictions on leverage (minimum capital requirements) and other balance sheet elements, and
5. Restrictions on geographic expansion.

The scope of change in these five categories of regulatory restrictions varies, as do causes of change. The most sweeping change is, of course, in category (1)—pricing restrictions have been virtually eliminated by legislation. Statutory action has also greatly relaxed restrictions on category (3), as new powers have been granted depository institutions and old limitations eliminated. Categories (2) and (5) have received little explicit legislative attention, but entry and expansion have nonetheless eased substantially. How has such deregulation affected the supply function for financial services? The first step in an attempt to identify such effects is to recognize how the existence of regulation impacts on the costs of producing and delivering financial services, both in the aggregate and for particular types of institutions.

Regulation affects the aggregate supply of financial services both directly and via its impact on the structure of the market. The latter, indirect effect stems from entry and expansion restrictions. Pricing and activity restrictions impact directly on the supply of the financial service so constrained, both in the aggregate and in the price-quantity mix of offerings of that financial service by particular types of financial institutions.

Pricing. Deposit rate ceilings have been virtually eliminated, but they clearly affected the financial services market in a highly significant manner. In the period from 1933 to 1980, commercial banks had a general monopoly on checkable deposits combined with prohibition of interest payment on such deposits. Competition for transactions accounts was thus limited to banks, and the competition among banks was necessarily nonprice in nature. The result was both operational inefficiency (wasted resources stemming from excessive branching and other aspects of nonprice competition) and inequity in the treatment of depositors. These costs mounted when market interest rates rose and were supplemented by the use of resources by individuals and firms to economize on cash balances and by the costs incurred by financial firms in efforts to innovate "around" pricing restrictions on transactions balances. Now that the latter have been removed (along with commercial bank monopoly of transactions accounts), depository institutions must incur the costs of adjusting to a competitive market for checkable deposits. In price competition, cost reduction is critical, and such economies are likely to be affected by reduction in the number of branches and via explicit pricing for deposit-related services. The effect is likely to be improved resource allocation and more equitable treatment of depositors. A less salutary effect is the incentive provided suppliers of checkable deposits to acquire higher return, higher risk assets as competitive pressures push up their cost of funds.

Market-rate pricing for deposits, combined with the increased depositor sophistication and technological developments previously discussed, has the potential for a marked further broadening of the market for both transactions and asset accounts. Money market mutual funds and cash management accounts have already significantly eroded this traditionally local market. Certainly the extension of the power to offer transactions accounts to nonbank institutions is a major market development. Depository institutions have two major advantages in competing for deposits in this broadened market—location convenience and deposit insurance. The rapid, substantial shift of funds from money market mutuals to the money market deposit account, when the latter was authorized, suggests that these are significant advantages.

Activity Limitations.   There is virtually no empirical evidence on the existence or magnitudes of economies in the joint production of financial services. As noted earlier, however, it appears intuitively apparent that such economies may have emerged as a major supply-side factor as new technological advances and the requisite equipment have been adapted to the production and delivery of financial services. To the extent that activity regulations limit the exploitation of economies of scope, such regulation results in operational inefficiency. To the extent that regulatory differentials exist so that some types of financial institutions can capture economies of joint production (by offering "packaged" financial services, for example) and others cannot, a competitive inequity emerges.

Competitive restraint is, of course, a natural consequence of activity regulation, as is limitation of portfolio diversification. The recent relaxation of activity restrictions for depository institutions (particularly for savings and loans) should serve both to increase competition and encourage diversification. The former effect serves to increase risk for depository institutions and the latter to decrease it, but both equity and efficiency are well served. By eliminating the need to innovate "around" these abandoned activity constraints, the costs of such innovations are avoided.

A high degree of activity constraints still hold for depository institutions, of which limitations on provision of securities and insurance services are salient examples. As an issue of competitive equity, these restraints are now intertwined with geographic constraints. This is true because of the new competition from nondepository institutions for financial services customers—institutions largely free of both types of restraints. The erosion of regulation aimed at keeping financial institutions in relatively separate product markets has made more urgent the need to address geographic restrictions of depository institutions.

Branching and Merger Restrictions. Constraints on entry and geographic expansion have acted to limit competition among depository institutions. In the process, it is quite likely that profitability of extant institutions has been augmented, and certainly possible that the supply of banking services in some areas has been affected in a fashion counter to consumer interests. This expansion-restriction aspect of the regulatory framework has tended to create local markets for financial services, with limited competition among suppliers of such services. Further, this framework encouraged "vertically integrated" operations in which local institutions both produced and distributed financial services.[2] It has also been argued that geographic restrictions have obliged banks to offer a less-than-optimal mix of services—a homogeneous product for heterogeneous groups of consumers.[3]

Relaxation of geographic restraints, in conjunction with continued deregulation of activity restraints, would make feasible new strategies for depository institutions in the provision of marketing services. Institutions may, for example, choose to focus primarily on producing *or* delivering financial services, rather than continuing to treat both functions as a joint process. Such a decision might stem from apparent availability of economies of scale and scope in production, or a locational advantage or opportunities for scope economies in delivery. A salient example is the origination and servicing of a mortgage loan separate and apart from the provision of funds for the loan. Credit card operations, discount brokerage services, and various trust activities are other examples of production-delivery separations in the provision process for financial services.

Depository institutions with permissible access to a nationwide market could feasibly elect to focus on specific types of financial services tailored to defined market segments or types of customers. The entry of brokerage firms (which already enjoy such access) into new lines of financial services has followed this pattern. Such depository institution strategies require, of course, that further relaxation of activity prohibitions parallel lifting of geographic constraints. We turn now to a more detailed assessment of the state of the new competition—its inter-industry and geographic aspects.

Deregulation and Nonbank Competition

One of the most significant aspects of the new competition is the expansion into the financial services industry by nonbank organizations.[4] These nonbank organizations frequently (traditionally) are nonfinancial in nature. Their impact on depository institutions has been great. Indeed much of the deregulation of depository institutions that occurred through 1983 reflects the growing competition from these nonbank firms. In turn, the deregulation of depository institutions that has already occurred (and that which appears likely to occur in the future) will have a substantial effect on the financial services offered by nonbanking firms.

Competition from nonbank firms with depository institutions occurs both in the credit and deposit markets. In the credit markets, the competition is especially intense in the market for consumer credit though the competition also encompasses business lending. Moreover, the competition has grown in intensity throughout the 1970s and early 1980s with nonbank firms obtaining a growing share of some of these markets.

Table 7–3 provides information on the combined retail mortgage, consumer installment, and revolving loans of the fifteen largest consumer lenders as of December 31, 1981. It is both interesting and important to note that only two of the largest five consumer lenders were banks. The largest consumer lender was General Motors, principally through its General Motors Acceptance Corporation (GMAC)

Table 7-3. Top Fifteen Consumer Lenders:[a] Combined Retail Mortgage and Consumer Installment and Revolving Loans as of December 31, 1981 ($ millions).

	Mortgage Loans	Installment and Revolving Credit	Total
General Motors	—	$31,077	$31,077
BankAmerica Corporation	$10,196	9,703	19,899
Citicorp	5,925	9,556	15,481
Sears	2,830	9,528	12,358
Ford Motor	—	11,892	11,892
First Interstate Bancorp	4,325	4,418	8,743
Security Pacific Corporation	3,835	3,799	7,632
Beneficial Corporation	3,785	3,078	6,863
Wells Fargo & Co.	4,606	1,977	6,583
National Steel	5,859	71	5,930
General Electric	2,460	2,792	5,252
Prudential/Bache/PruCapital	—	5,142	5,142
American Express	74	5,035	5,109
Merrill Lynch	—	4,725	4,725
Crocker National Corporation	3,354	1,192	4,546

a. Data for bank holding companies are domestic loans; nonbank company data are worldwide. National Steel's loans and some of Sears's loans are those of its savings and loan subsidiaries.

Source: Harvey Rosenblum and Diane Siegel, *Competition in Financial Services: The Impact of Nonbank Entry*, Federal Reserve Bank of Chicago, Staff Study 83–1, p. 17.

Table 7-4. Business Lending by Selected Nonbanking-Based Firms and Bank Holding Companies at Year-End 1981.[a]

	Commercial and Industrial Loans	Commercial Mortgage Loans	Lease Financing	Total Business Lending
	($ million)			
Fifteen Industrial/ Communications/ Transportation[d]	39,365	1,768	14,417[b]	55,550
Ten Diversified Financial[d]	3,602	3,054	1,581[b]	8,237
Four Insurance-Based	399	35,506	892[b]	36,797
Three Retail-Based	606	—	—	606
Total	43,972	40,328	16,890[b]	101,190
Fifteen Largest BHCs				
Domestic	141,582	19,481	14,279[b]	175,342
International	118,021	5,046	—	123,067
Total	259,603	24,527	14,279	298,409
Domestic Offices, All Insured Commercial Banks	327,101	120,333[c]	13,168	460,602

a. This table includes business lending data for thirty-two companies.

b. Includes domestic and foreign lending and may include leasing to household or government entities.

c. Includes all real estate loans except those secured by residential property.

d. Financing by banking and savings and loan subsidiaries has been subtracted.

Source: Harvey Rosenblum and Diane Siegel, *Competition in Financial Services: The Impact of Nonbank Entry*, Federal Reserve Bank of Chicago, Staff Study 83-1, p. 26.

subsidiary, while the fourth largest consumer lender was Sears and the fifth largest was Ford. Similar comparisons exist when the data are broken down into different types of consumer loans.

The importance of nonbank organizations as competition to depository institutions in business lending is illustrated by Table 7-4. As shown in that table, commercial banks and bank holding companies have most of the market for business loans. However, nonbank lenders, including insurance companies, retail-based companies, and industrial, communications, and transportation firms, hold over $100 billion in business loans. The competition from nonbank organizations is particularly intense for commercial mortgage loans, with two life insurance companies (Prudential and Aetna) holding the largest volumes of commercial mortgage loans as of year-end 1981.

Looking at the sources of funds for depository institutions, it is also evident that nonbanks offer extensive competition. Money market funds represent perhaps the most widely known subsitute for deposits, though with the authorization of money market deposit accounts depository institutions have an effective product to offer in competition with money funds. However, competition for deposits takes other forms. For example, many brokerage firms offer retail deposits of selected commercial banks and savings and loan associations to their customers, and some maintain a secondary market in these deposit instruments (see Table 7-5 for a listing of these arrangements). Such activities by brokerage firms tend to make the deposit market national in scope and to narrow the differences in deposit rates offered by depository institutions. It also increases the attractiveness of ownership by a securities firm of a commercial bank or of some other affiliation between banks and securities firms and further reduces the separation between these two industries.

The quantitative significance of these nonbank organizations in their competition with depository institutions clearly has importance for the future of depository institutions. These organizations that have entered the financial services industry are large in size, subject to only limited regulation, and frequently highly skillful in their marketing strategy. As the financial services industry becomes more competitive due to deregulation, the importance of marketing skill becomes greater, an area in which depository institutions traditionally have not excelled.

Given the increasing importance of these nonbank competitors also, it may be impossible in coming years to speak of a banking industry, or even a depository institutions industry. It may instead be appropriate to speak of a *financial services industry* that includes all depository institutions, other nonbank financial institutions, and many firms that offer financial services but are not traditionally considered to be financial institutions. The difficulty created by this merging of institutions for regulation is itself substantial. Indeed it may create pressures for further deregulation as it may be impossible to provide for equal and effective regulation in the industry. In par-

Table 7-5.   Depository Institution-Broker Relationships in the Distribution of Insured Retail Deposits as of August 1982.

Merrill Lynch (475 offices)
All-Savers Certificates for 15 thrifts nationwide
Retail CDs[a] for 20 banks and thrifts nationwide, including Bank of America
Secondary Market in Retail CDs of 2 banks and 2 thrifts
91-Day Negotiable CDs for Great Western Federal Savings and Loan, Beverly Hills

Dean Witter (8 Sears stores with financial center pilot programs and 320 Dean Witter offices nationwide)
Retail CDs[a] for 2 thrifts, including Allstate Federal Savings and Loan
Secondary Market in Retail CDs for City Federal Savings and Loan, New Jersey

Bache (200 offices in 32 states)
All-Savers Certificates for City Federal Savings and Loan
Retail CDs[a] for City Federal Savings and Loan and one S&L in Los Angeles

Shearson/American Express (330 domestic offices)
All-Savers Certificates for Boston Safe-Deposit & Trust Company
Retail CDs[a] for selected banks and thrifts

Fidelity Management Group (29 offices in 50 states)
All-Savers Certificates for 6 banks, including Security Pacific National Bank and First National Bank of Chicago

E. F. Hutton (300 offices in 50 states)
All-Savers Certificates for 15 regional banking companies

Edward D. Jones & Company (435 offices in 33 states)
All-Savers Certificates for Merchants Trust Company, St. Louis

Manley, Bennett, McDonald & Company (10 offices in 2 states)
All-Savers Certificates for First Federal Savings & Loan, Detroit

Paine Webber (240 offices)
All-Savers Certificates for 2 banks in California, including Bank of America

Charles Schwab & Company (Offices in 38 states)
All-Savers Certificates for First Nationwide Savings and Loan, San Francisco

The Vanguard Group (Offices in 50 states)
All-Savers Certificates for Bradford Trust Company, Boston

a. 3.5-, 4-, 5-year, and zero coupon certificates of deposit.

Source: Harvey Rosenblum and Diane Siegel, *Competition in Financial Services: The Impact of Nonbank Entry*, Federal Reserve Bank of Chicago, Staff Study 83-1, p. 34.

ticular, these developments have likely set the stage for eventual removal of geographic barriers in the financial services industry.

Geographic Expansion

The remarkable changes occurring in the financial services industry
due to economic and legal developments have substantial implications for the geographic expansion of depository institutions, especially for commercial banks that have been particularly affected by
legislative restraints on geographic expansion. The restrictive framework that has attempted to confine the operations of depository
institutions to a limited geographic area is rapidly eroding. As a
result, the geographic area over which depository institutions will be
able to offer their products has expanded and is likely to expand
even more in coming years.

It is important to note that a very substantial amount of interstate
operations by depository institutions already exists.[6] This interstate
operation of depository institutions occurs in a variety of forms. For
example, there are a number of bank holding companies that already
operate banking subsidiaries in more than one state. Most of these
organizations had operated interstate prior to the passage of restrictive legislation and were allowed to continue their operations under
"grandfather" clauses in the legislation. For example, First Interstate Bancorporation operates banking subsidiaries in eleven western
states, while Northwest Bancorporation operates banking subsidiaries
in seven states. Similarly, many savings and loan associations operate
in more than one state. For example, as of March, 1983, Home Savings Association of America operated in California, Florida, Illinois,
Missouri, and Texas.

Even more significant evidence of the interstate operations of
banking organizations is provided by an analysis of the nonbanking
activities of bank holding companies. In contrast to the bank subsidiaries of bank holding companies that are generally restricted in their
operations to a single state, the nonbank subsidiaries of bank holding
companies may operate without geographical limitation. Kaufman,
Mote, and Rosenblum point out that, as of 1981, Manufacturers
Hanover had 471 nonbank subsidiary offices located outside of New
York state. Security Pacific had 427 nonbank subsidiary offices

located outside of California, the state in which its banking subsidiaries were located.

Additional information on the interstate operations of the nonbank subsidiaries of bank holding companies is provided by looking at their geographical location. For example, of the 10,964 nonbank subsidiaries of bank holding companies, over 5,000 are located outside of the state in which the parent resides. Most of these interstate activities are concentrated in finance company offices. In fact, over 4,000 finance company offices are located outside the state in which the parent resides, accounting for about 80 percent of all interstate offices of nonbank subsidiaries of bank holding companies. The largest number of these offices are located in California (434), Pennsylvania (297), Florida (281), and Texas (243).

Commercial banking organizations also have expanded interstate by establishing loan production offices and Edge Act corporations. Both of these devices allow banking organizations to penetrate the wholesale or business market throughout the nation, with Edge Act corporations specializing in international banking activities. As of December 31, 1982, banking organizations operated over 200 loan production offices interstate and 143 Edge Act corporations. The interstate loan production offices were located throughout the country, though with a particularly large number in California (22), Illinois (21), Texas (19), and Colorado (14). In contrast, Edge Act corporations were highly concentrated in a few states, with New York (31), Florida (25), California (23), and Texas (17) dominating in terms of the number of offices.

Table 7-6 summarizes by state the number of interstate offices of out-of-state banking organizations, including "grandfathered" domestic banks, the operations of foreign banks, interstate savings and loans, loan production offices, and Edge Act corporations.[6] As shown in that table, the total number of such offices approached 8,000 in 1982, of which about 70 percent were interstate offices of nonbank subsidiaries of bank holding companies. The states with major out-of-state banking activity included California (787 offices) and Florida (621 offices). Clearly interstate banking already exists to a very considerable degree.

While many banking organizations have *circumvented* the barriers to geographical expansion, progress toward actual removal of these barriers has been relatively slow. In terms of *intrastate* barriers, a few states, including Illinois, Florida, Nebraska, Oklahoma, and Arkansas have recently reduced their restraints on geographical expansion of banking organizations. On an *interstate* basis, a number of states have recently passed legislation allowing out-of-state banking organizations to enter. For example, Alaska permits acquisition of existing banks by out-of-state bank holding companies. The acquired banks must have been in existence for at least three years; thus *de novo* entry is essentially prohibited. Delaware allows acquisition of a single office, limited purpose *de novo* bank with an initial capitalization of $40 million. At least 100 employees must be hired. South Dakota allows entry by out-of-state banks on terms similar to those of Delaware. Also, the six New England states have recently enacted reciprocal legislation that allows banks headquartered in any of the New England states to acquire other banks located throughout the region. This type of regional banking may indeed provide the model for the interstate banking movement of the future.

While economic, financial, and technological forces are clearly breaking down the barriers to interstate banking (and also to more intrastate expansion by banking organizations), the movement to full interstate banking and the complete elimination of the barriers to full interstate banking may require considerable time. There are, of course, substantial political pressures from some special-interest groups aimed at preventing the reduction or elimination of barriers to geographical expansion by banking organizations. Even if these political pressures were overcome (and it seems certain that they will be at some point), the question remains as to how rapidly banking organizations would actually proceed with interstate expansion. In this regard, it should be remembered that many banking organizations already have an interstate presence through nonbanking subsidiaries, loan production offices, and other means. Also, the apparent lack of major economies of scale in banking augur against any rapid interstate consolidation.

Despite these considerations, however, it seems likely that full interstate banking with some truly national organizations will eventually come to pass, although the timing is uncertain. The *manner* in which such expansion will occur is also uncertain. At the present time, it appears that interstate banking will occur through the action of state legislatures allowing reciprocal branching or creating regional banking zones, such as has already occurred in New England. Yet the development of these regional banking areas may, in turn, place pressure on the U.S. Congress to change the McFadden Act and the

Table 7-6.   Summary of Interstate Activity.

| | Grandfathered | | | | | | | | |
| | Domestic | | | Foreign* | | | Foreign Banks | | |
Location	Holding* Companies	Banks	Branches	Holding* Companies	Banks	Branches	Agency	Edge	Branch
Alabama									
Alaska									
Arizona	1	1	161						
Arkansas									
California				8	8	148	63	2	2
Colorado	1	3	7						
Connecticut									
Delaware	12	12	40						
District of Columbia									1
Florida	2	2	188				22	6	
Georgia							10		
Hawaii				1	1	15	2		
Idaho	2	2	107						
Illinois	1	3	4	1	1	1		3	36
Indiana									
Iowa	1	11	50						
Kansas									
Kentucky									
Louisiana							1		
Maine									
Maryland	1	2	30						
Massachusetts									4
Michigan									
Minnesota									
Mississippi									
Missouri									
Montana	3	25	48						
Nebraska	1	5	39						
Nevada	1	1	66						
New Hampshire									
New Jersey									
New Mexico	1	5	35						
New York	1	2	27	3	3	39	18	2	37
North Carolina									
North Dakota	3	34	110						

Table 7-6. continued

States* With Reciprocal Agreement	Preferred* Stock Deals Filed With Board	Interstate* S&Ls	Offices of 4(c) 8 Subs	Loan Production Offices	Edge Act Corporations	Total Offices per State
	1	1	107	1		108
√			4	1		5
			159			321
			3			3
		2	521	22	23	787
		1	158	14		182
	1		64	1		65
○			27	3	5	87
		2	2	3		6
□	1	7	372	6	23	621
	1	2	253	8	5	276
		2	39			57
		1	47			156
□		1	132	21	11	212
			99	1		100
□	1		42	2		105
		1	78			78
		1	61			61
			164	4	1	170
√	1		1			1
		2	82	7		121
√	2	1	68	6	3	81
			56	2		58
	1		34	5	4	43
			89			89
		1	75	6	2	83
		2	28	1		102
			28	2		74
		1	21			88
			20	1		21
			110	2		112
			44			84
√	4	3	156	16	31	331
			367	3		370
			23	1		168

(*Table 7-6. continued overleaf*)

Table 7-6. continued

| Location | Grandfathered | | | | | | Foreign Banks | | |
| | Domestic | | | Foreign* | | | | | |
	Holding* Companies	Banks	Branches	Holding* Companies	Banks	Branches	Agency	Edge	Branch
Ohio									
Oklahoma									
Oregon	1	1	169						7
Pennsylvania									6
Rhode Island									
South Carolina									
South Dakota	3	12	80						
Tennessee	2	2	27						
Texas								9	
Utah	1	1	35						
Vermont									
Virginia	1	6	63						
Washington	1	1	85						10
West Virginia									
Wisconsin	3	6	22						
Wyoming	2	4	4						
TOTALS	45	141	1,397	13	13	203	116	22	103

Notes: o — These states allow entry of limited-purpose banks; □ — These states allow expansion of interstate grandfathered banks; * — These columns are not included in total number of offices; A — Six of the foreign bank holding companies own only one bank but the bank is located outside the home state of the foreign banking organization.

Source: David D. Whitehead, "Interstate Banking: Taking Inventory," Federal Reserve Bank of Atlanta, *Economic Review* May 1983, p. 19.

Table 7 6. continued

States* With Reciprocal Agreement	Preferred* Stock Deals Filed With Board	Interstate* S&Ls	Offices of 4(c) 8 Subs	Loan Production Offices	Edge Act Corporations	Total Offices per State
	2		310	8	4	322
	1		76	3		79
		4	83	7	3	270
	2		320	7	2	335
			13			13
	1		229			229
○			16			108
			159	14		202
	1	5	289	19	17	334
√		1	37	1		74
			4			4
		1	227	1		297
		2	114	3	6	219
			40			40
			39		1	68
		1	10			18
10	20	45	5,500	202	143	7,840

Douglas Amendment to the Bank Holding Company Act in order to allow interstate branching or holding company acquisitions.

Product Line Expansion

Related to the ability of commercial banking organizations to expand geographically is their ability to increase their product line offerings to the public. Through 1983, at least, most of the expansion of product lines permitted for depository institutions focused on thrifts. In the effort to transform the nature of thrifts in order to make them economically viable, savings and loans and other thrifts were permitted to offer products that traditionally had been limited to commercial banks (in the case of transactions accounts) and products (such as consumer loans) in which banks were prominent lenders but thrifts were not (with the exception of credit unions). Similarly, nondepository financial institutions and certain nonfinancial institutions had entered into direct competition with banks through offering bank-like products. The best examples of this new competition is provided by Merrill Lynch, American Express, and Sears, although there are many others that are important.

The expansion in product line offerings permitted for commercial banks in this revolutionary era has been relatively slight. Probably the most significant new product permitted the commercial banking industry is the money market deposit account, though the reduction in Regulation Q ceilings generally may be viewed as giving banks a more competitive span of product offerings. Yet the banking industry has increasingly sought to test the limits of their legal authority to offer new products and at the same time to effect legislative changes that would allow them to offer a wider product mix.

The best example of banking organizations seeking new product lines perhaps is expansion into discount brokerage. This industry itself was created by the deregulation of exchange commission rates that occurred in the mid-1970s. However, it was not until the early 1980s that banking organizations began to offer discount brokerage services to their customers either through the acquisition of existing discount brokerage firms (such as Bank of America's acquisition of Charles Schwab and Chase Manhattan's acquisition of Rose and Co.) or through starting new firms (in which case most of the execution of the transactions was placed through an existing firm).[7]

Entry of banking organizations into discount brokerage represents the first step in the desired entry by these firms into the securities business. Such a step was legally justified on the grounds that the discount broker offers only execution of transactions, a function that some banks had provided for their customers for many years. Since it does not involve the underwriting or distribution of securities, it is argued, the action did not violate the separation of commercial and investment banking that was provided for in the Glass-Steagall Act. In fact, the banking industry has pressed Congress to modify or eliminate such divisions between investment and commercial banking.

It seems increasingly likely that this separation between investment and commercial banks will narrow even further in the future, and may disappear entirely at some point. At a minimum, it would appear that commercial banks would be allowed to provide investment banking services for debt securities. Banking organizations very likely will also be allowed to manage mutual funds and offer shares in mutual funds to the public as well as to offer a full range of brokerage services. Such a broadening of the banking product line would seem to be the logical extension of the entry by thrifts and non-depository institutions into the products traditionally offered by commercial banks.

IMPLICATIONS OF THE NEW STRUCTURE OF THE FINANCIAL SERVICES INDUSTRY FOR DEPOSITORY INSTITUTIONS

The case has now been made that innovation, deregulation, and the new competition have set in motion a profound alteration of the structure of the financial services industry. We conclude this chapter with a further and more focused assessment of the implications of the financial services revolution (and deregulation in particular) for the two major types of depository institutions—commercial banks and savings and loan associations.

Commercial Banks

There clearly will be numerous major effects on commercial banks from the transformation of the financial services market. While many of these effects are closely intertwined, making a separate discussion of each effect somewhat difficult, the following aspects of commercial banking can be identified as likely to be significantly affected: (1) profitability; (2) consolidation and the number of commercial banking organizations; (3) geographic limits to bank operations; and (4) product market limits.[8]

Profitability

An important issue in examining the potential short- and long-run consequences of the emerging new financial services framework is the effect on bank profitability. To the extent that bank profitability is reduced dramatically, as some observers have suggested, then the industry will likely face larger numbers of failures, more rapid consolidation, and more pressure to relax more quickly the restraints on products offered and limitations on the geographical scope of bank operations. On the other hand, if commercial banking organizations are able to adjust to the new environment and to maintain their profitability, the consequences for failures, consolidation, and other aspects of the banking industry will be much reduced. Also, the effects on the profitability of small banking organizations is crucial to the evolving banking structure.

There are sharp differences of opinion regarding the effects of deregulation and related changes on bank profitability. Based upon the workings of the competitive model as well as observations of deregulation's impact in other industries, it might be expected that the greater competition that accompanies deregulation would, on average, reduce sharply the operating profitability of commercial banks. The reduction in profitability, at least in the near term, would be produced principally by the increased cost of funds as, with the elimination of Regulation Q deposit rate ceilings, banks are forced to pay market rates of interest for their funds. While the effects of rising costs of funds would extend to all banking organizations, they would be most pronounced, it is argued, at small banks since these banks have a greater share of their deposits paying below market rates. As an example of the potential effects of deposit rate deregulation on the profitability of smaller banks, a recent study for the Texas Bankers Association of community banks projected a very substantial decline in income, with many community banks becoming unprofitable.[9] From a longer term perspective, of course, the growing competition in the credit markets from depository institutions and also from major nondepository institutions may limit the profitability of banking organizations.

In contrast to this view that removing deposit rate ceilings and other aspects of deregulation will sharply reduce bank profits, the argument is made that bank managements will learn to cope with these changes in the environment just as they have with other other changes in recent years. For example, banking organizations in past years competed for deposits by offering convenience in the form of large numbers of branches and longer operating hours and also by charging less than full cost for a number of banking services (checking accounts being the most notable though not the only example). This form of competition was a substitute for explicit price competition for deposits that was prohibited by Regulation Q. Yet as Regulation Q deposit rate ceilings are removed, it would be expected that this historical process would be reversed. Banks would seek to offset the rising cost of funds by reducing the number of branches, curtailing operating hours, and vigorously pricing their services on a full-cost basis for each service. While it is difficult to know how much of the increase in explicit interest rates could be offset by a reduction in implicit interest, Flannery has estimated that a figure of 45 percent of the increase in explicit interest could be offset by a reduction in implicit interest.[10] Moreover, the ability of banking organizations to pay market rates for their deposits should allow them to grow more quickly, so that the profits resulting from more rapid growth may partially or totally offset the shrinkage in margin caused by the rising cost of bank funds.

Additional evidence on the potential effects on bank profits of deregulation is provided by examining a time series of bank accounting profit during the 1970s and early 1980s, a period during which a substantial volume of bank deposits shifted from below-market to market-rate levels. For example, it has been estimated that the percentage of liabilities at commercial banks paying unregulated interest rates increased from 1 percent in 1965 to 37 percent in 1979 and to 50 percent in 1981. Even banks with total assets of $100 million or less were estimated to have almost 40 percent of their liabilities paying market rates by June 1981.[11] Yet, as Flannery pointed out, despite the growth of liabilities not subject to deposit rate ceilings, commercial banks have been able to maintain their return on assets quite well—net income as a percentage of assets was 0.77 percent in 1977 and 0.98 percent in 1982 (annualized rate of return for data for the first half of 1982) for all insured banks. Similar results were found for banks classified into those with under $300 million in total assets and those with over $300 million.

In a more comprehensive analysis of the effects of interest rate deregulation on bank profits, Kolari and Fraser examined the returns on assets and equity for a sample of over 1,000 banks over the period from 1964 through 1982.[12] They found no evidence that either small or large banks were unable to adjust to the gradual deregulation of interest rate ceilings on deposits. Even in the period from 1978 to 1982, during which interest rate deregulation occurred at a more rapid rate and during which interest rate volatility was great, banks were able to maintain their profitability, measured either in terms of return on assets or return on equity. In fact, smaller banks which might be most affected by the deposit rate deregulation maintained higher return on asset ratios than larger banks throughout the entire period studied.

In evaluating these ratios, it is important to note, of course, that the deposit rate deregulation that occurred in late 1982 and 1983 was more substantial and more rapid than those that occurred earlier. Hence the results of the studies of past profit performance may not be relevant to assessing the future impact of deregulation. It may be possible, though, to examine market-price information on bank stocks in order to determine market perceptions of the effect of deposit rate deregulation on the future earnings of banking organizations.

Fraser and Richards examined the market reaction to the introduction of money market deposit accounts (MMDAs) in December, 1982, and of "Super-NOW" accounts in January, 1983, for a sample of over 100 commercial banking organizations.[13] The sample was divided into multinational banks, regional wholesale organizations, and regional retail organizations. There appeared to be no substantial effect of the announcement of MMDA and Super-NOWs by the Depository Institutions Deregulation Committee. Indeed, whatever effect appeared to exist was positive, suggesting that deposit rate deregulation may benefit rather than harm commercial banks.

Banking Consolidation

The movement toward deregulation of depository institutions should contribute to the consolidation of banking resources. The speed with which such consolidation occurs will, of course, vary with the effects of deregulation and the new competition on the profitability of existing institutions. It will also vary with the extent to which existing laws that restrict branching and holding company acquisitions are reduced or removed. A substantial reduction in profit margins at depository institutions coupled with rapid removal of legislative barriers to geographic expansion would produce great consolidation in the number of depository institutions. In contrast, should deregulation not shrink profit margins and should legislative barriers remain intact, the pace of consolidation would be much slower.[14] However, substantial shrinkage in the number of depository institutions (and thereby an increase in the average size of the typical depository institution) appears highly likely. The question remains, though, of how far the consolidation will proceed and what the new structure of depository institutions will look like.

There are a number of possible scenarios that appear plausible in predicting the consolidation process. The least likely scenario appears to be such a degree of consolidation that the U.S. banking system will become, like its counterparts in Canada and Britain, dominated by a small number of banks, perhaps as few as fifteen or so. Given the history of the U.S. financial system, its current large numbers of banks, the distrust of concentrated economic and political power that has existed in the United States, and the lack of economies of scale that has been found in banking studies, it appears highly unlikely that the banking system will coalesce around a few major institutions. Among the more likely outcomes appear to be the following.

The bank consulting firm of Golembe Associates projects a potential 30 to 50 percent decline in the number of commercial banks. This would leave roughly 7,000 to 10,000 commercial banks in the United States, though a lesser number of independent entities. In contrast, the consolidation among savings and loans may be less substantial in view of the preregulation consolidation that has already occurred.

Additional evidence is provided by the consulting firm of McKinsey and Co. Drawing upon the experience with deregulation in other

Table 7-7.   Future Banking Structure.

	Type of Organization		
	(1) National Distribution	(2) Low-Cost Producer	(3) Specialty Firm
Money Center Banks	*		*
Regional Banks			*
Local Banks			*
New Entrants		*	
Nonbank Financial Institutions	*	*	

industries, they envision the banking and financial services industry as evolving into a three-tier structure (see Table 7-7). The first tier consists of a few national financial institutions offering a wide range of financial services (obviously this presupposes additional deregulation beyond that contained in the 1980 and 1982 legislation). This tier might include the largest ten commercial banks. It also might (and probably will) include major nonbank organizations such as American Express and Sears. These organizations would offer a wide variety of financial services to businesses, governments, and households. They would truly be department stores of financial services. The second tier consists of low-cost producers of specialized financial services (analogous to discount brokerage firms). Many of these firms would be new entrants into the industry using the latest technology. These firms might attain cost advantages that existing organizations could not match. Finally, the last tier consists of those firms that specialize in particular parts of the market where price sensitivity is least, and, in terms of number, would be the majority of firms. Most small organizations would serve these specialized niches in the market, competing with those organizations in the first tier that would also choose to serve this segment of the financial services market.

It also appears likely that there will be increasing separation between the manufacturing and the distribution of financial services, where manufacturing refers to products such as check processing, credit card processing, and stock transfers, and where delivery refers to activities involving direct contact with consumers of financial services such as teller services, lending, and personal trust services. Since the manufacturing of financial services is capital-intensive (and thereby subject to substantial economies of scale) while the delivery of financial services is labor-intensive (and thereby subject to only limited economies of scale), it appears likely that the type 3 firms will specialize in the delivery of financial services while the type 1 and type 2 firms will be more occupied with the manufacturing of financial services. Of course, there may also be a substantial degree of cooperation among the different types of firms, with some manufacturing financial services and then arranging for others to deliver the services to the ultimate consumer.[15]

The Future Role of Savings and Loan Associations

Savings and loans currently face remarkable changes in their deposit-taking and funds-providing functions. These changes may be attributable to the 1980 and 1982 legislation, but may more fundamentally stem from basic economic and financial factors such as high and volatile interest rates and rapid technological change. (A summary of the major changes in legislation appears in Table 7–8.) In any case, in contrast to past years when savings and loans management was constrained by law and regulation into a specialized role in the housing finance process, in future years the management of savings and loans has sufficient discretion to determine by its own decisions the nature of the institution. By these decisions, managements at savings and loans will determine the extent and significance of the future link between the industry and the mortgage market.

There appear to be three possible models that individual savings and loans could adopt:

1. the traditional or classic association;
2. the real estate related mortgage association;
3. the family financial center.[16]

If savings and loans adopt the traditional or classic association model, they would continue to gather funds principally from various types of savings and time deposits and would channel these funds into housing markets, principally into mortgages within their local market area. It has been estimated that under this model, savings and loans would have approximately 80 percent of their assets in home

Table 7-8. Changes in S&L Assets and Liability Powers Resulting from Recent Legislative Actions.

Liability Powers

1. Nationwide NOW Accounts for
   a. individuals and not-for-profit organizations — DIDMCA-1980
   b. governmental units — Garn-St Germain 1982

2. Federal S&Ls may offer demand deposits to persons or organizations that have established a "business, corporate, commercial or agricultural loan relationship with the association." — Garn-St Germain 1982

3. Authorizes new accounts to compete with money market mutual funds — Garn-St Germain 1982

   Garn-St Germain (11/15/82) indicated that effective 12/14/82 one account would have a $2500 minimum balance, no interest rate ceiling, an option to guarantee a fixed rate for one month, limited check writing facilities, and deposit insurance.

   A second account was authorized effective 1/5/83 identical to the 12/14/82 account but with unlimited transaction facilities. The account was subject to the reserve requirements on transaction accounts.

4. Authorizes establishment of Remote Service Units — DIDMCA-1980

Asset Powers

1. Expands 20 percent limit of DIDMCA to 40 percent of assets that may be invested in commercial real estate loans. — Garn-St Germain 1982

2. Up to 20 percent limit of assets may be invested in combination of commercial paper, debt securities, and consumer loans. — DIDMCA-1980

3. Expands limit in DIDMCA on consumer loans (including inventory and floor plan loans) from 20 percent to 30 percent of assets. — Garn-St Germain 1980

4. May issue credit cards — DIDMCA-1980

5. May offer overdraft loans on any transaction account — Garn-St Germain 1982

6. Permits investment in time and savings deposits of other associations — Garn-St Germain 1982

7. Limited investment in state and local obligations of any one issuer to 10 percent of associations's capital and surplus. Total investment in general obligations is not limited. — Garn-St Germain 1982

8. May make commercial loans up to 5 percent of assets until December 31, 1983 and up to 10 percent thereafter. May be direct loans or participations. — Garn-St Germain 1982

9. May invest in tangible personal property up to 10 percent of assets — Garn-St Germain 1982

10. May make educational loans up to 5 percent of assets — Garn-St Germain 1982

11. May make loans to Small Business Investment Corporations up to 1 percent of assets — Garn-St Germain 1982

Source: Robert Eisenbeis and Myron Kwast, "New Investment Powers for Savings and Loans, Diversification or Specialization," Federal Reserve Bank of Atlanta, *Economic Review* (July 1983), p. 55.

mortgages (a negligible amount in commercial mortgages) and would obtain about 10 percent of their funds from transactions accounts.[17] It is important to note that these associations would perform their traditional functions by choice, not by regulation, and would have the flexibility to alter their roles should economic and financial conditions change.

Another possibility is that savings and loans would become real estate related mortgage associations. As such, they would be active in the origination of many types of mortgages, some of which they would retain for their own portfolio, and they would finance their portfolios from a variety of savings and transactions deposits. They would also make extensive use of service corporations and engage in many aspects of builder/developer activity. Home mortgages would comprise only 40 percent of the total assets of this type of organization with commercial mortgages, construction loans, and real estate loans warehoused totaling 30 percent.[18] Savings and transactions accounts taken together would amount to less than one-half of the total sources of funds, with particularly heavy reliance on the nationwide money and capital markets through the issuance of mortgage-backed bonds and similar debt instruments. The organizations would be wholesale-oriented, dealing principally with business both in terms of funds sources and uses. (In contrast, the traditional model and also the family finance center model discussed below would result in savings and loans principally oriented toward serving retail or consumer accounts.)

The third potential model is that of the family finance center. With this model, the savings and loans would be a diversified department store of financial services offering a full range of deposits and credit services to consumers. Both its sources of funds and its uses of funds would be quite diverse as compared to traditional savings and loans. Home mortgages would account for about 60 percent of total assets, and transactions accounts would provide 35 percent of the total sources of funds.

It is important to note that savings and loans could adopt policies that embodied elements of each of these models. Also, since the functions of the organizations are now determined by management rather than by law and regulation, an individual savings and loan could alter its role as economic and financial conditions changed. The important question, of course, is which of these models will most accurately describe the savings and loan of the future.

Evidence from experience of state chartered associations in states that have previously allowed wider diversification for their savings and loans would suggest that the changes in the functions of savings and loans may not be as great as have been commonly projected. In fact, the state chartered associations in these states—principally Florida, Maine, and Texas—have made little use of their diversification powers and have remained as traditional or classical associations. This lack of interest in asset diversification in previous years may reflect principally the tax advantages available to savings and loans that invest primarily in qualified assets (residential mortgages, cash, and federal securities). These tax benefits are reduced as the qualified assets fall below 82 percent of total assets and are eliminated entirely when qualified assets fall below 60 percent. However, the authority in the 1982 legislation to invest in state and local government securities provides a means for savings and loans to reduce their tax burden and at the same time to diversify their assets. Also, the relevance of the experience of state chartered associations in taking advantage in past years of their asset diversification powers may not be great in the altered financial environment that currently exists.

A recent study by Eisenbeis and Kwast explored the question of whether thrifts would be better off as widely diversified financial service organizations or as organizations that continued to concentrate in areas where they have specialized expertise.[19] This study examined the performance of 254 commercial banks that chose to specialize in mortgage and real estate lending during the 1970s. These organizations held at least 65 percent of their loans in real estate loans for at least seven of the ten years from 1970 through 1979. The performance of these real estate banks was used as a proxy for the performance of thrifts. In each of the ten years of the study, the net return on assets of these organizations equaled or exceeded the return on assets of a comparable set of banks that did not specialize in real estate lending.

While any projections about the future operations of thrifts are hazardous and subject to a wide margin of error because of future economic, financial, and legislative variables, the following assessment appears reasonable:

1. Some savings and loans will continue in their traditional or classical role. In terms of total assets (though perhaps not numbers of

associations), these savings and loans may represent a minor fraction of the industry.

2. Other associations will take advantage of the new diversification powers and become wholesale-oriented, diversified real estate organizations, or retail-oriented, full-scale family finance centers. These organizations may be located in metropolitan areas with branches throughout a state or potentially throughout the nation. They are likely to be dominant in terms of total assets.

3. The savings and loan associations will likely continue their emphasis on home loans regardless of the model the organizations adopt. Savings and loans have personnel knowledgeable about the real estate market. Moreover, as discussed above, there remain tax advantages to holding a large portfolio of home loans. Even if savings and loans become principally real estate mortgage associations, it is expected that they will have 40 percent of their assets in home mortgage loans. And the total dollar value of mortgage loans held by savings and loans may in fact not decline, as asset diversification is partially or totally affected by more rapid expansion of total assets for the more competitive savings and loan industry. The link between savings and loans and the mortgage market may be weaker than in the past, but it is not likely to be broken.

4. This shift in the asset portfolio at savings and loans may reduce the fraction of the total flow of home mortgage credit provided by savings and loans. Moreover, many savings and loans may prefer to acquire participations in mortgage pools rather than locally originated loans. Yet it does not appear likely that such structural changes in the nature of the savings and loan industry will severely reduce the availability of mortgage credit to housing. As long as borrowers are willing to pay market rates to obtain mortgage credit it is likely that, in a deregulated environment, lenders will be available to provide the funds.

There remains one final, extremely important qualification to these expectations. The nature of the savings and loan industry (perhaps even its existence) is heavily dependent on the economic and financial environment of the next years.[20] If interest rates return to or surpass previous record levels, the structure of the industry will obviously be quite different from what it would have been if interest rates had remained at mid-1983 levels or declined from those levels. Yet the revolutionary economic and financial developments of the

1960s and 1970s, coupled with the profound legislative changes in 1980 and 1982, suggest quite strongly that the savings and loan industry of the future (and indeed the entire financial services industry) will be very different than in the past.

Failure of Depository Institutions

As discussed earlier, the increased competition that accompanies deregulation of depository institutions may contribute to an increased incidence of failure. Whereas at one time the regulatory authorities protected the managers of depository institutions from the consequences of their mistakes through an elaborate system of regulations, in the new deregulated financial environment managers of depository institutions have both the freedom to succeed and the freedom to fail. Successful innovations in the financial marketplace will be rewarded with above-normal profits. Unsuccessful innovations or failure to alter competitive products through emulating the successful innovations will result in below-normal profits and, in some cases, with substantial losses. While the effect of the deregulation movement on the average return on bank assets is perhaps debatable (though it appears likely that the average return will decline), the effects of deregulation on the variability of bank profits is less difficult to predict. It appears highly likely that the variability from high or low profit banks will be larger, and probably *much* larger than in past years as the ability to compete and offer new products produces major winners and major losers. In any case, any decline in average profits or increases in the variability of profits from high to low profit banks will contribute to an increased incidence of failure.

It is important to note that the effects of rising failure rates at depository institutions would be quite different depending on the size of the failed institutions. The failure of small institutions would be of concern principally to uninsured depositors though the amount of uninsured deposits of small banks is usually quite small. With a liberal chartering and branching policy the effects of small-bank failure on the availability of financial services to the public is unlikely to be very significant. Indeed, the great increase in the number of nonbank organizations that offer financial services in competition with depository institutions makes the failure of a single depository institution to be of less significance from the perspective of the public. The fact that Sears now offers financial services may make it less significant that a single bank or savings and loan fails.

The failure of a large bank or thrift is likely to be much more significant from the perspective of the entire financial system. Of course, large depository institutions are likely to have a much larger fraction of their deposits in uninsured form. Relatedly, the failure of a large depository institution is more likely to produce a spill-over into the entire financial system. While it is very unlikely that the failure of a small bank will produce a financial panic, the failure or the rumor of failure of one of the nation's largest banks may produce such an effect. In that regard, it is important to note that the period from the early 1970s through the early 1980s was one in which there were a number of failures among large banks. In fact, the two largest bank failures in United States history occurred in this period, with the failure of Franklin National Bank in 1974 and the failure of First National Bank of Midland in 1983 (the second largest failure in terms of total assets).

The information contained in Figure 7-1 does in fact show a sharp increase in the failure rate in the early 1980s, a fact consistent with the growing competition associated with deregulation. Yet the early 1980s also was a period of a lengthy and severe economic contraction that substantially affected the quality of the loan portfolio of depository institutions. It was also a period of high and volatile interest rates that affected the financial stability of all depository institutions and particularly those such as savings and loans that concentrated in long-term fixed-rate loans financed with short-term, interest-sensitive deposits. As a result, it is not possible to assert with certainty whether the increased failure rate was due to external economic conditions or to deregulation. Such a disentangling of causes awaits the return to stable interest rates and a sustained period of economic prosperity.

CONCLUSIONS AND IMPLICATIONS

The pace of change in the American financial system has quickened remarkably in the past decade. The transformation that is presently taking place began in the postwar economic expansion, but proceeded relatively slowly until the 1970s. The financial innovations of

Figure 7-1.   Bank Failures as a Percentage of All Banks.

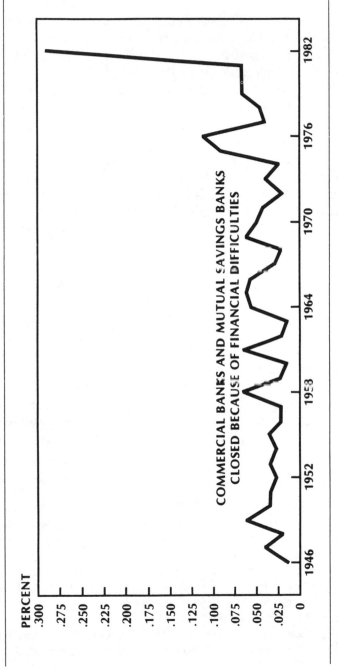

Source: Eugenie D. Short and Gerald P. O'Driscoll, Jr., "Deregulation and Deposit Insurance," Federal Reserve Bank of Dallas, *Economic Review* (September 1983), p. 13.

the 1960s were essentially means of circumventing the regulatory strictures of the 1930s—a predictable and nonrevolutionary consequence of a framework constructed in a very different era. In the 1970s, the financial and organizational innovative response to regulatory control was greatly spurred by economic change and became linked to technological advance. This union of events and forces led to significant steps toward dismantling of the regulatory structure forged in the 1930s. Thus deregulation became yet another force for change in the market for financial services.

The salient element of the evolving, transformed structure of the financial services industry is the new competition that characterizes the provision of financial services. Nondepository financial institutions and even nonfinancial firms have become strong contenders for a share of traditional banking markets. The market for financial services, because of both the new competition and new technology, has become more and more a national market, creating pressures for the removal of regulatory barriers to geographic expansion.

Depository institutions, thus, are confronted with a rapidly changing environment in which their future role is uncertain. While the continued existence of these institutions is not in question, their nature may change radically in future years. It is likely that there will be fewer independent depository institutions in the future, due to voluntary consolidation and some inevitable failures, but there may be more heterogeneity among these institutions as they exploit new freedoms in different ways. In the next and final chapter of this book, we seek to identify further the role of depository institutions in a rationalized financial system.

NOTES TO CHAPTER 7

1. See "Signals from the Future: The Emerging Financial Services Industry," Federal Reserve Bank of Atlanta, *Economic Review* (September 1983), pp. 20–32, for an interesting report of a symposium concerned with future prospects for the industry.

2. For an excellent discussion of the relationship between the production and delivery of financial services, see Dwight B. Crane, Ralph C. Kimball, and William T. Gregor, *The Effects of Banking Deregulation*, Association of Reserve City Bankers (July 1983).

3. George Kaufman and Larry Mote, "Implications of Deregulation for Product Lines and Geographical Markets of Financial Institutions," *Journal of*

Bank Research (Spring 1983), pp. 8–23. See also Webster Hull's comments, pp. 23–24.

4. See Harvey Rosenblum and Diane Siegel, *Competition in Financial Services: The Impact of Nonbank Entry*, Federal Reserve Bank of Chicago, Staff Study 83–1, for a detailed analysis of the growth and significance of nonbank competition in the financial services industry.

5. See David D. Whitehead, "Interstate Banking: Taking Inventory," Federal Reserve Bank of Atlanta, *Economic Review* (May 1983), pp. 4–20.

6. The table also includes interstate banking through states with reciprocal banking arrangements and interstate banking arrangements between banks whereby one bank has agreed to acquire an out-of-state bank when and if allowed by law.

7. These arrangements provide further examples of the growing separation between the manufacturing and distribution of financial services. The banks that have begun new discount brokerage operations are involved in distributing the product but generally not in the manufacturing, which is often left to an existing firm that can better realize the economies of scale.

8. To a considerable extent, many of these consequences for commercial banks also apply to savings and loans and other thrifts. For example, the anticipated consolidation among commercial banks and the resultant decline in the number of independent entities should occur for savings and loans as well as for commercial banks.

9. More specifically, the study projected a decline in net-interest margin due to conversion of NOWs and savings deposits ranging from eighty-two basis points, on average, for banks of from $10 to $24 million in total assets to seventy-eight basis points for banks with total assets of $500 million and over.

10. The issue of the time required for banks to reduce these implicit interest payments is an important one, though very little information exists upon which an informed judgment could be made. Changes in service charges presumably could be made quickly, though reducing an extensive branch network should be a much more time-consuming process.

11. The data for all banks comes from Gillian Garcia et al., *Financial Deregulation*, Federal Reserve Bank of Chicago, Staff Study 83–2, 1983, p. 20. The information on small banks comes from a Staff Report of the Board of Governors of the Federal Reserve System, "Charts and Tables for the DIDC Conditions Briefing," December 16, 1981. The report is referenced in "Deregulation and the Commercial Banking Industry," Association of Reserve City Bankers, 1983, p. 87.

12. Donald R. Fraser and James W. Kolari, *Size and Financial Performance in Banking*, A report prepared for the U.S. Small Business Administration, October 1983.

13.   Donald R. Fraser and R. Malcolm Richards, "Deregulation, MMDAs, Super-NOWs and Returns on Bank Securities" Paper presented at the 1983 meeting of the Financial Management Association.

A similar approach had been used in studies of the market-price reaction of the stock of banks to previous deregulation. For example, Dann and James showed that the removal of interest rate ceilings (on a temporary basis) for wild-card certificates and the introduction of six-month, variable-rate money market certificates produced significant negative returns for shareholders of savings and loans. However, James found that—in response to the suspension in 1970 of Regulation Q ceilings on short-maturity time deposits of $100,000 or more—the price of large, money center banks rose by about 5 percent and that there was no measurable effect on the price of small banks' stock. See: Larry Dann and Christopher M. James, "An Analysis of the Impact of Deposit Rate Ceilings on the Market Values of Thrift Institutions," *Journal of Finance* (December 1982), pp. 1259–70.

14.   The number of institutions will also be affected by policies of the regulatory authorities toward chartering. To the extent that deregulation is accompanied by liberal chartering policies (and the Comptroller of the Currency did adopt liberal policies from the late 1970s through the early 1980s), the number of independent institutions may remain substantial. However, the liberal chartering policies could be partially offset by rising economic barriers to entry produced by changing technology.

15.   See Crane, Kimball, and Gregor, *The Effects of Banking Deregulation*, for a more extensive discussion of the implications of this distinction for the future of depository institutions.

16.   These models are discussed in more detail in the following: Jack Harris, "Major Issues for Thrifts in the 1980s," Federal Home Loan Bank Board, *Journal* (February 1983), pp. 7–11; Leon T. Kendall, "Rebuilding the Business: It's Time to Decide Which Road to Take," *Savings and Loans News* (August 1981), pp. 50–56; and Richard Marcis, "Savings and Loan Planning for the New Competitive Environment," Federal Home Loan Bank Board *Journal* (July 1981), pp. 5–14.

17.   The estimate was made by the Mortgage Guaranty Insurance Corporation.

18.   Walker estimates through the use of an econometric model that mortgages as a percent of total assets at savings and loans will fall only by 10 percent from current levels and that consumer loans will total less than 7 percent of total assets. See: David A. Walker, "Effects of Deregulation on the Savings and Loan Industry," *The Financial Review* (Spring 1983), pp. 94–110.

19.   Robert A. Eisenbeis and Myron L. Kwast, "The Implications of Expanded Portfolio Powers in the S&L Institution Performance" Paper presented at the Western Economic Association Meetings, San Francisco, 1982. Also

see: Robert A. Eisenbeis, "New Investment Powers for S&Ls: Diversification or Specialization?" Federal Reserve Bank of Atlanta, *Economic Review* (July 1983), pp. 53–62.

20. In fact, in projecting the future of the industry, the Federal Home Loan Bank Board assumed three different interest rate scenarios. See: Richard L. Marcis and Dale Riordan, "The Savings and Loan Industry in the 1980s," Federal Home Loan Bank Board, *Journal* (May 1980), pp. 1–15.

8 THE OUTLOOK FOR FINANCIAL DEREGULATION

This book has been concerned with financial change—deregulation, reregulation, technical and organizational innovation, and the nexus of these developments in a rapidly transforming financial services industry. The primary focus of attention has been on depository institutions and their past, present, and potential future role in the financial system. In this concluding chapter, we seek not to offer a detailed summary, but rather to assess further the agenda of financial change and related implications. It is quite possible that the transformation of the regulatory and competitive structure of the financial system has only begun. Certainly, there is no dearth of reform proposals or market possibilities seeking implementation. A brief survey of various such proposals and possibilities is in order, with an eye to their implications for depository institutions and their potential import for the macrofinancial dimension of the economy. We begin with the pertinent legislative calendar, circa 1984.

THE FINANCIAL REGULATORY ARENA: CONFUSION AND STALEMATE?

It is clearly an understatement to assert that the financial regulatory scene is currently in a state of some confusion and disarray. Major

231

legislative initiatives in the Congress are apparently stalled. A senior member of the Senate Banking Committee, Senator John Heinz (R–Pennsylvania), has announced his intention of introducing legislation that would essentially halt deregulation and launch a rebuilding of the regulatory structure. The various financial regulatory agencies have publicly squabbled on issues of regulatory interpretation and "turf." The Comptroller of the Currency has extended his office's moratorium on consideration of "nonbank bank" applications. Congressional action to deal with the confused regulatory situation is as clearly needed as its likelihood (in the near term) is remote.

Legislative Issues

The Reagan administration, via the Treasury Department, has submitted to the Congress proposed legislation entitled the "Financial Institutions Deregulation Act of 1983." While this bill was only one of several legislative proposals in both houses of Congress in the fall of 1983, its content offers a useful framework for assessment of the issues that lawmakers must eventually decide (if only to ratify numerous *faits accomplis*).

The centerpiece of the administration bill is its powers provisions relating to bank holding companies (BHC). The bill would allow BHCs significantly expanded scope in allowable activities while simplifying their supervisory framework. Ownership of thrift institutions, insurance and real estate brokerages, insurance underwriting, real estate development (albeit with limited capital investment), and certain securities activities would all be authorized if conducted in separate affiliates. Securities affiliates of BHCs could underwrite municipal revenue bonds and sponsor and underwrite money market, stock, and bond mutual funds registered under the Investment Company Act. (The prohibition on underwriting of corporate securities would remain intact.) Beyond these specific authorizations, the regulatory prescription for allowable activities would be altered from "closely related to banking" to those of a "financial nature."

The bill would also establish the types of nonbank firms that may own banks by redefining the term "bank" to mean any institution insured by the FDIC (or eligible for such insurance) and that both accepts transactions accounts and makes commercial loans. The present definition of a bank in the Bank Holding Company Act contains only the latter provision. This definition spawned the emergence of the "nonbank bank" that either takes deposits or makes commercial loans, but does not conduct both activities. The revised definition closes this "loophole."

The administration bill (unlike its 1982 version) includes supervisory procedures that allay Fed concerns about the broadening of BHC powers. The Fed's position disagrees with the view that confining the new activities to nonbank subsidiaries would, in itself, serve to insulate the bank adequately from the risks and potential conflicts of interest inherent in such activities. Thus the Fed applauds provisions of the bill that prescribe criteria for its own authorization and supervision of nonbanking activities. Procedures would be altered, however, so that a formal review process of a proposed undertaking or acquisition of a nonbanking activity by a BHC would be necessary only when the Fed indicated disapproval. (At the present time, all such proposals are reviewed and the burden of proof is on the applicant to demonstrate a net public benefit—a process conducive to obstructive tactics by competitors.) The Fed could disapprove a proposed activity on the grounds that it was nonfinancial in nature or on the basis of various prescribed statutory considerations such as inadequate financial resources or jeopardized bank safety and soundness.

The bill would also require that nonbanking affiliates of BHCs be capitalized at least to the same extent as comparable competing businesses. Significantly, the provision in the present law that requires Fed evaluation of competitive conditions is deleted. Antitrust laws would, of course, be applicable, and the Justice Department would monitor proposed BHC acquisitions and entry into new activities. The bill would leave unchanged the provision included in the 1970 amendments to the Bank Holding Company Act that prohibits the "tying" of bank to nonbank services. (Such tying pertains to the offering of discounts on a package of bank and nonbank services.) This prohibition is intended to preserve "impartiality in the provision of credit" and proscribe potentially risky tying arrangements that could undermine bank stability. No such prohibition applies, however, to nonbank financial institutions and therein lies a potential future competitive inequity.

The administration bill made no progress in 1983. Near the year's end, Senator Jake Garn, Chairman of the Senate Banking Committee, introduced an alternative "compromise bill." The Garn bill would prohibit mergers between the largest banking organizations and non-bank financial institutions. As prescribed in the bill, a banking organization with more than 0.3 percent of total U.S. domestic deposits could not use more than 25 percent of its capital to acquire a non-banking financial institution. Garn's proposed legislation would allow nonbank financial firms to acquire "consumer banks" that would be allowed to take deposits and make consumer loans but would have only highly restricted commercial lending powers. The same geographic restrictions that apply to full-service banks would apply to such "consumer banks."

Garn's bill also includes a provision for payment of interest to financial institutions on reserve balances held with the Fed. The prohibtion of payment of interest on demand deposits would be repealed. State usury ceilings would be preempted. The Garn proposal omits a provision in the administration bill considered objectionable by the thrift industry—placing thrift holding companies and service corporations under the same activities scope regulations as bank holding companies. The proposed new law would also lend congressional approval to the creation of regional interstate banking zones.

The Garn bill addresses concerns about excessive concentration of financial resources and power via its merger limitations. But even to the extent that such concerns are allayed by the Garn version of the administration bill, there appears to be only a remote possibility of enactment of it (or some similar set of proposals) before 1985. Two principal ingredients for congressional procrastination—lack of widespread interest on the part of the general electorate but *keen* interest on the part of affected industries—are very much characteristic of these proposals. Further, many legislators doubtless find the issues involved rather esoteric and confusing. Also, 1984 is an election year. Barring development of another set of crisis circumstances, it is unlikely that Congress will act soon. Thus what Fed Chairman Volcker has termed a "pervading atmosphere of unfairness, of constant stretching and testing of the limits of law and regulation and circumvention of their intent, and of regulatory disarray" is likely to persist for some time.[1] Such "stretching, testing, and circumvention" of the legal and regulatory framework, however, has a way of preordaining the shape of eventual legislation.

Other Developments and Issues

Neither the Garn bill nor the administration bill addresses the issues associated with the organization and structure of the federal regulatory agencies and with deposit insurance reform. The latter has won little support to date. The former apparently triggered considerable disagreement among the members of Vice-President Bush's Task Group on Regulation of Financial Services. None of the federal agencies wished to relinquish existing regulatory powers nor did they wish to have their separate identities extinguished. The Fed, in particular, strongly resisted proposals that would eliminate its regulatory purview over bank holding companies and state member banks.

The Fed is an unpopular regulator among regulatees. The American Bankers Association has urged in a policy statement that the Fed's role be narrowed to formulation and implementation of monetary policy. The Association of Bank Holding Companies has made clear its desire for a different regulator than the Fed. Thrift holding companies and service corporations are strongly opposed to being placed under the Fed's regulatory purview. (Their opposition to that section of the administration's deregulation bill that would bring this about has apparently been successful.) The breadth and depth of opposition to the Fed's regulatory role thus suggests it is entirely possible that the Fed may eventually be stripped of at least some portion of its regulatory powers.

Proposals for reorganization of the federal regulatory agencies are numerous, but they can be roughly lumped into "functionally focused" and "institutionally focused" categories. The former set of proposals are based on the view that blurring of functions among financial institutions has rendered obsolete a regulatory focus by type of institution. The latter set of proposals would preserve the present institutional focus for regulation, but generally with some degree of consolidation.

The Bush task force (or at least a majority thereof) appears to favor a modestly consolidated institutional approach. In this reported compromise plan, a new Federal Banking Commission would be created to assume responsibility for most commercial bank regulation. The *label* of the Office of the Comptroller of the Currency would disappear, but the agency itself would be the core of the new commission. Most FDIC and some Fed bank regulatory powers would be absorbed by the commission, with the Fed retaining some purview over the largest multinational banking organizations. Thrift institutions would continue to be regulated by the Federal Home Loan Bank Board. The Securities and Exchange Commission would assume the task of enforcing securities laws and disclosure laws as they apply to financial institutions. The Justice Department would be responsible for antitrust law enforcement for these institutions. All such changes, of course, require action by Congress.

Deposit Insurance

There is an apparent lack of broad, influential support for deposit insurance reform. Commercial banks oppose consolidation of the insurance funds and are, at best, lukewarm regarding risk-related deposit insurance premiums. The failure of First National Bank of Midland in the fall of 1983, largely attributable to a "quiet run" of uninsured depositors concerned about energy loans gone sour, will not help the case for placing uninsured depositors at risk in the cause of enhancing market discipline over bank risk-taking. Congress appears to view the "deposit insurance crisis" as either nonexistent or simply surmounted. Without legislative endorsement, the ability of the deposit insurance agencies to implement change is quite limited. Barring developments that reignite concerns about deposit insurance, the near-term probability of significant action in this area is apparently quite low.

Brokered Deposits

The FDIC and FHLBB (FSLIC) may be more successful in spurring Congress to take action regarding brokering of deposits. The House Banking Committee is presently considering this issue and has received proposals from the five federal financial institution regulators. (The FDIC suggested denial of deposit insurance coverage to brokered deposits.) But the deposit insurance agencies can, and probably will, take steps to restrict money brokering even without new legislation. The role of brokered deposits in the failure of First National Bank of Midland (at the time of failure, about 13 percent of its deposits came from money brokers) adds impetus to the movement toward restriction.

At present, brokers in $100,000 CDs are unregulated and entry into the business is easy. It is estimated that money brokers "placed" about $120 billion in banks and savings and loan associations in 1983. About 40 percent of the nation's banks now use brokered funds. Clearly, brokered deposits are not merely a phenomenon stemming from abuse of deposit insurance; it appears that money brokers have emerged as significant agents for funds transmission from capital-surplus to capital-short areas.

In an October 3, 1983, letter to Congressman St Germain, Fed Chairman Volcker addressed the issue of brokered deposits. While agreeing that the placement of such deposits in failing depository institutions raised the cost to deposit insurance agencies of ensuing failures (as with Penn Square Bank and First National Bank of Midland) and that money broker activities undercut market discipline, Volcker pointed out that:

> ... In a banking system where individual institutions are subject to geo graphic limitations—in some cases they are limited to a single office—it is quite natural and, under appropriate circumstances, economically desirable that mechanisms develop to facilitate the transmission of funds from areas of excess savings of liquidity to those areas in need of funds for the legitimate banking and credit needs of consumers and businesses. Brokers have long played and continue to play an important role in this function, and, in so doing, have contributed to a more efficient use of our economy's liquid savings. ... In considering the activities of money brokers, therefore, the critical issue is to devise a regulatory response that will address the practices considered harmful without substantially impeding the legitimate role of the brokers.[2]

Volcker goes on to suggest that attention be focused on the type of money brokering that clearly exploits deposit guarantees—the splitting of brokered funds into $100,000 denominations. One possibility is to reduce or eliminate deposit insurance for such funds. Another is to mandate required public disclosures by depository institutions of their use of brokered funds. Volcker prefers the latter approach and points to the recent institution of such a requirement (in effect for the September 30, 1983, call report) for commercial banks.

Reliance on disclosure, however, is a frail reed for fully insured brokered deposits; the investors in this case don't care. And if uninsured depositors do care, there are now available a great many more pointed indicators of depository institution difficulty. If the money-brokering business continues to grow—and in the absence of regulatory or legislative action, it almost certainly will—it will doubtless become a major factor in bringing the issue of deposit insurance reform to center stage.

Assessment of Current Developments

In sum, the near-term outlook for major legislative and regulator initiatives for restructuring of the financial regulatory framework is highly uncertain. A backlash appears to have developed against such change after the relatively rapid pace of developments in the period from 1980 to 1982. Perhaps Congress is tired of banking-related issues. While reactionary efforts to roll back deregulation, in the absence of some unforeseen deregulation-spawned crisis, will almost certainly fail, forward motion has been slowed. Along with the usual interplay of special-interest considerations, lack of public interest, and political inertia, personalities are presently playing a significant (albeit short-term) role.

One such personality is that of Paul Volcker, clearly an extremely influential Fed chairman. Volcker's stewardship is likely to end in 1985, and the prospects for changes in regulatory organization, scope, and nature may be substantially altered. At the Federal Home Loan Bank Board, the replacement of Richard Pratt by Edwin Gray has resulted in a sharp change in the tone and content of the FHLBB's policy recommendations. Whereas Pratt lobbied strenuously (and, to a large extent, successfully) for new powers for thrifts to permit diversification and for sweeping change in general, Gray works to reaffirm and emphasize the traditional housing finance role of thrift institutions.[3] The result is likely to be some near-term retardation of the trend toward elimination of differences between commercial banks and thrift institutions.

In the longer run, however, more fundamental forces will shape financial regulatory change. There is little reason to believe that the economic and technological forces that have already triggered and shaped the changes of recent years have abated to the point of halting the financial services revolution. Further, the general public has now "had a taste" of deregulation of financial services and appears to like it. Certainly the effects of deregulation and the new competition on consumers of financial services are highly significant for the fuure course of events.

IMPLICATIONS FOR CONSUMERS OF FINANCIAL SERVICES

There seem to be at least two important implications of deregulation and the new competition for consumers of financial services. First, recognizing that consumers of financial services are both lenders (depositors) and borrowers (and use a variety of other financial services as well), it is increasingly likely that depositors will receive market rates on their deposits—both transactions and nontransactions—*and* that borrowers will pay market rates to obtain funds. Second, the proliferation of alternatives available to users of financial services will continue to expand. This substantial increase in the variety of financial services available may produce some degree of confusion in the minds of users of financial services that may, in turn, lead to the growth of specialized financial planning organizations that provide advice and fund management to consumers, especially those of substantial wealth.

The pricing of financial services at market rates should produce benefits to many (though not all) users of financial services. The benefits should be greatest for larger depositors in nontransactions accounts and should be the least for small depositors using transactions accounts. The elimination of Regulation Q deposit rate ceilings and the intensifying competition for funds will force depository institutions to pay full-market rates for each maturity range and each denomination of time deposits, producing a significant benefit to rate-insensitive depositors who, in past years, have often left funds at depository institutions paying below-market rates. While all such depositors will benefit, the greatest gain, of course, will accrue to those with the largest amount of such deposits. There may also be substantial benefit to rural residents who often received below-market rates on time deposits in past years.

Gains to users of transactions accounts, in contrast, will not be evenly distributed as depository institutions reprice this service from a "loss-leader" basis to a full-cost basis. Large depositors who hold transactions accounts both for making payments and also for savings purposes will benefit greatly from the deregulation movement. However, smaller depositors who use transactions accounts only for making payments and who have high-activity accounts will most likely face higher costs for those accounts. Also, to the extent that deregulation causes depository institutions to reduce costs through consolidation of their branches, the depositors (and to a lesser extent the borrowers) will face higher costs in the form of less convenience in their relationship with depository institutions.

Borrowers from depository institutions also will be affected by the deregulation phenomenon. While, as with the deposit relationship, it is difficult to anticipate all of the consequences of deregulation for borrowers, two in particular seem reasonably certain. First, while depositors will receive market returns for their funds, borrowers will pay full-market rates for their funds. In past years, some depository institutions paid below-market rates for their deposits *and* charged below-market rates for their loans. These less-than-market rates were most common in two areas: (1) mortgage lenders, where savings and loans often made single family loans at interest rates reflecting their subsidized (by Regulation Q ceilings and FHLB advances) costs of funds; and (2) borrowers in rural areas or other areas subject to limited competition (such that the deregulation movement might have particular significance for the agricultural sector of the economy). Second, the deregulation movement may and probably will lead to greater and greater use of variable rate loans. As depository institutions obtain an increasing share of their funds from accounts that not only pay market rates but also pay rates amenable to rapid adjustment as market rates change (the money market deposit account is an excellent example), they will increasingly seek to reduce their risk exposure by making their loan rates variable.

A particularly interesting dimension of the deregulation and new competition phenomenon concerns the implications for the alternatives available to individual consumers of financial services. Without question, the number and variety of financial services available, particularly deposit services but also including credit and other financial services, will be much greater after deregulation and the new competition than before. In past years, the range of deposit services was quite limited—transactions accounts were available from a commercial bank and only from a bank; savings and time deposits were available from all depository institutions, but there were only a very few types of accounts and the differences among the institutions in the types of accounts offered were quite small; and mortgage loans for the purchase of residential property were available primarily from local savings and loans. Now there are a vast array of deposit and credit accounts available from a large number of local and nation-wide financial institutions, both depository and nondepository.

Such an expansion in the choices available to consumers of financial services would seem to provide net benefits to these consumers. The benefits would include a better price for each financial service due to increased competition and a greater variety of services provided. Deregulation and the new competition should allow individual consumers to tailor financial services specifically to their needs; in other words, to customize the financial services they purchase. Yet, such proliferation of types of services and greater variability in the prices of the services increases the search costs to the consumer. These search costs might be reduced by the expansion of the services offered by professionals known as financial planners. These professionals might be independent of existing organizations and provide their service for an explicit fee, or they might be employees of existing financial institutions and earn their salary by generating deposit and credit business for the institution. Recent advertisements by many financial institutions that attempt to portray their employees as financial counselors are consistent with this trend. It may also be necessary for the financial institution to simplify the choices available to consumers of financial services by packaging a number of specific financial services into one type of account, such as has been done with the various cash management accounts.

These are only a few of the possible changes in store for consumers of financial services if present trends continue. And, as asserted previously, whether or not "present trends continue" may hinge, in part, on how the consuming public responds to these changes in the financial services marketplace.

Another arena in which deregulation and a changing financial environment will have significant repercussions is in the realm of monetary policy. Here, also, the nature of the effects has definite implications for the degree and nature of further regulatory and legislative change.

IMPLICATIONS OF DEREGULATION
FOR MONETARY POLICY

The principal focus of this book has been on the effects of deregulation and other changes in the financial environment on the operations of depository institutions in their provisioning of financial services to households, businesses, and governments. In that regard, we have concentrated on the effects of deregulation on the number and profitability of depository institutions, products offered by depository institutions, the geographical span over which these products are offered, and the implications of deregulation for failures of depository institutions. There are also important implictions of deregulation in the financial industry for the conduct of monetary policy. Indeed, deregulation may have some very important implications for both the way monetary policy is conducted and also for the effectiveness of monetary policy. These implications are important for our evaluation of the future of depository institutions, since the future of depository institutions will be greatly affected by the course of monetary policy.

There are at least four ways in which financial deregulation may affect the conduct and operations of monetary policy. Financial deregulation may affect (and probably already has affected) the way in which the Fed seeks to curtail total spending, causing the Fed to place greater emphasis on interest rate movements and less on the availability of funds. This aspect of deregulation is likely to produce greater volatility in interest rates in future years, at least as compared with what would have occurred without deregulation. Second, deregulation, and especially the money market deposit accounts and the Super-NOWs that were authorized by the Garn-St Germain Depository Institution Act of 1982, raise important questions about whether the Fed will be able to continue its present emphasis on the growth of monetary aggregates as policy targets. The significant problem of monetary aggregate measurement created by these changes greatly complicates the operations of the Fed and may produce a retreat or an abandonment of the policy implemented in October, 1979, of emphasizing control of the monetary aggregates as an intermediate target of monetary policy. Third, the deregulation movement raises important questions about the ability of the Fed to *control* the monetary aggregates, principally due to the potential effects of deregulation on the monetary multiplier. Fourth, and perhaps most important for a longer term perspective, the deregulation movement—and particularly the Depository Institutions Deregulation and Monetary Control Act of 1980—has sharply increased the monetary policy powers of the Federal Reserve.

Prior to deposit rate deregulation, the Federal Reserve sought to affect the volume of spending in the economy (and thereby production, employment, and purchasing power) by affecting the availability of funds at commercial banks and other depository institutions as well as the cost of those funds. In periods of rising interest rates, the Fed would refrain from raising the Regulation Q ceilings on rates paid by banks for funds. As open-market rates increased above the permissible deposit rate ceilings, the ability of banks to fuel new loan expansion was curtailed, thus forcing some banks to reduce their lending. The effect would be the most significant in large banks that practiced liability management in order to fund their loan demand, though it might be important also at smaller banks. Thus the Fed could reduce the volume of spending by, in effect, curtailing the *availability* of funds to potential borrowers from banks and other depository institutions.

It should be pointed out that this argument is most relevant to the containment of excessive demand and inflationary pressures. The effects of changing relative spreads between deposit rate ceilings and open-market rates would be less in periods of falling rates. Also, the strength of the argument is reduced somewhat by two factors. First, credit is available from sources other than commercial banks and other depository institutions. In fact, as discussed earlier, the availability of credit from nondepository institutions has increased substantially during recent years due, at least in part, to the restrictions placed on depository institutions. Second, depository institutions have found ways to circumvent the Regulation Q ceilings by acquiring federal funds, Eurodollars, and other nondeposit sources not subject to rate ceilings. Deposit rate ceilings appeared to be quite successful in curtailing the availability of funds at depository institutions in 1966 and again in 1969, though the importance of this policy instrument diminished in the 1970s and early 1980s as the portion of bank liabilities subject to deposit rate ceilings declined sharply.

With the phase-out of Regulation Q (virtually eliminated by October, 1983), depository institutions are able to pay competitive market rates for virtually all their funds. Strong demands for credit by business and other customers of depository institutions can be met by acquiring funds through the issuance of deposits at market rates of interest. Hence, rising rates need not lead to reduced availability in the supply of funds. As a result, it may be that interest rates may have to rise further in periods of rising rates than they would have during the era of Regulation Q in order for the demand for funds to be significantly curtailed. Hence, the deregulation of deposit rate ceilings may contribute to greater volatility in interest rates.

Deposit rate deregulation also may substantially affect the ability of the Fed to set growth rates for its intermediate targets. For example, if the Fed desires some growth rate in nominal gross national product, it can set a desired growth rate in M1 and M2, *provided* that it knows or can predict the velocity of circulation of these monetary aggregates (since nominal GNP is the product of the money supply and the velocity of circulation). Yet the introduction of new deposit instruments as a result of deposit rate deregulation may alter the traditional velocity relationship and make it much more difficult to predict nominal income from knowledge of the quantity of M1 and M2.

The best example of this potential problem created by deposit rate deregulation is the experience with the new money market deposit accounts and Super-NOWs in early 1983. The MMDAs in particular have been extremely successful, attracting over $350 billion in the period from late 1982 through mid-1983. The Super-NOWs, while less successful, have also obtained a substantial amount of funds, exceeding $30 billion by mid-1983. MMDAs are counted as part of M2, while Super-NOWs are treated as part of M1.

The growth rate of M2 increased substantially in early 1983, reflecting the inflow of funds into MMDAs from non-M2 sources. Given the historical velocity relationship between M2 and nominal GNP, the Federal Reserve might have anticipated a sharp increase in the growth rate of the economy (though probably not until some months later, given the lags that appear to exist between monetary changes and real economic activity). However, the financial innovation that the MMDA represented may have altered the velocity of money (as measured by M2 velocity) with the result that past magnitudes of velocity were not useful for policy purposes. If so, the Fed must now anticipate the effect on velocity of this financial innovation, a task that is difficult to accomplish and subject to substantial potential error.

The same problem existed with the effects of the Super-NOWs and MMDAs on M1 velocity, though prediction of the direction and magnitude of the effect is more difficult than in the case of M2. Shifts into Super-NOW accounts from non-M1 sources tend to raise the growth rate of M1, while shifts into MMDAs from M1 sources tend to lower the growth rate of M1. The net result of these conflicting forces is far from clear, though it appears that more funds shifted into M1 than out of M1 during early 1983.

As more and more transactions accounts begin to pay interest, the demand for money and hence the velocity of circulation of money may be altered. In past years, when transactions accounts did not pay interest, the demand for money by wealth holders was interest-sensitive; the public wished to hold more money at lower interest rates and to hold less money at higher interest rates because the spread between interest-earning assets and noninterest-earning transactions accounts was changing directly with interest rate movements. However, with the public able to receive market interest rates on their transactions accounts, the interest sensitivity of the public's demand for money will be altered. In fact, the demand for money may no longer respond significantly to changes in the level of interest rates, perhaps introducing a further complication in the conduct of monetary policy.

Presumably, though, these problems for monetary policy are transitory. Once the MMDAs and the Super-NOWs have become established and once the process of deposit rate deregulation is complete, the velocity relationships should stabilize and the Fed should once again be able to use historical velocity and projections of future velocity in formulating monetary policy. Similarly, the demand for money function should stabilize as interest-paying transactions accounts become the norm. However, the transition period may be lengthy (years rather than months), and during this transition period the Fed may find that deregulation has produced serious problems for its operations. If so, the Fed's posture toward further deregulation may become one of resistance.

The third potential problem created by deregulation for monetary policy concerns effects on the ability of the Fed to control the volume of money. The total amount of money at any point in time is the product of the quantity of reserves and the multiplier. While the ability of the Fed to control the quantity of reserves is not perfect, it is generally concluded that the Fed can control reserve growth within reasonably narrow limits. However, to control *money* growth the Fed must be able to predict the value of the money multiplier, a variable over which it has no direct control. Yet there are reasons to believe that financial deregulation has made the money multiplier more volatile and less predictable.

The value of the money multiplier is heavily affected by the average reserve requirements against all deposits. This average reserve requirement ratio is itself determined by the mix of deposits. Personal time deposits have a zero percent reserve requirement, nonpersonal time deposits have a 3 percent reserve requirement, and transactions accounts have a graduated reserve requirement, rising from 3 percent to 12 percent. Sharp changes in the mix of deposits have been occurring concomitant with financial deregulation and are likely to continue to occur. Such changes in deposit mix necessarily produce changes in the value of the money multiplier. Shifts into MMDAs will affect the average reserve requirement ratio for depository institutions, though the exact magnitude of the effect will vary with the source of those funds. Presumably this instability of the multiplier is temporary (as with the instability in velocity), yet the multiplier may not return to its more stable and predictable position until the financial innovations associated with deregulation are completed.

Each of the three items discussed above tend to complicate and perhaps weaken the power of monetary policy. Yet there is one important aspect of deregulation that has strengthened the power of the Federal Reserve in its conduct of monetary policy. The DIDMCA of 1980 extended the power of the Fed not only to all commercial banks but to all depository institutions. Hence, the effects on the supply of money and credit produced by shifts in deposits among member and nonmember banks and between banks and savings and loans are eliminated by this aspect of deregulation. Since the passage of DIDMCA in 1980, a change in the legal reserve ratio affects all accounts in a given category almost instantaneously and in precisely the same way. The magnitude of the effects upon required and excess reserves is the same for all institutions. Thus reserve requirement changes by the Fed become a potentially more important tool of economic stabilization.

Interest Payment on Required Reserves

The system of reserve requirements, however, may be itself a target of significant future change. Proposals for change range from minor technical adjustments to the abolition of reserve requirements.[4] One long-argued and increasingly persuasive idea is payment of interest on reserve balances at Federal Reserve Banks. This has long been urged as a means of improving monetary control and stability. Incentives to evade reserve requirements via unsettling financial innovations (specifically, development of transactions accounts outside the depository system) would be eliminated. Increases in reserve requirements would be much more acceptable as a policy measure, as would elimination of lagged reserve requirements. The Fed has publicly urged payment of a market-related rate of interest on reserve balances for a number of years (most strongly during its "membership crisis" of the 1970s).

Payment of interest on reserves is likely to be eventually approved by Congress. The principal obstacle remains the Treasury's reluctance to lose a large portion of the lucrative transfers from the Fed that it presently enjoys (over $10 billion a year) to such payments—opposition made more vehement of late by the Treasury's huge present and projected deficits. Despite this opposition, this special tax on banks is likely to be eventually eliminated due to deregulation (especially the demise of Regulation Q) and the new competition from nondepository institutions not subject to reserve requirements. The issue has evolved from one of simple equity to one of concern about the financial health and viability of depository institutions. Concern about the impact on Treasury revenues is likely to result in phased, rather than immediate, implementation, but eventual congressional action—probably in conjunction with legalization of interest payment on demand deposits—is quite probable. The Fed is presently urging such a course of action.[5] As mentioned earlier, Senator Garn has introduced legislation that includes such a provision.

The Fed and Deregulation

In recent years, the Fed has arguably been less enthusiastic than its sister agencies about the wave of change sweeping the nation's financial structure. In particular, the Fed's conservatism in performing its regulatory mandate over bank holding companies has led to unrest among the latter. We will not seek to assign speculative weights to the factors that presumably underlie the Fed's cautious stance, but we will venture to identify a few of them.

The Fed is doubtless concerned that its regulatory purview will be a casualty of deregulation; certainly, it is under attack. The personality factor mentioned previously is perhaps at work—views of "the Fed" at this point in time are, to a major degree, the views of Paul Volcker. More constructively, the Fed's basic mission is monetary and financial stability, and it is rightly concerned that such stability not be endangered by precipitous change. Put more critically, financial deregulation makes the job of the Fed more difficult and, like any institution, it views with a somewhat jaundiced eye developments that complicate its operations and render more difficult accomplishment of its objectives. For all these reasons (whatever their respective weights), the Fed can hardly be expected to join the vanguard of a movement to construct a brave new financial order as quickly as possible. But neither is it likely to actively resist attempts to construct a more rational financial system, provided such efforts are legislated and implemented with the degree of deliberation that the Fed deems due. For example, consider the September 13, 1983, call of Chairman Volcker for Congress to take action regarding geographic constraints on depository institutions. After citing the de facto existence of a large measure of interstate banking in the form of Edge Act subsidiaries, loan production offices, credit card operations, grandfathered holding companies, interstate acquisitions of failing depository institutions, and bank holding company nonbank affiliates, Volcker asserts:

> But these developments are uneven and haphazard. . . . Present law forces banking services to be fragmented, even within many metropolitan areas. . . . A closely integrated economy requires and deserves more uniform rules in this important area. It is reasonable to ask whether rules that prohibit New York or St. Louis banking organizations from establishing offices across a river, but permit them to sell insurance in Arizona, serve a national purpose. Similar doubts arise about the logic of proposals that allow a bank in Providence, Rhode Island, to purchase a bank two states and 150 miles away in southern Vermont, but that a bank 30 miles away, in Albany, New York be prohibited. We also have the anomaly of states welcoming foreign banks with-

in their borders, while prohibiting entry of U.S. banks from neighboring states.

Volcker thus urges outright alleviation or elimination of interstate banking barriers as eminently preferable to the present pattern of "end runs" and regional interstate banking arrangements. In this regard, the Chairman and his agency are "hawks," but dovish (or other fowl-like sentiments) are likely to prevail.

CONCLUSIONS AND IMPLICATIONS

Many of the laws governing this nation's financial system were enacted under circumstances and prevailing philosophies far different from those that exist today. Many of these laws stem from the banking crisis of the 1930s, others reflect concern for "states' rights" (to preserve the dual banking system), some (such as the Glass-Steagall Act) are attributable to desires to separate banking from certain activities deemed to be deleterious to the banking system, and still others are philosophically grounded in fears of concentration of financial power. Viewed in this fashion, the numerous legislative restrictions have a distinctly anachronistic flavor. Why then is the statutory framework proving to be so resistant to change? Why are the McFadden Act, the Glass-Steagall Act, and the Bank Holding Company Act still essentially intact despite the recent years of ferment, crisis and near-crisis, and technological and organizational innovation in the financial system?

Do these various statutes enjoy support from empirical investigation of their effects in objective research studies? No. Do impartial scholars in banking and financial fields of study offer widespread professional endorsement of these laws? No. Does the experience of other countries indicate the existence of clear perils in the absence of the restrictions embodied in these various items of legislation? No. Then why is the Congress so evidently unwilling to repeal or significantly amend these laws? This does not appear to be a question for which the answer is imbedded in conceptual or empirical investigation of financial markets phenomena.

A number of authors have attempted to develop analytical frameworks that explain congressional action (and inaction) in the realm of financial reform. Perhaps the most useful is the dialectical framework associated with various writings of Edward J. Kane and Robert A Eisenbeis.[6] The Kane-Eisenbeis framework recognizes that regulatory restriction confers benefits as well as costs on regulated firms, thus providing economic incentives for the preservation and extension of regulatory constraints as well as their change and removal. And lobbying efforts by firms bearing net regulatory *costs* to change or remove restrictions may be softened and even negated by successful efforts on their part to reduce or eliminate these costs by financial innovation. The latter may result in regulatory disequilibrium and cost/benefit changes that set forces in motion for legislative and regulatory change.

George Benston makes much the same argument in what he calls the "private interests rationale" for regulation:

> ... The private interests rationale explains regulation as an interplay between the benefits to private interests from legislation, the breakup of coalitions as individual producers seek to benefit by avoiding the regulations, and the efforts of outsiders to offer consumers better and unregulated substitute products as the costs to consumers of the regulations and technological change increase the profitability of innovations.[7]

Benston also offers the "continuing constituency rationale" to explain the durability of regulatory laws. Such laws soon acquire a constituency of benefitting parties dedicated to their preservation and even extension. The regulatory agencies themselves are a salient example.

While this framework is plausible, its predictive powers are quite limited. One can easily identify who benefits and who loses from particular laws. Commercial banks as a group gain from restrictions on thrifts and nondepository financial institutions. Small independent banks benefit from geographic restrictions. Nondepository financial institutions benefit from both geographic and activity constraints on bank holding companies. But the whole cost/benefit spectrum inherent in any given regulatory arrangement among all affected institutions is not observable. Thus, there is no basis to evaluate potential tradeoffs among interested parties in attempts to forge a new regulatory framework. For example, what geographic restraints are commercial banks willing to accept in exchange for reduced activity constraints, or vice versa? What restrictions will banks accept in exchange for the imposition of new restrictions on the banking activities of nonfinancial depository institutions? It is unlikely that the institutions themselves can supply answers to these questions. This is why legislators who are waiting for financial institutions to agree on a new regulatory framework and submit it to the political process will have a very long wait indeed.

Thus the Kane-Eisenbeis-Benston framework (or any other known theory) offers no clear guide as to whether deregulation will proceed or be reversed or to what degree or when this will transpire. Unlike competitive market solutions to economic problems that emerge independently of the blueprints of individual market participants, the political process can remain blocked indefinitely. Market forces grind away inexorably, continually coping with the intricate decision calculus of the marketplace. There is no counterpart in the political arena; the Kane-Eisenbeis-Benston dialectic is, at best, to the political arena what, say, a supply and demand chart is to the workings of the stock market.

Further substantive and sweeping *legislative* change in the U.S. financial regulatory framework will likely come only when a new crisis emerges or is perceived to emerge. The crisis may arise independently of the existing framework but render it (in real or perceived terms) no longer viable as in the 1930s model. Or a crisis stemming from the interplay between the regulatory framework and financial innovation, or between the regulatory framework and economic-technological change (the 1970s model), may make legislative action imperative. The shape of change then will be determined by the nature and severity of the crisis and the interplay among fiercely lobbying regulated institutions seeking to bend the impending changes in a way most beneficial to their own situation.

Conjecture that crisis and the goals of special-interest groups will shape the future course of the legislative framework governing the financial services industry is a poor substitute for a crystal ball. There appear to be a few reasonably predictable parameters in the equation, however. Dual banking will likely be with us for a considerable period; this victory for states' rights is clearly an enduring one. This country is unlikely to ever have British-Canadian-style banking concentration; the fear of concentration of financial power is too deep-seated. No changes in deposit insurance or otherwise will be permitted that consciously raise the spectre of widespread bank runs; those 9,000 bank failures in the 1930s are an indelible memory. The future of depository institutions as the principal component of the U.S. financial system appears secure indefinitely—for both economic and political reasons. And, finally, the safest prediction of all is akin to that treasured aphoristic response to a request for a stock market forecast, "The market will continue to fluctuate"—change will continue.

NOTES TO CHAPTER 8

1. Statement by Paul A. Volcker, Chairman, Board of Governors of the Federal Reserve System, before the Committee on Banking, Housing, and Urban Affairs, U.S. Senate, September 13, 1983. Printed in *Federal Reserve Bulletin* (October 1983), pp. 757–769.
2. Letter of October 3, 1983, from Paul A. Volcker, Chairman, Board of Governors of the Federal Reserve System, to Hon. Fernand J. St Germain, Chairman, Committee on Banking, Finance, and Urban Affairs, U.S. House of Representatives, released in public testimony, October 27, 1983.
3. See Gray's statement before the Senate Banking, Housing, and Urban Affairs Committee on August 13, 1983, in *Federal Home Loan Bank Board Journal* (October 1983), pp. 2–9.
4. An excellent case for significant modification of the reserve requirement burden on depository institutions is made by Stuart I. Greenbaum, "Legal Reserve Requirements: A Case Study in Bank Regulation," *Journal of Bank Research* (Spring 1983), pp. 59–74. While many previous observers have questioned the usefulness of reserve requirements, Greenbaum argues that they are less than useless and are downright harmful to monetary control and stability.
5. See Statement of J. Charles Partee, Member, Board of Governors of the Federal Reserve System, before the Subcommittee on Financial Institutions, Supervision, Regulation, and Insurance of the Committee on Banking, Finance, and Urban Affairs, House of Representatives, October 27, 1983.
6. See, for example, Edward J. Kane, "Accelerating Inflation, Technological Innovation, and the Decreasing Effectiveness of Banking Regulation," *Journal of Finance* (May 1981), pp. 355–367; and Robert A. Eisenbeis, "Regulation and Financial Innovation: Implications for Financial Structure and Competition Among Depository and Non-Depository Institutions," *Issues in Bank Regulation* (Winter 1981), pp. 15–23.
7. George J. Benston, "The Regulation of Financial Services," in George J. Benston, ed., *Financial Services: The Changing Institutions and Government Policy* (Englewood Cliffs, N.J.: Prentice-Hall, 1983), pp. 28–63.

ILLUSTRATION OF EFFECTS OF PRICING DEPOSIT INSURANCE ACCORDING TO RISK

The effects of pricing deposit insurance are shown here for a hypothetical bank. Period 1 in the table predates any deposit insurance reform. The bank's position is revealed by its balance sheet, which is a simplified version of an actual financial balance sheet. The bank can invest in U.S. Treasury bills (T-bills), conservative loans, or risky loans; rates of interest earned on such assets are 8 percent, 10 percent, and 12 percent, respectively. The bank issues checking accounts, passbook savings accounts, and large certificates of deposit (purchased funds); interest rates paid on such accounts are 0 percent, 5 percent, and 8 percent, respectively. Net-interest income is the difference between interest received and interest paid. Net interest is "profit," exclusive of noninterest expenses. In this example, insurance expenses will be treated as if they are interest expenses.

"Reform" consists of pricing risk at the margin. In Period 2, deposit insurance reform is introduced. It is assumed that depositors are now exposed to possible losses, at least at the margin. The effective cost of purchasing deposits (marginal funds) increases for the hypothetical bank. The effective cost may rise for either of two reasons (or both): the bank will pay a higher return to depositors for the additional risk to which they are exposed, or the bank will incur costs as a result of excess deposit insurance. These costs will be incurred because depositors are now taking into account the risk of loss. This, in turn, compels the bank to internalize more fully the

EFFECT OF DEPOSIT INSURANCE REFORM ON A HYPOTHETICAL BANK
(Thousands of dollars).

Period 1. Before Reform

Assets		Liabilities	
Cash	5,000	Noninterest-bearing accounts	2,500
T-bills	15,000	Passbook savings	5,000
Conservative loans	10,000	Purchased funds	40,000
Risky loans	20,000	Capital and surplus	2,500

Interest Earned		Interest Paid	
T-bills (8 percent)	1,200	Passbook savings (5 percent)	250
Conservative loans (10 percent)	1,000	Purchased funds (8 percent)	3,200
Risky loans (12 percent)	2,400		
	4,600		3,450
		Net-interest income	1,150

Period 2. After Reform

Interest Earned		Interest Paid	
T-bills (8 percent)	1,200	Passbook savings (5 percent)	250
Conservative loans (10 percent)	1,000	Purchased funds (10 percent)	4,000
Risky loans (12 percent)	2,400		
	4,600		4,250
		Net-interest income	350

Period 3. After Portfolio Adjustment

Assets		Liabilities	
Cash	5,000	Noninterest-bearing accounts	2,500
T-bills	15,000	Passbook savings	5,000
Conservative loans	20,000	Purchased funds	40,000
Risky loans	10,000	Capital and surplus	2,500

Interest Earned		Interest Paid	
T-bills (8 percent)	1,200	Passbook savings (5 percent)	250
Conservative loans (10 percent)	2,000	Purchased funds (8 percent)	3,200
Risky loans (12 percent)	1,200		
	4,400		3,450
		Net-interest income	950

cost of incurring additional risk. Private costs now more closely reflect social opportunity costs. The costs show up as reduced net-interest income for the bank.

In Period 3, the bank adjusts its portfolio in order to reduce its interest expenses. It will reduce the percentage of risky loans in its portfolio so long as interest expenses fall more rapidly than earnings. In this example, net-interest income rises again but remains $200,000 less than its level before reform. This difference represents the effects of subsidizing risk-taking. Before reform, profits of the hypothetical bank were higher. The financial system, however, was less stable. The bank's portfolio adjustment reduces its exposure to loss. In the aggregate, changes made by individual institutions would improve the stability of the financial system.

BIBLIOGRAPHY

Akerlof, George A. "The Market for Lemons: Quality, Uncertainty, and the Market Mechanism." *Quarterly Journal of Economics* (August 1970), pp. 488–500.

Altman, Edward I., and Arnold W. Sametz. *Financial Crises: Institutions and Markets in a Fragile Environment.* New York: John Wiley & Sons, Inc., 1977.

Baker, Donald I. "Competition, Monopoly and Electronic Banking." *The Economics of a National Electronic Funds Transfer System,* Federal Reserve Bank of Boston Conference Series #13, 1974, pp. 47–64.

Baker, James C. *International Bank Regulation.* New York: Praeger Publishers, 1978.

Baker, James C., and M. Gerald Bradford. *American Banks Abroad: Edge Act Companies and Multinational Banking.* New York: Praeger, 1974.

Barnett, Robert E.; Paul M. Horvitz; and Stanley C. Silverberg. "Deposit Insurance: The Present System and Some Alternatives." *Banking Law Journal* (April 1977), pp. 304–332.

Benston, George J. "Economies of Scale in Banking." *Journal of Money, Credit, and Banking* (May 1972), pp. 312–314.

Benston, George J. "Economies of Scale and Marginal Costs in Banking Operations." *National Banking Review* (June 1975). Reprinted in *Studies in Banking Competition and the Banking Structure.* The Administrator of National Banks, United States Treasury, 1966, pp. 355–394.

Benston, George J. *Corporate Disclosure in the U.S.* Lexington, Mass.: D.C. Heath & Co., 1976.

Benston, George J. "Deposit Insurance and Bank Failures." Federal Reserve Bank of Atlanta, *Economic Review* (March 1983), pp. 4–17.

Benston, George J., ed., *Financial Services: The Changing Institutions and Government Policy*. The American Assembly. Englewood Cliffs, N. J.: Prentice-Hall, 1983.

Benston, George J. "Federal Regulation of Banking: Analysis and Policy Recommendations." *Journal of Bank Research* (Winter 1983), pp. 216–244.

Benston, George J. "The Regulation of Financial Services." In George J. Benston, ed., *Financial Services: The Changing Institutions and Government Policy*. Englewood Cliffs, N. J.: Prentice-Hall, 1983, pp. 28–63.

Benston, George J., and Gerald A. Hanweck. "A Summary Report on Bank Holding Company Affiliation and Economies of Scale." Federal Reserve Bank of Chicago, *Bank Structure and Competition*, 1977.

Benston, George J.; Gerald A. Hanweck; and David B. Humphrey. "Operating Costs in Commercial Banks." Federal Reserve Bank of Atlanta, *Economic Review* (November 1982), pp. 6–21.

Benston, George J.; Gerald A. Hanweck; and David B. Humphrey. "Scale Economies in Banking: A Restructuring and Reassessment." *Journal of Money, Credit, and Banking 14* (November 1982), pp. 435–456.

Berger, Frederick. "The Emerging Transformation of the U.S. Banking System." *The Banker* (September 1981), pp. 25–39.

Binhammer, H. H., and Jane Williams. *Deposit-Taking Institutions: Innovation and the Process of Change*. Ottawa, Canada: Economic Council of Canada, 1976.

Bleeke, Joel, and James Goodrich. *Capitalizing on Opportunities Created by Deregulation of the Banking Industry*. Chicago: McKinsey & Company, Inc., September 1981.

Blunden, George. "The Supervision of the U.K. Banking System." *Bank of England Quarterly Bulletin* (June 1975), pp. 188–189.

Board of Governors of the Federal Reserve System. *All Bank Statistics, United States 1896-1955*. Washington, D.C., p. 37.

Board of Governors of the Federal Reserve System (Staff Report). "Charts and Tables for the DIDC Conditions Briefing," December 16, 1981.

Buser, Stephen A.; Andrew H. Chen; and Edward J. Kane. "Federal Deposit Insurance, Regulatory Policy, and Optimal Bank Capital." *Journal of Finance* 36 (March 1981), pp. 51–60.

Cargill, Thomas F. "The Impact of Deregulation on the Financial System." *Issues in Bank Regulation* (Winter 1981), pp. 10–14.

Cargill, Thomas F., and Gillian Garcia. *Financial Deregulation and Monetary Control*. Stanford, Ca.: Hoover Institution Press, 1982.

Carron, Andrew S. In *The Plight of the Thrift Institutions*, Studies in the Regulation of Economic Activity. Washington, D.C.: The Brookings Institution, 1982.

Cheng, Hang-Sheng. "Financial Reform in Australia and New Zealand." Federal Reserve Bank of San Francisco, *Economic Review* (Winter 1983), pp. 9–24.

Christophe, Cleveland A. *Competition in Financial Services.* New York: First National City Corporation, 1974.

Colton, Kent W. *Financial Reform: A Review of the Past and Prospect for the Future.* The Office of Policy and Economic Research, Federal Home Loan Bank Board, Washington, D.C.: September 1980.

Cooper, Kerry, and Gerald Keim. "The Economic Rationale for the Nature and Extent of Corporate Financial Disclosure Regulation: A Critical Assessment." *Journal of Accounting and Public Policy* (September 1983), pp. 189-205.

Crane, Dwight B.; Ralph C. Kimball; and William T. Gregor. *The Effects of Banking Deregulation.* Association of Reserve City Bankers, (July 1983).

Dann, Larry, and Christopher M. James. "An Analysis of the Impact of Deposit Rate Ceilings on the Market Values of Thrift Institutions." *Journal of Finance* (December 1982), pp. 1259-70.

Diamond, Douglas W., and Philip H. Dybvig. "Bank Runs, Deposit Insurance, and Liquidity." *Journal of Political Economy* (August 1983), pp. 401-419.

Edmister, Robert O. *Financial Institutions: Markets and Management.* New York: McGraw-Hill, 1980.

Edwards, Franklin R. "Banks and Securities Activities: Legal and Economic Perspectives on the Glass-Steagall Act." In L.G. Goldberg and L.J. White, eds., *The Deregulation of the Banking and Securities Industries.* Lexington, Mass.: Lexington Books, 1978, pp. 273-291.

Edwards, Franklin R. *Issues in Financial Regulation.* New York: McGraw-Hill, 1979.

Edwards, Franklin R. "The New International Banking Facility: A Study in Regulatory Frustration." *Columbia Journal of World Business* (Winter 1981), p. 6.

Edwards, Franklin R., and J. Scott. "Regulating the Solvency of Depository Institutions: A Perspective for Deregulation." In Franklin R. Edwards, ed., *Issues in Financial Regulation.* New York: McGraw-Hill, 1979, pp. 65-105.

Eisenbeis, Robert A. "Financial Innovation and the Role of Regulation: Implications for Banking Organization, Structure, and Regulation." Working paper, Board of Governors of the Federal Reserve System, February, 1980.

Eisenbeis, Robert A. "Regulation and Deregulation of Banking." *The Bankers Magazine.* (March-April, 1981), pp. 25-33.

Eisenbeis, Robert A., and Myron L. Kwast. "The Implications of Expanded Portfolio Powers in the S&L Institution Performance." A paper presented at the Western Economic Association Meetings, San Francisco, 1982.

Eisenbeis, Robert A. "Regulation and Financial Innovation: Implications for Financial Structure and Competition Among Depository and Nondepository Institutions." *Issues in Bank Regulation* (Winter 1981), pp. 15-23.

Eisenbeis, Robert A. "New Investment Powers for S&Ls: Diversification or Specialization?" Federal Reserve Bank of Atlanta, *Economic Review* (July 1983), pp. 53-62.

Federal Deposit Insurance Corporation. *Deposit Insurance in a Changing Environment*, A Study of the Current System of Deposit Insurance Pursuant to Section 712 of the Garn-St Germain Depository Institutions Act of 1982, Washington, D.C., 1983.

Federal Reserve Bank of Atlanta. "Signals from the Future: The Emerging Financial Services Industry." *Economic Review* (September 1983), pp. 20–32.

Federal Reserve Bank of Minneapolis. "Are Banks Special?" *1982 Annual Report*, pp. 2–24.

Federal Reserve Bank of New York. "The Depository Institutions Act of 1982." *Capsule* no. 27 (January 1983), pp. 4–6.

Fieleke, Norman S. "International Lending on Trial." Federal Reserve Bank of Boston, *New England Economic Review* (May–June 1983), pp. 5–13.

Fischer, L. Richard; Elizabeth G. Gentry; and Petrina M. E. Venderamo. "The Garn-St Germain Depository Institutions Act of 1982." The Consumer Bankers Association, Arlington, Va., 1982.

Fischer, Gerald C., and Carter H. Golembe. "The Branch Banking Provisions of the McFadden Act as Amended: Their Rationale and Rationality." In *Compendium of Issues Relating to Branching by Financial Institutions*, Subcommittee on Financial Institutions of the Committee on Banking, Housing, and Urban Affairs, United States Senate, 94th Congress, 2nd Session. Washington, D.C.: U.S. Government Printing Office, October 1976.

Flannery, Mark J. "Removing Deposit Rate Ceilings: How Will Bank Profits Fare?" Federal Reserve Bank of Philadelphia, *Business Review*, (March–April 1983), pp. 13–21.

Flannery, Mark J., and Jack M. Guttentag. "Problem Banks: Examination, Identification and Supervision." In *State and Federal Regulation of Commercial Banks*, Federal Deposit Insurance Corporation, Washington, D.C., 2 (1980), pp. 169–226.

Ford, William F. "Banking's New Competition: Myths and Realities." Federal Reserve Bank of Atlanta, *Economic Review* (January 1982), pp. 3–11.

"Foreign Banks in America." *Euromoney* (August 1983) Supplement, p. 6.

Fraser, Donald R. "Deregulation and the Future of Depository Institutions." *The Bankers Magazine* (January–February 1983).

Fraser, Donald R., and James Kolari. *Size and Financial Performance in Banking*. U.S. Small Business Administration, Washington, D.C.: October 1983.

Fraser, Donald R., and R. Malcolm Richards. "Deregulation, MMDAs, Super-NOWs, and Security Returns in the Banking Industry." Paper presented at the 1983 meeting of the Financial Management Association.

Fraser, Donald R., and Gene C. Uselton. "The Omnibus Banking Act." *MSU Business Topics* (Fall 1980), pp. 5–14.

Friedman, Benjamin M., and Peter Formuzis. "Bank Capital: The Deposit-Protection Incentive." *Journal of Bank Research* 6 (August 1975), pp. 208–218.

Garcia, Gillian et al. *Financial Deregulation.* Federal Reserve Bank of Chicago, Staff Study 83–2, 1983, p. 20.

Garcia, Gillian et al. "The Garn-St Germain Depository Institutions Act of 1982." Federal Reserve Bank of Chicago, *Economic Perspectives* (March–April 1983), pp. 3–31.

Gestrim, B. V. "Understanding Banking in Canada." *Bankers' Magazine* (Winter 1976), pp. 50–56.

Gibson, William E. "Deposit Insurance in the United States: Evaluation and Reform." *Journal of Financial and Quantitative Analysis* 7 (March 1972), pp. 1575–94.

Goldberg, Lawrence G. "Bank Holding Company Acquisitions and Their Impact on Market Shares." *Journal of Money, Credit and Banking* (February 1976).

Golembe Associates, Inc. "How Many Commercial Banks in 1990?." *Golembe Reports*, vol. 1980–6.

Golembe Associates, Inc. "Deposit Insurance—A Sense of History and a Shattered Illusion." *Golembe Reports*, vol. 1982–2.

Golembe Associates, Inc. "Regulatory Reform—Some Observations on the Bush Task Group." *Golembe Reports*, vol. 1983–1.

Gramley, Lyle E. "Financial Innovation and Public Policy." Paper presented at the Financial Institutions Conference, Northwestern University, Evanston, Illinois, April 23, 1981.

Greenbaum, Stuart I. "Legal Reserve Requirements: A Case Study in Bank Regulation." *Journal of Bank Research* (Spring 1983), pp. 59–74.

Greenbaum, Stuart I., and Charles F. Haywood. "Secular Change in the Financial Services Industry." *Journal of Money, Credit and Banking* 3 (May 1981), pp. 571–89.

Guffey, Roger. "After Deregulation: The Regulatory Role of the Federal Reserve." Federal Reserve Bank of Kansas City, *Economic Review* (June 1983), pp. 3–7.

Harris, Jack. "Major Issues for Thrifts in the 1980s." Federal Home Loan Bank Board, *Journal* (February 1983), pp. 7–11.

Heggestad, Arnold A., ed. *Regulation of Consumer Financial Services.* Cambridge, Mass.: Abt Books, 1981.

Hoffman, Diether H. "German Banks as Financial Department Stores." Federal Reserve Bank of St. Louis, *Review* (November 1971), pp. 8–13.

Holleman, Leon. "Japan's New Banking Laws." *The Banker* (January 1982), pp. 37–39.

Horvitz, Paul M. "Failures of Large Banks: Implications for Banking Supervision and Deposit Insurance." *Journal of Financial and Quantitative Analysis* (November 1975), pp. 589–600.

Horvitz, Paul M. "Commercial Bank Financial Reporting and Disclosure." *Journal of Contemporary Business* (Summer 1977), pp. 59–75.

Horvitz, Paul M. "Reorganization of the Federal Regulatory Agencies." *Journal of Bank Research* (Winter 1983), pp. 245–263.

Humphrey, David B. "100% Deposit Insurance: What Would It Cost?" *Journal of Bank Research* 7 (August 1976), pp. 192–198.

Isaac, William M. "Are There Too Many Depository Institutions?" Paper presented to the 89th Annual Convention of the Ohio Bankers Association, Columbus, Ohio, May 20, 1980.

James, Christopher. "An Analysis of Inter-Industry Differences in the Effect of Regulation: The Case of Deposit Rate Ceilings." *Journal of Monetary Economics* 12 (1983).

Jessee, M. A., and S. A. Seelig. *Bank Holding Companies and the Public Interest.* Lexington, Mass.: Lexington Books, 1977.

Kahane, Yehuda. "Capital Adequacy and the Regulation of Financial Intermediaries." *Journal of Banking and Finance* 1 (1977), pp. 207–218.

Kane, Edward J. "Accelerating Inflation, Technological Innovation, and the Decreasing Effectiveness of Banking Regulation." *Journal of Finance* (May 1981), pp. 355–367.

Kane, Edward J. "Changes in the Provision of Correspondent Banking Services and the Role of Federal Reserve Banks Under the DIDMCA Act." *Carnegie-Rochester Conference Series on Public Policy* 16 (1982), North Holland Publishing Company, pp. 93–126.

Kane, Edward J. *The Gathering Crisis in Federal Deposit Insurance: Origins, Evolution, and Possible Reforms.* (Forthcoming).

Kareken, John H. "Deposit Insurance Reform, Or Deregulation is the Cart, Not the Horse." Federal Reserve Bank of Minneapolis, *Quarterly Review* (Spring 1983), pp. 1–9.

Kareken, John H., and Neil Wallace. "Deposit Insurance and Bank Regulation: A Partial-Equilibrium Exposition." *The Journal of Business* (July 1978), pp. 413–438.

Kaufman, George. "The Depository Institutions Deregulation and Monetary Control Act of 1980: What has Congress Wrought?" *Journal of Midwest Finance Association* (1981), pp. 20–35.

Kaufman, George, and Larry Mote. "Implications of Deregulation for Product Lines and Geographical Markets of Financial Institutions." *Journal of Bank Research* (Spring 1983), pp. 8–23.

Kendall, Leon T. "Rebuilding the Business: It's Time to Decide Which Road to Take." *Savings and Loan News* (August 1981), pp. 50–56.

Kennedy, H. Patrick. "The Role of Foreign Banks in a Changing U.S. Banking System." *The Banker* (February 1982), pp. 101–103.

Khoury, Sarkis J. *Dynamics of International Banking.* New York: Praeger, 1980, pp. 38–85.

Klein, Michael A. "Monetary-Control Implications of the Monetary Control Act." Federal Reserve Bank of San Francisco, *Economic Review* (Winter 1981), pp. 6–21.

Koehn, Michael F. In *Bankruptcy Risk in Financial Depository Intermediaries: Assessing Regulatory Effects.* Lexington, Mass.: Lexington Books, 1982.

Kreps, Clifton H., Jr., and Richard R. Wacht. "A More Constructive Role for Deposit Insurance." *Journal of Finance* 26 (May 1971), pp. 605–614.

Laurent, Robert D. "Reserve Requirements, Deposit Insurance, and Monetary Control." *Journal of Money, Credit and Banking* 13 (1981), pp. 314–324.

Lawler, Thomas A. "On the Nature and Causes of Financial Innovations by Nondepository Firms." Paper presented at the 1981 Western Finance Association Meeting.

Leff, Gary. "Should Federal Deposit Insurance Be 100 Percent?" *Bankers Magazine* (Summer 1976), pp. 23–30.

Lipsey, R.G., and R.K. Lancaster. "The General Theory of Second Best." *Review of Economic Studies* no. 63 (1956–57), pp. 11–32.

Luetkens, W.J. "Austrian Banks Temper Their Steel." *The Banker* (January 1982), pp. 109–110.

Maisel, Sherman J. *Risk and Capital Adequacy in Commercial Banks.* National Bureau of Economic Research, University of Chicago Press, 1981.

Marcis, Richard. "Savings and Loan Planning for the New Competitive Environment." Federal Home Loan Bank Board, *Journal* (July 1981), pp. 5–14.

Marcis, Richard L., and Dale Riordan. "The Savings and Loan Industry in the 1980s." Federal Home Loan Bank Board, *Journal* (May 1980), pp. 1–15.

Martin, Preston. "Some Causes and Consequences of Financial Innovation." Paper presented before the Securities and Exchange Commission Conference on Major Issues Confronting the Nation's Financial Institutions and Markets in the 1980s, Washington, D.C., October 7, 1982.

Mastropasqua, Salvatore. *The Banking System in the Countries of the EEC.* Germantown, Md.: Sizthoff & Noordhof, 1978.

Mayer, Thomas. "A Graduated Deposit Insurance Plan." *Review of Economics and Statistics* (February 1963), pp. 114–116.

McCord, Thomas. "The Depository Institutions Deregulation and Monetary Control Act of 1980." *Issues in Bank Regulation* (Spring 1980), pp. 3–7.

McNeill, Charles R. "The Depository Institutions Deregulation and Monetary Control Act of 1980." *Federal Reserve Bulletin* (June 1980), pp. 444–453.

Merton, Robert C. "An Analytical Derivation of the Cost of Deposit Insurance and Loan Guarantees: An Application of Modern Option Pricing Theory." *Journal of Banking and Finance* (June 1977), pp. 3–11.

Morgan, E. Victor; Richard Harrington; and George Zio. *Banking Systems and Monetary Policy in the EEC.* London: *Financial Times*, 1974.

"New Life in Italian Banking." *Euromoney* (August 1983), pp. 90–131.

Ogilvie, Nigel. "Foreign Banks in the U.S. and Geographic Restrictions on Banking." *Journal of Bank Research* (Summer 1980), pp. 72–79.

Orgler, Yair E., and Benjamin Wolkowitz. *Bank Capital.* New York: Van Nostrand Reinhold, 1976.

Park, James W. "The Mississippi Deposit Insurance Crisis." *Bankers Magazine* (Summer 1977), pp. 74-80.

Pigott, Charles. "Financial Report in Japan." Federal Reserve Bank of San Francisco, *Economic Review* (Winter 1983), pp. 25-45.

Polakoff, Murray. *Financial Institutions and Markets*, 2nd edition. Boston: Houghton-Mifflin, 1981.

Porter, Richard D.; Thomas D. Simpson; and Eileen Mauskopf. "Financial Innovation and the Monetary Aggregates." *Brookings Papers on Economic Acitivity* (1979), pp. 213-229.

Porzecanski, Arturo C. "The International Financial Role of U.S. Commercial Banks: Past and Future." *Journal of Banking and Finance* 5 (December 1981), pp. 5-16.

Prest, A.R., and P.J. Coppock. *The United Kingdom Economy.* London:Weidenfeld and Nicholson, 1978, pp. 67-72.

Puglisi, Donald J., and Anthony J. Vignola. "Funds Deployment and Money Market Deposit Accounts." Federal Home Loan Bank Board *Journal* (September 1983), pp. 9-15.

Raviv, Arthur. "The Design of an Optimal Insurance Policy." *American Economic Review* 69 (1979), pp. 84-96.

Revell, Jack. *The British Financial System.* London: Macmillan, 1973.

Rhoades, Stephen A. *Structure-Performance Studies in Banking: A Summary and Evaluation.* Washington, D.C.: Board of Governors of the Federal Reserve System, Staff Economic Study (92), 1977.

Robertson, Ross M. *The Comptroller and Bank Supervision.* Washington, D.C.: Office of the Comptroller of the Currency, 1968.

Robinson, Stuart W., Jr. *Multinational Banking.* Leiden, Holland: A.W. Sizthoff, 1972, p. 67.

Rockoff, Hugh T. "The Free Banking Era: A Re-examination." *Journal of Money, Credit and Banking* 6 (May 1974), pp. 141-167.

Rockoff, Hugh. *The Free Banking Era: A Reexamination..* New York: Arno Press, 1974, p. 3.

Rolnick, Arthur J., and Warren E. Weber. "Free Banking, Wildcat Banking, and Shinplasters." Federal Reserve Bank of Minneapolis, *Quarterly Review* (Fall 1982), pp. 10-19.

Rose, John T., and Samuel H. Talley. "The Banking Affiliates Act of 1982: Amendments to Section 23A." *Federal Reserve Bulletin* (November 1983), pp. 689-699.

Rose, Peter S., and Donald R. Fraser. *Financial Institutions*, 2nd edition. Dallas: Business Publications, Inc., 1984.

Rose, Peter S., and William L. Scott. "Risk in Commercial Banking: Evidence from Postwar Failures." *Southern Economic Journal* (July 1978), pp. 90-106.

Rosenblum, Harvey, and Diane Siegel. "Competition in Financial Services: The Impact of Nonbank Entry." Federal Reserve Bank of Chicago, Staff Study 83-1, 1983.

Scott, Kenneth E., and Thomas Mayer. "Risk and Regulation in Banking: Some Proposals for Federal Deposit Insurance Reform." *Stanford Law Review* 23 (May 1981), pp. 537-582.

Sharpe, William F. "Bank Capital Adequacy, Deposit Insurance and Security Values." *Journal of Financial and Quantitative Analysis* (November 1978), pp. 701-718.

Silber, William L. *Financial Innovation.* Lexington, Mass.: Lexington Books, 1975.

Silber, William L. "Towards a Theory of Financial Innovation." In William L. Silber, ed., *Financial Innovation.* Lexington, Mass.: D.C. Heath & Co., 1975.

Silber, William. "The Process of Financial Innovation." *American Economic Review* (May 1983), pp. 89-95.

Sinkey, Joseph F. "On the Cost of Deposit Insurance When There are Surveillance Costs." *Journal of Business* 51 (July 1978), pp. 439-452.

Sinkey, Joseph F. *Problem and Failed Institutions in the Commercial Bank Industry.* Contemporary Studies in Economic and Financial Analysis, volume 4. Greenwich, Connecticut: Jai Press Inc., 1979.

Sinkey, Joseph F., and David A. Walker. "Problem Banks: Identification and Characteristics." *Journal of Bank Research* 5 (Winter 1975), pp. 208-217.

Smith, Paul F. "Structural Disequilibrium and the Banking Act of 1980." *Journal of Finance* (May 1982), pp. 385-398.

Sprenkle, Case M., and Bryan E. Stanhouse. "A Theoretical Framework for Evaluating the Impact of Universal Reserve Requirements." *Journal of Finance* 36 (1981), pp. 825-840.

Stigler, George. "The Effectiveness and Effects of the SECs Accounting Disclosure Requirements." In H.G. Manne, ed., *Economic Policy and the Regulation of Corporate Securities.* Washington, D.C.: The American Enterprise Institute, 1969.

Talley, Samuel H. "Bank Holding Company Performance in Consumer Finance and Mortgage Banking." *Magazine of Bank Administration* 52 (1976), pp. 42-44.

Temby, Warwick, and John L. Goodman, Sr. "Coping with Volatile Financial Markets: Australia's Experience." Federal Home Loan Bank Board *Journal* (March 1983), pp. 2-5.

Texas Bankers Association. "The Impact of Deregulation on Small and Medium-Sized Texas Banks." Austin: Management Analysis Center for the Texas Bankers Association, 1983.

U.S. Congress, House Committee on Bank, Currency and Housing. *FINE-Financial Institutions and the Nation's Economy, Discussion Principles,* 94th

Congress, 1st Session, Washington, D.C.: U.S. Government Printing Office, 1975.

U.S. Congress, House Committee on Banking, Finance and Urban Affairs. *Financial Institutions in a Revolutionary Era*, 97th Congress, 1st Session, October 1981, Washington, D.C.: U.S. Government Printing Office, Committee Print 97-8.

U.S. Senate, Committee on Banking, Housing and Urban Affairs. *International Banking Act of 1978*. Washington, D.C.: U.S. Government Printing Office, 1978.

U.S. Treasury. *Studies in Banking Competition and the Banking Structure*. Washington, D.C.: Office of the Comptroller of the Currency, 1966.

Waite, Donald C. "Deregulation and the Banking Industry." *The Bankers Magazine* (January–February 1982), pp. 26–35.

Walker, David A. "Effects of Deregulation on the Savings and Loan Industry." *The Financial Review* (Spring 1983), pp. 94–110.

Walmsley, Julian. "International Banking Facilities—We Have Lift Off." *The Banker* (February 1982), pp. 91–96.

Weaver, Ronald L., and Andrew M. O'Malley. "The Depository Institutions Deregulation and Monetary Control Act of 1980: An Overview." *Banking Law Journal* (February 1981), pp. 100–116.

West, Robert Craig. "The Depository Institutions Act of 1980: A Historical Perspective." Federal Reserve Bank of Kansas City, *Economic Review* (February 1982), pp. 3–12.

Whitehead, David D. "Interstate Banking: Taking Inventory." Federal Reserve Bank of Atlanta, *Economic Review* (May 1983), pp. 4–20.

Wojnilower, Albert M. "The Central Role of Credit Crunches in Recent Financial History." *Brookings Papers on Economic Activity* (1980), pp. 277–326.

Wolkowitz, Benjamin. "Bank Capital: The Regulator Versus the Market." In L. G. Goldberg and L. J. White, eds., *The Deregulation of the Banking and Securities Industries*. New York: Lexington, Mass.: Lexington Books, 1979.

Zimmerman, Gary C. "The Pricing of Federal Reserve Services Under MCA." Federal Reserve Bank of San Francisco, *Economic Review* (Winter 1981), pp. 22–40.

INDEX

ABOUT THE AUTHORS

Dr. Kerry Cooper is Professor of Finance and coordinator of the Ph.D. Program in Business Administration at Texas A&M University. He previously served as Head of the Department of Finance at Texas A&M and was a Senior Fellow at the University of Manchester Business School in 1980. He is coauthor of five books and has published articles in leading finance, accounting, economics, and other business journals. He is an Associate Editor of *Financial Management* and serves as a reviewer for several journals. Dr. Cooper holds B.S. and M.S. degrees in accounting from Louisiana State University and a Ph.D. in economics from the University of Texas.

Donald R. Fraser is the Dresser Industries Professor of Finance at Texas A&M University. His teaching responsibilities include undergraduate and graduate courses in financial management, financial institutions, and financial markets. Prior to joining Texas A&M in 1972, he was employed by the Federal Reserve Bank of Dallas and by Bell Telephone Laboratories. He has also taught at the University of Arizona, where he received his Ph.D., and at the University of Texas at El Paso. He has extensive consulting experience, primarily with commercial banks and bank holding companies, as well as substantial experience in Executive Development Programs offered by Texas A&M. His over 100 articles have appeared in the *Journal of Finance*, the *Journal of Financial and Quantitative Analysis*, the

277

Journal of Financial Research, the *Journal of Bank Research*, as well as in other finance and business publications. In addition, he is the coauthor of four books, *Financial Institutions, Financial Institutions and Markets in a Changing World, The Financial Marketplace*, and *Money, The Financial System and Economic Policy*. Dr. Fraser has been honored on four separate occasions for outstanding research by the College of Business Administration at Texas A&M, and has been awarded Graduate Faculty Research Fellow status. In addition, he was selected for a Texas A&M University Faculty Distinguished Achievement Award in Teaching during the 1979–80 year. He served as visiting scholar at the University of Sussex, England, from January–May, 1982.